Barcode in Back

W9-ANT-703

PEOPLE OF THE
SEVENTH FIRE

RETURNING LIFEWAYS
OF NATIVE AMERICA

PEOPLE OF THE
SEVENTH FIRE

EDITED BY

Dagmar Thorpe

PHOTOGRAPHY

Lawrence Gus

FOREWORD BY

Vine Deloria, Jr.

AKWE:KON PRESS, CORNEL

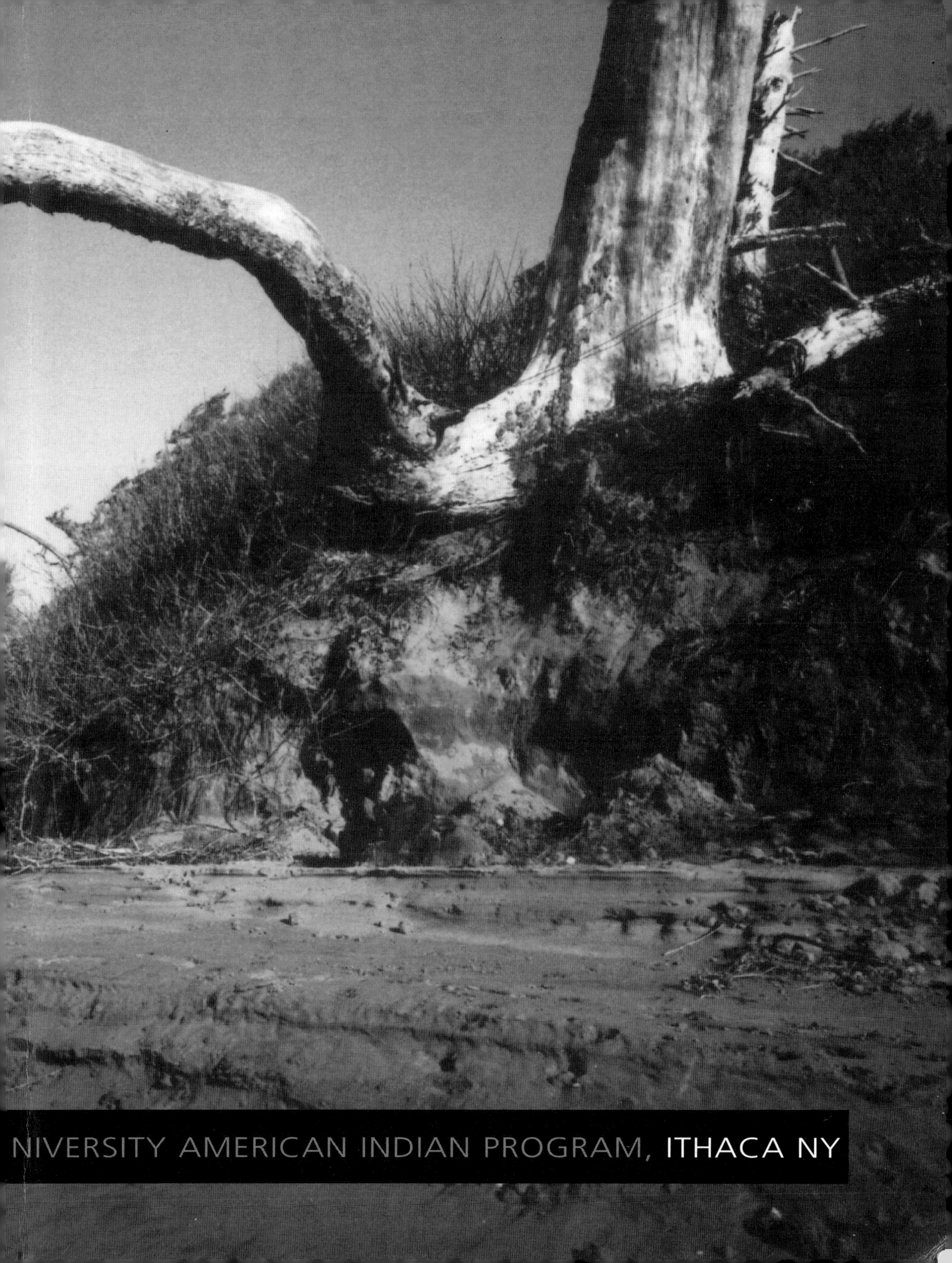
NIVERSITY AMERICAN INDIAN PROGRAM, ITHACA NY

Akwe:kon Press, Cornell University American Indian Program, Ithaca, New York 14853 USA
Copyright © 1996 by Akwe:kon Press
All photos copyright © 1996 by Lawrence Gus, unless otherwise noted

AKWE:KON PRESS
EDITOR-IN-CHIEF José Barreiro
EXECUTIVE MANAGER Tim Johnson
EDITORIAL ASSISTANT Brendan White

AMERICAN INDIAN PROGRAM
DIRECTOR Jane Mt. Pleasant

BOOK DESIGN AND PRODUCTION Jennifer Bedell
COPY EDITORS Gabrielle Sándor, Jennifer Hanna Martínez
ASSISTANT BOOK PRODUCTION Brendan White

LIBRARY OF CONGRESS CATALOGING-IN-PUBLICATION DATA
People of the seventh fire/edited by Dagmar Thorpe; photography,
Lawrence Gus; foreword by Vine Deloria, Jr.
p. cm.
ISBN 1-881178-02-1 (alk. paper)
1. Indians of North America—Interviews. 2. Indian philosophy—North America. 3. Indians of North
America—Social life and customs. I. Thorpe, Dagmar.
E98.I54P46 1996
970.004'97—dc20 96-25058 CIP

Photographer Lawrence Gus would like to extend special thanks to Cindy Hahn and Leica Camera, Inc., for the generous use of Leica Rangefinder cameras and lenses.

Contributors to the development and publication of People of the Seventh Fire are gratefully adknowledged: Penny Cabot, Richard Prentice Ettinger, Jr. and the Ettinger Foundation, W.K. Kellogg Foundation and Andrea Rabinowitz.

Proceeds from sales of People of the Seventh Fire will feed a revolving fund for Akwe:kon Press books.

Cover: left section of the giant canvas mural, Survival, by Leland Bell. Courtesy of Laurentian University. Photo by Christian Elliott.

CONTENTS

For those who show us the way,

My daughter, Tena,

Future generations of all life,

And the Thakîwa way of life

'People of the Seventh Fire' refers to an Anishinaabe prophecy which speaks of the emergence of a new people who will retrace the steps of their ancestors. It is said that if the people are strong in their belief, the sacred fire of the Anishinaabe people will be rekindled.

—Jim Dumont (Ojibwe)

ACKNOWLEDGMENTS

eople of the Seventh Fire was made possible by contributions from the W.K. Kellogg Foundation of Battle Creek, Michigan, founded in 1930 to "help people to help themselves. As a private grant making organization, it provides seed money to organizations and institutions that have identified problems and identified constructive action programs aimed at solutions." Special thanks go to Valorie Johnson, program associate to the vice-president, who supported this work and the vision it contains. I also gratefully acknowledge the support of Vine Deloria who served as advisor. This book was created through *LifeWay: A Resource for the Support of Traditional People*, a project of the Tides Foundation, San Francisco, with appreciation to Drummer Pike, president, and Brad Erickson, Ed Lee, and Miyoko Oshima of the Projects Program.

I appreciate the contributions of all those interviewed for this book. I also want to recognize those individuals who have helped me along this journey: my mother, Grace Thorpe, and daughter, Tena Malotte; Mary and Carrie Dann, Pearl Dann, Eunice Silva, Florence Vega, and Corbin Harney; Oren Lyons, Audrey Shenandoah, Thomas Banyaca, Janet McCloud, Robert Antone, Cheryl Antone, David Risling, Priscilla, Mark and Vicky Vigil, Clayton and Margaret Brascoupé, Bruce Elijah, Jerry and Wendy Flute and their family; Gary and Rita Holy Bull, Henri Mann, Jim Dumont, Jeanette Armstrong, Tessie Williams, Donna House, Renee Senogles, Diane Hill-Miller, Marie-Helene Laraque, Janine Jamison, Pam Colorado, Wilma Mankiller and Charlie Soap, Katsi Cook, Jerry and Elizabeth Mander, Denise Quitiquit, Doug Tompkins, Ann Roberts, Diane Feeney, Edith Buchi; Albie and Susan Wells and the Windcall Fellows Program; J. Patrick Lannan, Barbara Dalderis, and Lannan Foundation; Harriet Barlowe, Ben Slater, and the Blue Mountain Center; Richard P. Ettinger, Roneen Ettinger, Andrea and Alan Rabinowitz, Penny Cabot; Dan Bomberry, Bill Wahpepah, Carl and Sophia Butler, Carol Mack Patterson, Valerie, Murial and Jessica Patterson; the McKosato sisters, Liz, Pat, Carmen, Anna, Wanda and Harvey Ross; Henrietta and Sandra Massey, Francis Scott, Vera and Austin Grant, Jr., and Roderick Wakolee.

I extend my appreciation to Kathy Smalley for assistance with the computer, Gordon Whittaker for the spelling of Sauk words, and to Rebecca Kelner for transcribing the interviews. I thank José Barreiro, editor of the Akwe:kon Press, for his collaborative efforts and support.

F O R E W O R D

Vine Deloria, Jr.

(Dakota)

lmost eighty years ago, John Collier, recently discharged from his post in the California educational system, drove into Taos to spend Christmas with Mabel Dodge (later Luhan). The people of the Pueblo were celebrating their winter dances and Collier stood transfixed as the dancers methodically performed the Red Deer Dance. Later he would reflect that he caught a glimpse of the Red Atlantis, a way of life that created personalities so strong they could survive any obstacle placed in their path. Collier went on to become Commissioner of Indian Affairs and secured passage of the Indian Reorganization Act which allowed a measure of self-government for Indian tribes and reservation peoples.

Collier's original vision was filtered throughout by the behavior and beliefs of the Southwestern Indians and at times he expected all the other tribes to behave in a similar manner. But the statutory framework he put in place was sufficiently flexible and Indian communities, once freed from the onerous burdens placed on them by the Indian agents who controlled the reservation, began to prosper and to seek restoration of their original lifeways. Between the original vision and our time, federal policy has shifted back and forth between the harshness of unilateral severance of federal services and recognition and generous support of Indian aspirations. No one alive today has not suffered, in some degree, from the ever-changing federal policies of the intervening decades.

With the new found freedom of the 1930s people began slowly to perform dances which had previously been prohibited, to practice religious ceremonies that would have meant jail sentences before, and to talk of the old way of doing things. Although the situation in Congress today appears life-threatening to many Indian communities, the events of the immediate past have provided a much larger stage upon which Indian fortunes can be determined. We see now some institutions, tribally controlled schools and reservation colleges, that seem to be permanent parts of Indian life. We also see a real flowering of Indian concern for their lands and sacred places, even as some tribes turn away from traditional teaching and embrace destructive projects that would have been instantly rejected by their ancestors. The present is confusing, but in this confusion we also find many signs of hope and a continuity with the generations of many centuries ago. We can see the old trail that began at the creation and now leads us into the future.

This collection of stories is an important part of the rising of the Red Atlantis. It reflects a thoughtful odyssey through Indian Country and through the struggle to achieve a new Indian identity as seen in the lives of reservation people who have a vision. The collection is broken into four parts which illustrate the various attitudes now to be found in Indian Country. Book One covers "The Spirit of the People Has Survived Despite all We have Endured" stories—life experiences of people who have fought hard to maintain religious and cultural values. Inevitably, because culture is so vulnerable to political change, we see that the lives of these people cannot escape the conflicts that plague so many American communities today. We come to understand that winning and losing are but temporary resting places. What is important is that these people stood up when it was time to stand for something.

Book Two presents life stories under the theme "Who We Are As a People is Within Us Waiting to be Awakened." Here we encounter the substance of Indian life, memory and values—the connection of the people to creation and the responsibility that entails. The respect and response to the creation was the foremost value in the old ways of every tribe and considerable time was devoted to the practice of rituals, ceremonies and social customs that would ensure that the people remembered and revered the creation of our world, its life forms, and its passage of time.

Book Three reflects that "Practicing Our Ways of Life is What Strengthens the Spirit of the People." Beliefs are merely sterile propositions unless and until they become part of our spontaneous behavior. Different Indian nations developed customs and practices to ensure that they came to represent what they believed. What is most remarkable is that there was such a similarity in how the people maintained a spiritual posture in a world in which there were no easy ways of living. While today we are forced to celebrate distinctions in order to overcome the stereotypes that suggest that all Indians are the same, we nevertheless admit to ourselves, and indeed are delighted to learn, that there are great areas in which we have the same rituals and ceremonies and that even our ancient historical experiences are much the same.

Finally, Book Four looks forward into the future: "Developing Community Projects which Enliven and Strengthen Who We are As Peoples." Culture is a constantly changing set of behaviors that both feeds on itself and transcends its roots. Simply bringing back the old ways, or preserving them, is insufficient for survival in today's world. More relevant is the ability to adapt to new technologies and attitudes while maintaining a basic philosophical attitude that represents the continuing values of the people. When some of the Indian people were finally restricted to reservations, they were deprived of traditional plants, animals, and sacred sites. So many changes and adaptations were made but the basic substance of the practices and beliefs were treasured and used to confront the new situations that people faced. Today we must adhere to traditional values but we must demonstrate that they have relevance for the new conditions in which we live.

Although this collection of life stories brings focus to the amazing variety of people adhering to and perpetuating traditional ways, the book can also be read as a personal experience of its author, Dagmar Thorpe. In a great many ways she is representative of the younger generation of Indians now influencing federal policy and reservation planning. As Indian youngsters have matured, they are often thrown into the larger society knowing they are Indians but placed in situations in which they cannot find the proper way to express their inner selves. They attach themselves to causes with great energy and often bring about great changes but they still continue to seek the quietude that the traditional community has. Too many of them give up the search when they discover that not everything is institutionalized and formal. If they are alert, then they go back to their origins, to the elders, and begin to build a new appreciation of what it is that makes Indian communities capable of withstanding insurmountable odds and maintaining themselves.

Dagmar has been through the activist years, and indeed was an active and effective supporter of the Western Shoshone claim, which is still not settled to the satisfaction of many people. She has traveled to many Indian communities, here and in Canada, and has learned from an amazing variety of elders, perfecting both her understanding and commitment to traditional ways. She has been an invaluable member and supporter of the recent set of conferences conducted by the American Indian Science and Engineering Society to revive interest and respect for traditional knowledge. Indeed, these conferences could not have been held without her advice, support, and hard work.

So many of these interviews are part and parcel of Dagmar's life and learning experience. As she has gone from community to community, she has been as important bearer of glad tidings–that elders are not alone, that in every Indian community in the land they are patiently preserving the nuances of the stories which are so important for proper understanding of the ways of the people. These interviews are not, therefore, interviews as much as they are a shared learning experience and a celebration of the joy that comes when people communicate meaning on the deepest personal level.

As the reader understands the process by which this collection of interviews came into being, and places this collection in the context of this century, the importance of this book will become obvious.

I N T R O D U C T I O N

Dagmar Thorpe

(Sauk/Thakiwaki)

I came home to the Sac and Fox Nation in 1993. Until that time I was, in Lyn Risling's words, "dormant," I was asleep to my culture. Although some of my relationships with Native people had great depth, it was not until I returned to my own culture that I discovered and understood the formidable obstacles working against a continuation of the Sac way of life. For the first forty-six years of my life, I lived in the non-Native world. When I awoke to my culture, I walked from that world into a reality filled with brilliant light and vivid color, where I recognized the Creator from the depths of my soul.

Why did I choose the path of being Sauk, or *Thakîwaki*, as we call ourselves? Several years ago, a white friend said to me, "The only difference between you and me is a little blood." At first, I was angry. But the comment caused me to think. "How *am* I different?" I asked myself. I have a Thakîwaki name, I was named into the Thunder Clan, and I am a citizen of my nation. My bloodline goes back to the original Thakîwaki from which our people came. But what else makes me different?

I came to understand that being Sauk is more than having Thakîwaki blood in my veins. I had to ask myself if I was really a part of the Sac and Fox community. Did I participate in Sauk ceremonies? Did I understand and follow the original instructions to the Sauk people? Did I understand Sauk history and its effect on our people? Did I work to help future generations of Sauk people? I had to honestly answer myself with the word no. In the early 1990s, I was drifting in and around Indian Country and traveling occasionally through my homeland as a visitor. I had been working to advance Native concerns for twenty-seven years and had been involved with the traditional Western Shoshones' efforts to regain their homeland for twenty. Yet I was removed from my own identity as a Thakîwaki woman because I was not in a true relationship with our people.

Throughout the years I worked in support of traditional Native people, I had assumed that those traditional people would be the ones to bear the responsibility of maintaining their traditional ways of life. I saw myself as a helper, one who played a distant role in the lives of those who would perpetuate the identity of the Native peoples. As time has gone by and I have seen many elders pass on, I have come to realize that no matter what has torn each of us from our Native identity—issues of blood quantum, education, bureaucratization, relocation, or assimilation—it is still our responsibility to pick up our way of life and live it. If we do not do this, we will have no future. There is no one else who can do it for us.

How we perceive ourselves defines who we are and how we live. To place ourselves within the realm of the assimilated is to invite cultural death. I have observed an interview conducted with several members of a tribal council who told the interviewer that their nation had lost its language, customs and lifeway, and had become assimilated into the mainstream. This was stated as though the truth of their identity as a people no longer existed, as if traditional people inhabit another world. This limits all their efforts to work on behalf of their people.

Each nation has a unique language, set of teachings and ceremonies, and a way of life given to them by the Creator through the combined efforts of hundreds of thousands of their ancestors. From a traditional Native perspective, the European invasion intruded upon the natural evolution of their lives. Each race, nation, community, family and individual possesses unique characteristics which help to create a healthy environment through which their gifts can be revealed. Although this natural way of life still lies beneath the surface of most Native people and communities, it is submerged in layers of freeways, speeding cars, water diversion dams, and jet streams, and cluttered with the industrial development, buildings, and toxic waste of a technologically advanced but naturally regressed society.

What is within this lifeway of Native people that must be continued and why is it important in the contemporary world? The Native ways of life are spiritually guided. The basis for understanding spirituality is rooted in the lifeway of the human beings who experience it. An understanding of spirituality comes through the practice of a natural lifeway harmonious with all of creation. In the contemporary world, this understanding is critical. A perception of life which is limited to material reality and excludes spiritual reality makes it easier for an individual to justify destructive thought and action, because the impact of such behavior on the spirit within life is not seen, felt, or understood.

There are some in this generation who are able to intellectually articulate what distinguishes the Native philosophy of thought from the non-Native philosophy. Yet few are able to embody their Native philosophy as a way of life, and the Native world view only becomes reality when it is lived. Spirituality is not an abstract or a theoretical phenomenon; it is as real as the physical bodies we inhabit. To deny the spirit is to deny our relationship with the Creator and all of life.

We as Natives have reached the time where we must awaken to what and who we are, and practice our identities. Some characterize this time as a crossroads. We can choose the road to the renewal of our way of life, or we can choose the road that will lead to the end of our peoples. I believe, however, that this generation will put an end to the legacy of pain which has forced us away from who we are. The disruption of our traditional practices has caused disharmony and violence to come into every dimension of our lives. Yet many of us are returning peace, stability, and well-being to our communities by learning to apply our original instructions to our contemporary lives and practicing our traditional ways in the contemporary world of the twentieth century.

I have been a Native activist since the Alcatraz occupation of the late 1960s. I was not a major player at Alcatraz, just one of the thousands, new to activism and my Indian identity. I am a person who early in life exemplified the assimilated Indian. I am fair-haired and blue-eyed; I was born in Japan, raised in a white suburb of New York, and grew up knowing little of my identity as a Sauk except for the awareness that I was the granddaughter of Jim Thorpe. My mother enrolled me as a member of the Sac and Fox Tribe of Oklahoma when I was born. We are also Potawatomi and Kickapoo. I was given the name Kôhtatoa ("woman with the power of a frightening thunderclap") by the elders of the Thunder Clan.

The Thakîwaki, or Sauk, and Mesquakie, or Fox, are Algonquin-speaking peoples originally from the northeastern United States. Thakîwaki means "people of the outlet" or "people coming forth" and Mesquakie means "people of the red earth." These two distinct Native American nations are united in Oklahoma as the Sac and Fox Nation.

Our oral history tells us that we originated near the Saint Lawrence River in Canada. Following the settlement and invasion of Europeans on the East Coast, which also resulted in pressures from other Native nations, the Sauk moved from near Saginaw Bay in Michigan to Green Bay, Wisconsin; then to Sâkînâke, at the convergence of the Rock and Mississippi rivers; and were then forcibly removed to Iowa and Kansas. The fight of the Sauk people to keep the Sâkînâke homeland resulted in a war, forced on Black Hawk, which was to be the last war fought by Native Americans for homelands east of the Mississippi.

The Sac and Fox relinquished a vast area encompassing parts of Illinois, Wisconsin, Michigan, Missouri, Minnesota, and Kansas. Most of the Mesquakie moved to Tama, Iowa. In 1869, 387 Sac were removed to Indian Territory and settled on 750 square miles of land purchased in what later became Lincoln, Payne and Pottawatomi counties in Oklahoma. They were joined later by approximately 200 members of the Mokohoko Band which had resisted a forcible move to Oklahoma.

Today, the population of the Sac and Fox Nation of Oklahoma is 2,300. There are 956 tribal members living within the jurisdictional area of the original reservation which covered 480,000 acres in Lincoln, Payne and Pottawatomi counties in north-central Oklahoma. This land base was reduced by 80% through the Indian Land Allotment Act. Subsequent land sales have reduced our homeland to 16,000 acres.

The family of my great-great-grandmother, Nôtenôkwa ("woman with the power of the wind before a storm"), a Thunder Clan member of Black Hawk's band, was forcibly removed from Illinois to Iowa to Kansas. She married an Irish blacksmith named Hiram Thorpe; their son, Hiram Thorpe Jr., moved with other Sac and Fox from Kansas to Oklahoma Territory, where he married Charlotte Vieux, a Potawatomi. One of their sons was my grandfather, Jim Thorpe. His Sauk name was Wâthêhaka, or "the one who goes forward on a bright path." He was born in Sac and Fox territory near Prague, Oklahoma, on a land allotment near where my mother, daughter and I now live. He went to Indian boarding schools from his sixth year. My grandfather won the pentathlon and decathlon competitions of the 1912 Olympic Games and has been called the greatest athlete of the century. His Olympic medals, stripped from him because he played minor league baseball one summer, were restored to him posthumously in 1982.

He married Iva Margaret Miller and one of their daughters was my mother, Grace Thorpe. My grandmother and grandfather divorced and my mother grew up from the age of two in Indian boarding schools and orphanages in Oklahoma and Kansas. She joined the Women's Army Corps during the Second World War and married my father, Fred Seely. My mother has worked actively for Native rights most of her adult life and is now a well-known anti-nuclear activist. Of the first cousins from my grandfather's first marriage, I am the only one who has chosen to be Sauk. Although the others are proud of their ancestry, I am the only one who has chosen to live it.

When I came home three years ago, I shifted my focus from gathering experiences to feeling and living life more deeply as a Thakîwaki woman. I could not have done this without the teachers that have helped me to understand our way of life. As I reach more deeply into this truth, I become more and more convinced that learning and practicing our lifeways is the only way we will survive as Native peoples.

Yet, as a Thakîwaki woman, I cannot separate myself from the dysfunction which results from the collective memory of multi-generational violence and the devastation of our people. This unresolved grief obstructed the truth of who I am and the lifeway which is mine to follow. To heal the life around us, we must first heal ourselves; healing our wounds heals our hearts and allows us to hear the guiding voice of the Creator. Facing the truth of who we are and overcoming our pain through focus, guidance and discipline is the beginning of the way to healing. Healing cannot be accomplished in one great stride; we find the truth of our lifeway through persistence and the effort of many small steps.

My guidance has come through prayer, self-observation and traditional teachings. When I first came home, I believed that our lifeway was only to be found in participating in our ceremonies, singing our songs, learning our original instructions, and following our teachings. I diligently participate in all of these activities and am learning our language. Over time, however, I have come to realize that it is the way in which these aspects of our tradition are applied every day that is the way of life. As Jim Dumont says, "The lifeway is the entire path which the spirit walks through life."

The continuation of our lifeways is dependent upon the renewal of Native worldviews which manifest themselves in traditional culture, spirituality, economics, and government. Returning to the belief systems upon which our lifeways are based forms the essence of a powerful movement which can bring about healing and empowerment of Native individuals, communities, and nations. Native people are revitalizing traditional governmental, educational, economic, spiritual, and socio-cultural systems; protecting existing ways of life, homelands, environment, and rights; reinstating traditional land management and use practices; reintroducing indigenous species of plants and animals and traditional agriculture and foods; developing language and cultural immersion projects; instituting community healing projects which have significantly reduced alcohol and drug use and suicide; adapting Native principles to tribal judicial, environmental, and ethical laws; and exploring and developing solutions for Native challenges through collaborative efforts among the diversity of Native peoples.

Despite the overwhelming obstacles of environmental degradation, deprivation of land and resource rights, seizure of tribal homelands, and internalized oppression, many still stand firm in their lifeways and continue to speak their languages, practice their ceremonies, and apply traditional knowledge in daily life. By the tens, hundreds and thousands, Native traditionalists have stood in the way of bulldozers, cattle chutes, and nuclear waste dumps to preserve and protect a way of life that for too many has become nothing but a nostalgia-laden memory. For those who live the ways of their people, traditions are a part of living reality. Practicing and teaching these traditions is vital to the survival of the Native nations, for in them are found the collective memory and knowledge of our ancestors which form the essence of our identities and strength.

People of the Seventh Fire reflects a personal journey through Native America. In January of 1993, I began an exploration of the realities of traditional Native American people in order to help develop strategies to assist in their specific efforts to revitalize our languages, cultures, and ways of life. Working with traditional people since the late 1960s in a variety of projects, I had realized that language and tradition form the foundation upon which all living culture is based. I wanted to examine projects which focused on the renewal and practice of Native thought, knowledge and ways of life, and the ways in which Native values may be applied to contemporary issues. As my work took shape in the form of conversations with Native people from all corners of the United States, this intellectual abstraction found roots in the living, breathing reality of the people I met.

My intent in writing this book was to share the thoughts and experiences of Native people who speak their traditional language, practice their traditional lifeways, and struggle daily within their communities to maintain their culture for future generations. I have known some of the people I interviewed for as long as twenty years; others I had never met. I sought diverse voices to express all the faces of Native experience—voices of individuals rooted in their communities, practicing their ways of life, and working for the continuation of Native life.

The interviews were intended to give these individuals the freedom to address the issues they chose to share with other Native Americans. They are presented, as much as possible, in their entirety; they have been edited only as much as was necessary to adapt the spoken word to the printed page. These people celebrate the strength of our ancestors and express the principles and lessons universal to human experience in the specific context of each person's life and background. I ask you, the reader, to immerse yourself in the telling of these experiences, and to listen to the voices that speak the words you read.

This book is primarily intended for Native Americans interested in understanding the ways in which we strengthen the spirit of our people, as well as for those institutions and individuals who presently, or who may in the future, support the efforts of traditional people in this work. These voices are offered as living examples of ways in which we can reawaken the spirits of our families and communities, and demonstrate how the unique gifts we have been given can contribute to the strength and vitality of our peoples.

THESPIRITOFTHEPEOPLE

HASSURVIVEDDESPITE

ALLWEHAVEENDURED

Book One contains interviews with Native people who were raised traditionally and, for the most part, have remained in their communities. Individuals like these are the ones we look to for the knowledge of our people when we return home. They are the ones who continue the fight for our languages, lifeways, lands, and environment, and they are continually assaulted on all sides in their efforts to do so. In many cases, their work has secured homelands for their people. They are the Black Hawks, Crazy Horses and Chief Josephs of our day; they defend the lifeways of their people and help preserve them for the generations to come. Their common theme is that in order to remain Native people, we must live within our beliefs. Native nations are defined by the ways of life given to us by the Creator. If we become disconnected from our lifeways, we become estranged from the spirit of our peoples. This disconnection can occur whether we live within our communities or not. Within these voices is the true feeling of our peoples continued from the beginning of time. As Native people we are challenged with finding this true voice within ourselves and giving it expression in all that we do.

The speakers emphasize that as Native people, our existence is interdependent with our instructions, beliefs, and worldview. This point is stated clearly by Carrie Dann who says, "We are losing our communications with the Creator and our spiritual helpers. If we refuse to recognize them, we walk outside the path we are supposed to walk on. If we do not walk on this path, we will lose our language, religious belief, and culture." Danny Billy emphasizes by saying, "If I lose these teachings and way of life, I am nobody anymore." Within these thoughts is contained the challenge before us as Native people. The spirit of our peoples has survived despite all we have endured, but it is the responsibility of this generation to carry this forward for those yet to come.

We Don't Hear The Spiritual Little
People Anymore, We Don't Hear
The Water Babies Cry.

C H A P T E R   O N E

An interview with Carrie Dann

(Western Shoshone)

Upwind and north of the Nevada test site and a
waste dump, to the south of a proposed monito
spent nuclear fuel rods, to the west of a propo
to the east of supersonic testing of military airc
Nation. In its heart, surrounded by gold mines,
ily. It is one of the last Western Shoshone stron
relentless hunger of the American market for its land and res

On that high desert ranch of sage and rabbit brush, agair
mountains, Mary, Carrie, Richard and Clifford Dann, together
and their families, are united in the truth that the Shoshones
the United States. They have withstood the killing of their p
mind away people"); the environmental devastation of the lan
the gold miners; the military and their proposed MX missile
Western Shoshone people who will stand with them.

In 1974, Mary and Carrie Dann were riding horseback, rounding up their cattle on lands which the Western Shoshone have lived on since their creation as a people, when they were served notice by a federal official that they were trespassing. The Dann case went through the United States legal system all the way up to the Supreme Court. Not once during the lengthy court proceedings was the issue of Western Shoshone ownership to their homelands heard.

The Dann sisters assert that the United States has never taken Western Shoshone lands in a manner permissible under its own laws–not by consent, conquest or treaty–while the Treaty of Ruby Valley recognized their rights. The Indian Claims Commission was set up to compensate Indians for lands ceded by them to the United States. The Commission asserted they took Western Shoshone lands by gradual encroachment. In this case, the Commission was used as a means for the outright seizure of lands and extinguished all their rights to them despite repeated attempts by the Shoshone to withdraw from the case.

The Western Shoshone have refused since 1980 to accept the 26 million dollar judgment which the United States has placed in a trust account. The Western Shoshone have exhausted the courts and appealed to the United States government for a negotiated settlement without success.

In 1993, Mary and Carrie Dann were awarded the Right Livelihood Award for their efforts to defend their homeland and way of life.

⋈•⋈•⋈•⋈

"REALITY IS LIVING A NATURAL LIFE."

Everything depends on technology. You switch a button here and you switch a button there. You don't have to do anything. Something else does it for you. Technology can do anything nowadays. If it does not work, you get somebody to come in and make it work. Then life goes on. Most people don't do anything with their hands. Everything is so easy. You get through with your housework in a half an hour. You wash dishes. You turn the water on and it is right there. You know this is not reality. Many people do not know what it is like to go out and work with their hands, think about what they are doing, instead of pushing a button. What you do with your own hands as a human is real life.

You go down to the grocery store for your food, come back, zap it, and there is your food. You get your food this way instead of growing it or looking for your native foods. I find it real hard to live this life because everything seems so convenient. In my own home, I have to heat my water to wash dishes. I work for what I do. I don't know if you would call it work, I would call it survival. You learn how to do these things.

Reality is living a natural life in a way that respects all living things instead of chasing them away or destroying them. A real life respects all kinds of life regardless of what it is. In the traditional way of thought everything has a purpose. Everything has a reason to be here. We feel that the Creator put everything here, so that things would be balanced. When we destroy a species, regardless of what it is, then we are destroying ourselves. We can see reality when we look at the use of water. To us, water is sacred. In today's world, we see the destruction of water by chemical contamination, mining and pollution. When you destroy water, you are destroying yourself. Water takes care of life. If there is no water, there is no other life–even insects would not be here. That is part of the reality. When we destroy these things, then we are destroying ourselves, whether we know it or not. The old people teach us to respect life, because all life has a purpose.

"YOU LOSE YOURSELF WHEN YOU LIVE IN THE FAKE WORLD."

Today, what we call the real world is a fake world. In today's society, the only thing that is important to people is humans. Man's satisfaction is the only important thing. That is not so in real life. In real life, all things are equally important, including humans. Whether we like it or not, we are in a fake world. All you can do is your best to live in the real world where you walk with dignity and treat all things, no matter what kind of life they are, with respect. These are the instructions of the Creator.

You lose yourself when you live in the fake world. When you live in the fake world, you think this is what life is all about. A lot of our young children today do not know the real world. All they know is the fake world. Our young people turn to the fake things like drugs, alcohol and cigarettes. They get addicted to these things. This is the fake world because when you live like that, you are no longer caught up with life. All you do is go and seek enjoyment, going to the casinos, all kinds of fancy dancing. There is no reality in it. It is make believe.

There are a lot of things that the young people can do without. Technology is taking jobs away from people. What is taking jobs away is all this technology. Let's live in the real world and give a person a job, instead of giving a machine a job.

There is too damn much money floating around in this area because of the big employment like the mining companies. They are making so much money that it controls their lives. There is no desire to live in the real world. Many of the people who work in the mines know damn well that they are ripping Mother Earth apart. The only thing that is important is the fact that they are making good money. That is what controls our lives today: money, money, money. That is what the fake world is. It is reliant upon the money that buys all of these fake things.

Everything is convenient in the fake world. I like to make good use of my time. It's boring when everything is convenient. You just work for a little while and you get the rest of the time to think about what to do next. Then you go downtown and lose yourself in the lights and get in trouble. In the fake world there is so much time on your hands. Everything is easy as long as you have the money. As long as our young people are working in the gold mines, they will never realize what real life is about.

When you live like this, you can easily lose your identity as a Western Shoshone. A lot of our young people don't identify themselves as Western Shoshone. Maybe they are the right color but their thoughts and actions are not Western Shoshone. Some of our people have started to look at themselves and question, "Is this what life is all about?" Some people have gone back to the sweat lodge. A lot of my people have taken up Christianity. The Bible does not tell you the truth, it contradicts itself in many places. Our own Bible people (as I call them) think that those of us who practice our traditional religious beliefs are going to hell.

A true Western Shoshone is a person who follows their traditional religious beliefs and lives them. You can't be a Western Shoshone and walk outside of your belief. Your beliefs, language and culture make you who you are. When you have your own language and beliefs, then you are who you claim to be, a Western Shoshone. You have to live it. You can't just say it and not live it.

It is pretty damn tough to be a Western Shoshone in the contemporary world. In this area, when I am visiting my daughter, it would be pretty damn hard. First of all, you cannot build a fire for your sweat. It is against the county ordinances and laws, against the county this and county that. People in authority seem to think that if you are not a Christian, then you are not a person. They think you are practicing heathenism. If you are going to be Western Shoshone, you have to live within how you believe. So you have to disobey what the county ordinances say to follow your belief. In this area there not many strong enough to stand up for the traditional ways. If they are, then they are very quiet and let things stay as they are. You have to live within your culture. You have to live according to your beliefs.

"YOU CAN'T BE A WESTERN SHOSHONE AND WALK OUTSIDE OF YOUR BELIEF."

"ONCE YOUR CULTURE DIES, YOU ARE NO LONGER A WESTERN SHOSHONE."

It is wrong for the white society, from the local to the highest part of the United States government, to not respect our ways and claim to have taken our land, our Mother away from us. That is genocide, because we cannot survive as a people without our ways and our land. Once our land goes, our culture dies, then we are no longer Western Shoshone. When indigenous people forget who they are, they cease to be indigenous people. They become caught up in the western world and give up all their rights and beliefs as indigenous people.

We have been fighting the United States for twenty-two years. No country has the right to buy my beliefs. They are not to be bought. We will not sell them. This land is my Mother and they are not going to buy that from me. If they take the land away from us, that is genocide. They will kill us as humans with distinct beliefs, culture, and languages. This is not what we want to do, we will have to be forced to do it. We are trying to preserve our way of life, so that our grandchildren and future generations can have something to look forward to. All we find is that no matter where we go, we are blocked by the people that came to our country and say "This is mine." We don't want any damn money from them. They can't buy my land. My land is not for sale. They can't buy my rights. My rights are not for sale. To them, the land is real estate. To me, it is my Mother. Nobody has the right to buy our Mother and say, "We have taken it from you." Then, throw us a few pennies and say, "Here, I'll shove it down your throat." When they take our land, they destroy our religious belief. Why don't they just outright exterminate us? They believe because they are stronger, they

Below: Carrie Dann with her sister Mary.

can refuse to let us use our own land. All necessities of life come from this earth. If they are going to deny us that, that is genocide.

What has kept us going is trying to be who we are and practicing our ways. You don't know how close we have come to giving in. Our beliefs keep us fighting. When we think about giving up, we think of the children. How is that little baby going to grow up? I think about Patricia and about how her husband works at the gold mine. We talk about this. I have told my son-in-law, "Listen, it is wrong to have children and at the same time destroy their environment." We all have to look at ourselves, especially mothers and fathers.

It is hard to practice your own ways in today's world. U.S. Congress had to pass an act in 1978, the American Indian Religious Freedom Act, before we could practice our religious beliefs with some recognition. We are the only people that have to have an act permitting our religious freedom. In other words, this is like them saying this is the "Coyote Act" and the coyote cannot do or say certain things until we pass this act. They don't recognize that we are human beings with thoughts, minds and abilities. We are not human in their minds. People with political or economic power don't want to recognize us because we live our own ways.

When you live firmly in your own beliefs, this in turn takes care of you. When you are walking your own path, you can only be right, although it is true that in today's society, you can't walk that way and make a good living.

There is very little left of our healthy environment. Being upwind from the Nevada test site, I think it is even worse. We get all this radiation blown in on us. The reports you read are really scary. We hear about all these people dying of cancer in Crescent Valley and vicinity. It is real sad. In our area most of the native foods are gone. If there are any, they are few and far between. You have to really look. Some of the things are totally gone. That is the environment we are bringing up our children in.

We want the public to understand we are humans with distinct beliefs and the right to live on our lands. We don't own the land, we are just caretakers. The industrialized western world cannot understand that Indigenous people are so close to the earth. We should not be forced to accept what they are offering us in dollars and cents. We don't want that.

It makes it hard to live your own lifestyle and to keep believing that this Earth is your Mother. How do you live with the earth as your Mother when they keep telling you, "We have taken the land from you." The United States says that it is wrong for other big countries to take over other little countries. But then they say it is all right for the United States to destroy Indian people, our lifestyle and culture by simply saying, "We decided that you people don't own this land because you are not Christian, you are subhuman. Because we are stronger and mightier than you, we have taken it from you. All you can have is what we want to give you." That is not right either.

I have been thinking about the history of man. Most of the books written by lawyers or historians say that the lands of indigenous people were taken by the United States. How can the United States take land from indigenous people? They are either God or they are oppressors. They came here because they were oppressed. When they got here they became the oppressors of the Indian people.

"YOU HAVE TO BE STRONG ENOUGH TO STAND ABOVE IT AND LIVE WITHIN YOUR BELIEFS."

The saddest thing I find is that the Indians recognize themselves as colonized and their lands as colonies of the United States. I am talking about the people here in Elko Colony, in Battle Mountain Colony, or in Ely Colony. When you can call yourself a colony, you are saying that you have been colonized by people who came across the water. Once they get our lands, Indians have nothing. You have to be strong enough to stand above it, live within your beliefs, and believe in your Mother. They say that they can do anything through Congress or their court system. But if an act of Congress and their court system is against the laws of our Creator, then it is wrong. How are you going to make that right? The only way you can make it right is by simply living the life that was handed to you by the Creator.

"THE HOMES OF OUR SPIRITUAL HELPERS ARE BEING DESTROYED"

People do not seem to understand that in our way of life, there are all kinds of spiritual helpers. When I first went to our ceremonies, they talked about the beautiful lakes and the little water babies. They talked about how the spiritual people each have a home. You look at the destruction of our lands and you wonder what is happening to the homes of our spiritual helpers. Where are those blue lakes where they used to live? What happens to these little spiritual people? No matter where you look there is a man, usually a white man. They destroy everything for us. They destroy our spiritual people, our little spiritual animals. They have no concept of life. They only know that their life must go on but our life must die. There are all kinds of spiritual little people in the forest, and their forest is being clear-cut. What happens to them? Don't they have a right to live? They are the Creator's little people and they have a purpose.

We get away from our way of thinking and start believing in only Jesus Christ. That is not the way of our people. We believe in our spiritual helpers who may be people, animals, insects, plants. No matter where we look, these things are being destroyed—the waters which they drink, where they live. The people used to talk about the underground connections from waters to waters. Some of these little animals in their spiritual way travel these byways underneath the crust of the earth. All of this is being destroyed.

How do you stay who you are? How do you stay an indigenous person when you know that the civilized society is out there destroying these things for you? How do you protect the spiritual creatures? I really don't know. I know that we don't hear our spiritual little people out there anymore. You don't hear the water babies cry. They are being destroyed. When they destroy the water babies, they are destroying our way and our culture. These things help us live day to day. How do you keep in touch with Western Shoshone reality when all these things are being destroyed? I want to cry when I think about all these things being destroyed right before my eyes.

No court is going to rule in favor of the indigenous people. There is no way in hell. We tried that. In our case, I found out we did not have constitutional rights. We thought the United States represented freedom. Everybody talks about the United States, where people can express themselves, where people have a right to live freely. It is not that way, not for us, anyway. Is it because we are indigenous, is that why? Simply because we are tied to this earth? They will never rule in our favor, never. It is their court system. They are not going to take from themselves to tell us, "You are right."

There is no equal ball game in a white man's society because it is ruled by greed. They see something and look at it as a belonging. They say, "It is mine." The earth is no one's personal belonging. When all of these political leaders die, do they take this earth with them? They are creatures of the earth but don't respect the earth. They are controlled by greed because we have something that they want, which is the earth, our Mother.

You have heard our old people talk about how these people wanted to get rid of all the Western Shoshone. They tried poisoning, killing each other and blaming us for it. The old history never stops. If something goes wrong, they will point at an Indian and say, he is the one that did it.

We have no Constitutional rights. The Constitution is the greatest law that was ever made. It is probably the greatest law because it was modeled by Indian, Iroquois, people. It was part of the Creator's instructions. It was copied by what they call "the founding fathers." They still are not living the Constitution the way it was meant to be. They changed the original Indian law and made it fit the way they wanted it. Indians don't have rights. We found that out when we went to court. There is no such thing as equal justice and there never will be as long as they want our land. There will never be equal justice because they are not willing to talk about our land on equal terms. They say it is not our land, it is their land. It is only greed, it is power. So what do you do? Where do you go? The only thing is to try to make more people aware of what is happening. But how are they going to become aware? They too live with greed and injustice. What do you do? I don't know. I wish somebody would tell me.

"YOU HAVE TO WALK
THE STRAIGHT PATH
ACCORDING TO THE
INSTRUCTIONS OF
THE CREATOR."

You have to live a real life even though we do have modern conveniences. When you live in what I call the real world, you have to be able to live according to the instructions that have been given to you by the Creator. It is something born in you or taught to you. There are certain things you have to do and certain things that you can't do. If Western Shoshone don't follow these instructions, there is no future for anybody. The original instructions given to the Native people tell us to protect the environment. That is supposed to be our duty–to never destroy any species because they all have a reason to be here on this earth.

We have to live according to the instructions given to us or we will go down the wrong path. We have only got two choices: either we walk the right path, or we walk the wrong path. I believe in our way and if we take the right path and know our own traditions and skills, we will survive, one way or the other. The ways of survival are right there before us, but we have to look and listen.

If we lose communication with our spiritual people and the Creator, who are we then, anyway? You may have the bronze coloring of an Indian, but if you don't know who you are and where you came from, who are you? Some people don't know who they are. People say, "I don't know where we come from." You have to walk the straight path according to the instructions of the Creator. I speak from a lot of anger and resentment toward our own people for the way they act. The American government does not look upon indigenous people as humans. I also have a lot of resentment about that.

Many of the political issues I have been involved with, like the Western Shoshone land rights, have instilled bitterness in me. I know they lied to us and cheat us. I think it makes me a bitter person. I try not to let it be like that. Sometimes anger gnaws on you, until it controls you. I know it controls me. I think that if only our own people would look at themselves, understand who they are, why they are, and act like Western Shoshone, maybe I wouldn't have this feeling of disrespect for them.

I look at my own people as having been misled. How do you understand people who want fifteen cents an acre for your Mother Earth? How do you understand people like that? What they do reflects on all of us, not just on one of us. You know the government is not going to look at us traditional Western Shoshone. They are going to look at their own creations, the IRA tribal councils, which are subservient to their trustee, the federal government, and work with them. The livelihood of the tribal councils depends on the federal government. These people live off the federal government. The federal government controls their wards by providing a few bucks here and a few bucks there. It is really a tough world. It is hard to understand your own people, let alone the United States government.

To live in the Western Shoshone reality, we have to know who we are, where we come from, and where we are going. We have to live within our beliefs. One of the greatest things that we could be doing is training our young people to be who they are, Western Shoshone. My daughter says to me, "You are going to have to teach my little girl this and my little girl that." How do I teach her? This is reality. We teach our children in a proper manner, in our language and within our own beliefs and culture.

We cannot ever forget who we are, where we come from, our duties to this earth and to preserve all life. We have to walk within that circle. If we walk outside, we are walking on the wrong path. We will destroy our own people and the earth as well.

One year it rained so much in the fall and springtime. We went out in the country and saw flowers growing that I had never seen in my life. They came back to life because they had the right ingredients and water. All we have to do is look and find them. We have to try and get people to understand where we are come from. Hang in there and keep fighting for what we believe.

"HANG IN THERE AND KEEP FIGHTING FOR WHAT YOU BELIEVE."

CHAPTER TWO

An interview with Danny Billy

(Seminole)

T wo hundred citizens of the traditional Seminole Nation, living in villages scattered throughout southwest Florida, persist in following their way of life in defiance of the dominant culture. They depend economically in part on subsistence hunting, fishing, and craft sales; build and use traditional structures for living and community gathering; speak the Seminole language and educate their children in the ways of their people as has been done for thousands of years.

Although the Seminoles hold a legal claim to five million acres, their right to live freely on their homelands has been disregarded by the agencies of government and corporate developers which continue the rapid destruction of the Everglades. The Seminole Nation is among the few Native nations to resist federal attempts to enclose them in reservations and remain one of the strongholds of Native traditionalism in its purest form. Danny Billy, spokesperson for the traditional Seminole Nation, states their philosophy this way: "You cannot live in the modern way and think in the traditional way. The way you live affects the way you think."

The Nation is committed to maintaining their traditional ways and beliefs. Crucial to this way of life is the Green Corn Dance which "defines who we are and what we are as traditional people. It is the heart and soul of our way of life." This ceremony had been held for 250 years in a remote area of cypress swamp and pine forest north of Lake Okeechobee. In the last several years, this land has been sold and most of it cleared, ditched, drained, and plowed up for citrus groves and other agricultural uses. Indigenous plants and animals, always plentiful under the stewardship of the Seminoles, are disappearing at an alarming rate. Marshes and waterways which provided habitats for endangered animals are gone. Seminole leaders search among the remaining wild lands, marshes, and forests north of Lake Okeechobee for a tract of land to secure as a permanent ecological preserve where they continue their traditional way of life, including the Green Corn Dance.

All photos in this chapter by Mark Madrid.

I became spokesperson for the people because of an incident that happened in the mid-1980s. We are not federally recognized or part of the Indian Reorganization Act reservations. We do not receive any federal aid. We work for what we get. The reservation people, the Seminole Tribe of Florida, Inc., were making a deal with the water district to sell a portion of their reservation for water rights. The written agreement was with the State, which was the negotiator between the water district and the Seminole Tribe. The agreement abolished all other land claims, any rights that any Indian tribe or nation had in the state of Florida. The Tribe agreed because they were going to be paid a lot of money. I don't know if they were blinded by the money, but they were going to go for it.

I was reading a newspaper one morning and caught what was going on. The way the agreement was written by the state was ambiguous but their intention was to wipe out any land claims. I caught wind of it and called our attorney at the Indian Law Resource Center. At the time I was not the spokesperson for my people. I had been to some of the meetings when I was younger. There was a span of four or six years when we had no representation. It all started up again when the Seminole Tribe wanted to sell a portion of their reservation which included our land claims. The way they had written it, the claim of any Indian in the state of Florida would be wiped out if the agreement went through.

I told some of my brothers and sisters, who were the first people to hear about it. They called a meeting. I heard everybody speak, the council, the elders and some of the young people. I listened to the things the people said about our teachings on right and wrong and our way of life. If this agreement went through, it would be the end of those things. I voluntarily started reading some of the letters and articles for them. I was not really appointed, I just started working with them. They put me in that position. That is how I became a spokesperson for my people.

"THEY SAY THAT WHEN YOU GO TO THE WHITE MAN'S SCHOOL, YOUR THINKING BECOMES LIKE HIS THINKING."

I graduated from high school but I don't have any college education. During those times, when I was still young and going to school, my mother always made sure that I used the Indian medicines. Every four months she put me on the medicine. They say when you go to the white man's school, your thinking becomes like his thinking. She put me on the medicine to keep me in line with our way of life while I was learning the non-Indian ways. I was fortunate to have what my mother gave me during those years when I was young and did not know what was better and right. She was my guide through my childhood and young adulthood.

When I was young, my older brothers, my mother and grandmother used to take me to my grandfather to listen to the teachings and the medicines. It seemed like he knew everything you wanted to know about. We would go down there and spend the nights and days with him. He would talk about anything you wanted to talk about, dances or ceremonial songs. I remember falling asleep or wanting to play, while I was sitting there listening. Whenever I fell asleep my mom would push my head, "Wake up." I would wake up and listen. The next thing I knew I would fall asleep again. Even though I did not hear all of it, I guess I was taking in what he taught to me. I don't remember seeing him speak, but I can still remember that he was teaching me. Even when I was off playing, I was listening to him from a distance.

I was fortunate to have people like that around while I was growing up. When I got to the point where I started becoming a spokesperson for my people, those teachings and ways helped me. They help me to walk on a fine line, so I don't wander onto that other road. I don't get mixed up in all this political stuff that we have to face every day. You got to walk your road and at the same time try to communicate with the other road. When you criss-cross these roads, you get into trouble. All those teachings they teach you when you are young to keep you in line on your road.

This helps me when I get confused about things that non-Indian people and Indian people who have criss-crossed those roads talk about. It is hard for them to come back and understand the way of the Indian people. It gets hard when those kinds of people cross my road. They don't understand who they are, what they are, and what they stand for when it comes right down to it. They are so much into that other road that their way of thinking is manipulated. It is complicated for them to understand their own ways of life. When I talk to people like that it throws me off a little bit. My strength comes from the teachings, the medicine and the way I grew up. Even to this day, we still live in the village and lead traditional lives.

A lot of Indian people have misunderstandings about their way of life. You can talk about the ways, the teachings, and what we need to do, but there are little things that are in between all of those things that people don't realize are important. The little things are the ones that matter the most. I had a visitor down in my village three weeks ago. She had a problem with her father. She was telling me that her father is a healer and helps a lot of people. When it comes to his family, the help wasn't there, and she was asking me why it was happening. She was getting sick from it.

"YOU HAVE TO KNOW YOUR PEOPLE FIRST."

I was telling her that that is what happens. You can reach way out there, help and heal people, and talk about these good things and traditional ways. In reality, you are not living that yourself because you have to take care of what is at home before you do that. Your foundation is the most important, your home, family, sisters, brothers, your own village or community. That is where you have to start because that is your strength. That is where you have to go back to revive yourself for the energy that you need in order to help other people in the distance. Once you lose that connection, you get into trouble and get sick yourself. You start losing faith in your own people, your home foundation. The people you are trying to help look to where you are coming from, your home base. Sometimes they question why you are talking about all these things you are not doing at home. That is the kind of question that pops into people's minds.

When you travel and help people you have to realize that it is the little things that matter. That is where you started from, your home. You have to know your people first, your brothers and sisters, your mother, father, and grandparents, before you start expanding your emotion, heart and mind to other people, other nations. If you don't do that, you will get into trouble. That is what I was telling her. She could see where her father was making these mistakes because he was not taking care of the home base, the foundation, where he was coming from. He was supposed to do medicine for her but he wasn't and she was getting sick.

We send our young children to public and boarding schools at a time when we should be teaching them our own way of life. When they are still young with a clean mind to learn our languages, the laws of our own ways, the songs, medicines and the ceremonies, that is what they should be learning. When you push them away at that young age, they learn a new way of life. That is where the damage comes in because they are learning a way of life that is not their own. When they get to an age where they can understand, they are going to have a hard time coping. At the same time they are going to have a hard time learning their own ways because they have grown up with another way. Mothers and fathers make a big mistake in not taking their young ones to learn their ways and language first before they go into public schools.

The thing we have to understand is that our way of life starts with teaching the young ones our language, laws and ceremonies at an early age. It is going to be hard to try and learn after they have grown up in another way. It is hard because by the time our children are at an age where they can understand and want to come back, they are too old to spend the quality time they need to learn. All the time we did not take to learn from our elders is the time we needed. Now that we are coming back to them and trying to learn, they are old and they are passing away. We are losing the laws, ways and teachings of our people.

But there are still some people out there who know each different nation's teachings, laws and languages. If you want to be who and what you are, you have to take the time to listen to those elders, so that you can learn those ways. When we were young, just born, we couldn't do anything for ourselves. When we were waking up and crying and barely moving, we couldn't do anything for ourselves. Our parents and our grandparents took care of us during those times. The teachings began when you first came out of your mother and woke up.

All those times, they sat up all night making sure that we slept well, dry and clean. They went sleepless nights. Sometime they were tired but they knew they had to take care of us and put us in this world the right way. When we get to an age where we can take care of ourselves, the roles are reversed—we have to look after them. They can't take care of themselves. That is the reason why we have to walk the walk to go to them, to learn these things from them. If we don't make the walk to hear the teachings, the laws of our own people, in reality we don't think too much of our own ways. When you don't do that, you are not taking that time to listen to those people.

When we talk about the environment and our way of life, it is all connected. When red people talk of our ways, land claims, and rights to self-determination, some white people look at us as greedy, wanting everything. They don't realize where we are coming from. They don't have common sense. When we talk about saving our rights, we are protecting them, too. We are the caretakers of the Creator's creation. It is our job to follow the instructions that he has given to us. If we don't do our job, then we are going to get fired. If we don't follow our own ways, our laws and ceremonies, the Creator is going to say that we are not doing our job and will clear everything and start all over again.

The survival of our people and all people in creation depends on our language, tradition and way of life. Those people are hurting themselves when they try to manipulate us into

their way of life. They are hurting themselves when they try to force the missionaries on us and when they try to take our way of life away. As the saying goes, they are creating their own death bed with the death of our people. They are not listening to what we are saying. When we go into court and fight for our rights and lose the case, not only do we lose, but everybody loses. No matter what color they are, no matter what part of the world they are from, everybody loses. The thing that we want to protect, that we are fighting for in our courts, has been overruled against us. The thing that we wanted to protect is gone forever because it is going to be destroyed.

A lot of people don't understand what they are doing because they don't fully understand where they are coming from. In order to understand where you are coming from, you have to born and taught with it. Even with our own people, some have been sent to school and come back wanting to learn. They have a hard time understanding some of the teachings. When you were born and raised in that way of life, you can understand it with common

"YOU HAVE TO START BY TEACHING THE YOUNG ONES."

sense. Everything is thought out with common sense. The complication comes in when you are not born with it. You don't understand it. You make it hard on yourself. When things are taught, told or shown to you, you start to question, you ask why. When you start asking questions, you lose your faith in your belief. Some things have no explanation. You have to understand that that is the way it is and believe in it. When you have grown up with those things, you understand.

You have to start by teaching the young ones the ways of life when they are clean in their minds. Once they have grown into this other world, it is hard to come back and learn every single bit of it. Our way of life is in the teachings. Every day, from the time you are born to the day you pass on, there is always a teaching. You never learn everything. People who say they know everything are lying because nobody knows everything. That is why it is important to support our way of life, in all the communities and nations. If there are the grassroots people within those communities or nations, the main concern with my people is to connect with them. We can understand each other and where we are coming from better than we can communicate with people who are trying to work within the political system.

"YOU CAN WORK ON THE WAY OF LIFE WE ARE TALKING ABOUT WITH JUST THE HEART AND THE MIND."

Sometimes, when I go to meetings, I have a hard time understanding what they are trying to accomplish. I am in the political system to a degree, but my heart and my thinking are in the roots of our way of life. I have a hard time understanding the political process that they go through to do some of the things that they do. Even as far as writing down notes or tape-recording, I can't comprehend that. I can't understand why you have to do that. You can work on the way of life we are talking about with just the heart and the mind. The way they want to do it gets into paper, pencils and computers. I personally don't like to get into that because that is where you are crossing to the other road. I can't understand why they want to do it that way.

Our way is still here. We can still communicate, understand and work with each other in our own way. I guess the hardest thing for me is why some of our own people can't understand who and what we are. They want to expand into the white man's way of doing things and distance themselves from the thing they are fighting for.

It is hard for me to sit through these meetings and listen to people talk. I can understand to a degree but when it comes down to it, I use the teachings that we were brought up with. When you get into these technologies, it's the white people's way of life and they know how to control it. They will have all the information you put on these computers and papers. They can get into things that you don't want them to get into. If we use our own way of communication then they will not be able to do this.

"WE HAVE BEEN FOLLOWING THE WAY WE ARE SUPPOSED TO FOLLOW."

A lot of people would listen to me and say "He is out of sync. He is out of this time or era." That is who we are, we can't get away from that. We are not going to give up everything we have, who and what we are. We can't comprehend living somebody else's way of life. We were given our own language, law, and form of government. We continue to live according to those ways, so we can protect and continue to the next generation. We take care like our ancestors did. We are not going to drop all that and adopt another way of life and another point of view.

We have a hard time understanding these other ways because we have been following the way we are supposed to follow. Don't misunderstand me, a lot of our teachings have been lost through the generations due to wars and oppression. In my travels visiting Native communities and nations across this continent, I see we are fortunate because our people fought to a stalemate with the United States government. Many of our ceremonies, medicines and teachings are still there.

We are losing our young ones. They are not listening because they are too much into the other society. For me, at the age I am, I can see both sides. I can see the elders' and the young people's side. I am the communicator of both the young and the elders. When the young ones can't understand what the elders are saying, I can explain it to them. When the young ones speak, the elders can't understand what they are saying, even in our own language. They are losing the ability to communicate in our own language. I can understand some of the things that they are talking about and relate to them in the right way, so that the elders can understand what they are saying.

You intend to keep all these things intact but as the white man's cities and communities converge upon our area, the young have more contact with the outside world. They get more interested in learning other ways. They can be manipulated into that society. There are things out there that they are interested in and that they want to do. Their responsibility is to continue our generations of people, our way of life and the teachings and the ceremonies and the songs. That is where I think the grassroots traditional people of our communities and nations are losing those young ones. They are being drawn to the cities and the easy life.

My oldest brother has this saying that explains it real clearly. He says, "The way of life of the red people is like a clay cup and the way of life of the white man is like a Styrofoam cup." The clay cup takes a lot of care because if you drop it, it is going to break. The Styrofoam cup does not take much caring; if you drop it, it doesn't break. You have to be real careful with the clay cup because if you put something hot in it, it will burn you. Compared to the Styrofoam cup which you use once and throw away, it takes a lot of work to keep a clay cup intact. The Styrofoam cup is the white man's way. They have no rules or regulations in their way of life. They say they do but in reality they do not.

The red man's way takes a lot of caring because everything around you helps you to live, breathe and walk on this earth. That is the difference between the clay cup and the Styrofoam cup. In the white man's way, there are no set rules for a way of life except for their own made-up rules. They make the laws, regulations and restrictions and figure they made them, so they can break them. But it is not okay for other people to do that. Their way of life is a double standard.

According to our ways, the laws are not made by people. The language is not made by people. Our ceremonies are not made by people. These things are gifts from the Creator. Our instructions, laws and way of life were given to us. We know for a fact that if we don't

"EVERYTHING AROUND YOU HELPS YOU TO LIVE, BREATHE AND WALK ON THIS EARTH."

follow these instructions, we are going to be punished. We have to maintain those laws and follow that way of life in order to survive as who we are. We have to help creation on this earth to continue.

In the other world, the white world, they take and they give nothing back. In some areas, they cut all the trees to make money. They don't think about where they are going to cut when there are no more trees. They don't realize the purpose of that tree in that area. They just don't care. They don't understand what is going to follow and that is a scary way of doing things. They think if they save one little area, that is going to help. It is not. The Creator made creation and put everything in its rightful place to maintain it. It is like the body of a person. If you remove an organ that is supposed to be in the body, the body starts deteriorating. It is the same thing.

The deterioration has already begun. The sinkholes in Florida are happening because the veins of the earth are being dried up. Even uranium has a purpose in making the earth function and continuing the life cycle. They are destroying all of these things, moving them from where they originated and putting them in another place. When they burn gas, it goes into the air, where it is not supposed to be. The different elements of the earth are in those places for a reason. If they continue to do those things, life as we see it on this earth is not going to be here any more. The end of creation is not far off. In our teachings, they tell us these things. The white professors and scientists go to university for many years to find out the way things work, things red people knew from the time of creation.

That is where another problem comes in. Some of our own red people think we need to reveal all this information to the white man but that is not the way it is. All those instructions go back to our way of life. That is our way of life. That is our identity, that is who we are. When you start giving away those things, you are not that same person anymore. You are selling yourself, giving yourself away. Some of these things we can talk about with other people but there are a lot of things we can't. It is for our own good.

We have a closer relationship with grassroots people of different communities and nations than we have with Native people in the political arena. I have a hard time understanding some of them. They are red people but when they talk about things, I can't see where they are coming from. I can't see their roots. Sometimes they say good things but when you look at them on the outside and the inside, they are different. They are not talking from the heart and they are not talking from the mind. A lot of my work comes in understanding where a person is coming from when I speak to them. I watch the body language, facial structure, and movements even if they are just walking or talking to somebody else. You can see people and understand them that way. It takes a lot of teaching to learn to do that. That is what I focus on when I try to understand people.

I play devil's advocate because I always try to see the negative side. Everybody talks about the positive and the good things but you know that somewhere along the line there is going to be a problem. So I try to ask, what happens if this doesn't go through? What happens if we have a breakdown? What happens if what we are talking about doesn't come through? What happens if this person is not telling us the truth? What happens if he takes all this information and gives it to the wrong people? What happens if these people take the information and use it against us later?

Dreaming of things that are going to happen in the future is good. At the same time, we have to face reality in order to reach our goals. We want to talk about good and peaceful times, anything that is positive, but that is not our reality. We are still being oppressed to the point that we are losing our way of life. Our lifeway is who and what we are.

It is like I was saying about walking the two roads. You walk the fine line when you are dealing with white people. They are very tricky. That is why we call them "forked tongue" or "two heads." These people have ways of manipulation, they buy people, and they are good with trickery. They are connivers. I do my best to watch out for them. I have gone to meetings and talked like this and not made people happy. That is just the way it is. I am not going to sit there, lie and make things rosy for everybody so that they can feel good coming away from that meeting. If I am given the opportunity to speak, I speak on the reality, not on these dreams.

Your work has to come from your heart and your mind, for the love of your people, not the love of fame and fortune. I get upset when they talk about money because that is the very thing that is destroying our way of life. In this day and age, I know we need some money to function and travel. When you get to the point of choosing your way of life according to a system of money, you are in trouble. You are not who you are anymore. I see a lot of people in that position nowadays. They talk about the tradition and ways and laws but when it comes down to it, it is money that is making people talk like this. The things I do and say are what I believe, what I live, and for the people I dedicate my life to.

This is personal. If I lose these teachings and this way of life, I am nothing. I'm not anybody anymore. I see it from that point of view. When I represent my people, I don't look for fame and fortune. On this trip, I came with nothing. I was fortunate that the people here provided me with an airplane ticket. As far as money for food, I came with nothing. I came because I knew that what I was doing was for the survival of my people as who and what they are. That is what keeps me going.

You know when you do the right thing, somewhere down the line you will get a reward in return, not in money. It is a good feeling that I get from helping people. When I see a person sitting there not feeling well or happy, I dedicate my time to that person. I talk to them to make them happy. If there is anything I can do for that person within my skill and ability, I am more than welcome doing that. Strength comes for me from seeing people happy. The high for me is to see that person who was sad continue what they need to do.

The only thing that I don't like about meetings is the last day when you have to say, "We'll see you again, until next time." The things I do in life for my people energize me. They keep me going. If I go home and don't do anything or just sit around, I get concerned, I feel like I am not doing my job. I need to be doing something. I am always on the go because of the energy it gives me to do the work I need to do.

My immediate family depends on me for a lot of things, not only to speak for them or carry their words to other places, but within the community, within my own family. I am the next in line of my mother who passed away. Every decision or question that is asked comes to me. They look to me for direction. It is hard when you are a spokesperson and the head of the family.

When I do something for somebody and they feel happy and good inside, I feel the same way. When I see somebody sad or hurt, I am hurt and sad. My energy comes from the joy and the smile on the faces of people able to laugh when we are oppressed almost to the point of extinction. We work hard to a point where we get worn out or what people call "burned out". We have to take the time to enjoy ourselves and the company of our own people. It is amazing because despite everything that has happened to us, we still exist as who and what we are and at the same time, we enjoy and laugh with each other. My energy comes from those times.

Our people need to take the time to nourish themselves and cleanse themselves of all of the things they are working on. If you don't, you are going to get burned out and sick. You may end up dying because of the stress and problems that exist among our different communities and nations. It builds within the system of the body and deteriorates your thinking and physical being. It is good to take the time to break away and to cleanse yourself and replenish your energy. I am replenished when I see the people happy, enjoying each other, or playing games with each other. That is purification. We all need to purify ourselves in our own way.

The main thing that my nation, community, family and myself try to accomplish is maintaining and effectively passing on our own way of life, laws, tradition, and ceremony to the next generations. To make sure it all stays intact, so that the next generations, who are not here yet, will have the understandings and the ways we have. Hopefully, they will do the same. In the political arena, we do what we can to protect those ways, so that our people can continue without the interruption of the outside world. This is hard. It needs a lot of caring. It is my purpose to watch out for those things that interrupt or intervene with our way of life. It is a hard road to walk but if you look at it with common sense, it is not hard at all. You are who you are, you know what your laws are, you know what your way of life is, and so you just follow it. That is it. The thing that makes it hard is when the outside intervenes, crosses your path, or tries to take your ways away from you.

That is where I come in. I try to keep all these threats away from the people, so they can live the way of life the Creator intended for them. We want to be who we are. We have our own way of life. We have our own laws. We have our own government and self-determination. We have our own way of dealing with our problems within our own communities and nations, and with other nations. We have our own way of understanding the structure of the earth, the elements of the earth and the environment. We feel like the outside world has no understanding of these things. Yet, they are trying to take our way of life away, manipulate and assimilate us into their world. We are fighting to live our way of life as it is.

"YOU KNOW WHAT YOUR WAY OF LIFE IS, SO YOU JUST FOLLOW IT."

We Are Becoming Yankee-Doodle-

CHAPTER THREE

An interview with Tommy Porter

(Akwesasne Mohawk)

Tommy Porter is one of the leaders of a group of traditional Mohawks from Akwesasne, a nation of the Haudenosaunee Iroquois Confederacy, who are securing a community in which to reestablish their traditional lifestyle on lands they once occupied in Mohawk Valley. *"Kanatsiohake,"* the Mohawk name for this area in New York State, has been established on a land base of several hundred acres with an intent to expand to 1000 acres. Families from Akwesasne, Kahnawake, and Tyendinega who are followers of the traditional, spiritual, and political beliefs of the Rotinonshonni are relocating to Kanatsiohake. They represent a spiritual movement by Mohawk people who believe the key to their survival is securing new lands and propagating an environment conducive to the relearning and sharing of their traditional beliefs.

The families of Kanatsiohake feel that the events of the past several years in their home community of Akwesasne have weakened the ability of traditionally-minded Mohawk people to practice their lifestyle and pass the language, culture, and spiritual and political beliefs on to their children. In traditional Mohawk belief, it is the responsibility of each individual to make decisions based on the "seven generations" philosophy. Cultural and spiritual preservation being the cornerstone of Mohawk future, some feel that the future seven generations have little chance of healthy survival. Kanatsiohake represents the fulfillment of a Mohawk prophecy which describes a movement of young Mohawks who will lead their people to safety.

The Mohawk way of life is practiced in Kanatsiohake. Community members use Mohawk for everyday expression to halt the language's slide towards extinction. The community works with the Iroquoian tradition of farming, raising beef, planting orchards, white corn, and berries, and seeding fish. Homes for families will include alternative energy technologies. Following the first three years of this implementation phase, an Onkwehonwe Spiritual Center is planned to provide teaching in Native spirituality and culture.

All photos in this chapter by Sally White.

When the Europeans first came here, the Mohawk Indian people had our principal villages and communities in the place which they call the Mohawk Valley. The Mohawk Valley is a geographic area which encompasses the region of present-day Albany, the capital of New York. We call that area *"Skanetate"* in Mohawk. Later Americans anglicized this pronunciation and the area became known as the town of Schenectady, though the word actually means the whole Albany region. This is the original Mohawk homeland and it goes clear across one hundred miles almost to Utica.

The lands at Akwesasne [St. Regis Reservation] are almost two hundred miles north of this original Mohawk homeland and were the traditional hunting grounds of the Mohawks of these villages. To avoid further killing and bloodshed, this is where we went.

The English colonizers here in the Americas tried to take over this entire country and they used certain Mohawks, namely Joseph Brant, to do it. They took him, a full blooded Mohawk, to England, and anglicized him. They took him to England and taught him how to be a soldier in the British Army. They gave him fancy dinners and he rubbed elbows with kings and queens and the hierarchy of English society. They babied him, pampered and nurtured him. They made his ego get so big he wasn't a Mohawk anymore. Then they sent him back to try to enlist the support, through whatever means, of the Iroquois peoples, to fight on the side of the British.

In the war between the English and the American colonists, the Six Nations government officially declared neutrality The English insisted Joseph Brant override the Iroquois confederacy itself, and they were successful because of the years they invested in him. He provided money or opportunities to the Iroquois men who would fight with him and the British against the colonists. In other words, he created mercenaries in defiance of the Chiefs of the Six Nations' neutral stance. He infuriated the colonists and caused the new Americans, the new United States, to hate the Mohawk people, any Iroquois. General Washington ordered General Sullivan to wipe the Iroquois from the face of the earth as a result of Joseph Brant. The English were able to use their pawn to terrorize the colonists' towns and burn them down. The colonists, who saw one Indian as every Indian, began to retaliate and burn our houses and shoot down our people as animals.

That is part of the reason why the Iroquois had to leave the Mohawk Valley. According to the treaties, the colonists weren't supposed to be there, encroach upon those lands nor build towns there. That's a general history of how, under forced conditions, we left the Mohawk Valley and went to Akwesasne. Others went to Kanawake, other Mohawks went to Toronto, others ended up at Six Nations with Joseph Brant. This reminds me of the Jewish people who were scattered all over the world for two thousand years and then returned to reclaim their homeland. We have only been scattered for two hundred years and are trying to do like the Jewish people did—go back to our sacred homeland where the Creator gives us the right to be.

When the Mohawks left the Valley, certain elders made predictions that one day our grandchildren, our great-grandchildren would return home. I don't know if it is a prophecy, but I could say it has all of the elements. It takes about half an hour to recite, so I will just generalize. It involves the two snakes, the silver and the gold snake, which were found and nourished by the Indian people and became monsters. They grew bigger and bigger. They nourished these two snakes, one silver and one gold, until the snakes became so big they attacked the Indian people and took over our land.

We were told that the gold and silver snake would destroy our people and cause them to argue. They would cause them to question the way they value things and make decisions. And when that happened, people would become panicked and they would argue with each other about who had the best idea to destroy this great evil. There would be great arguments about what is evil and what is not. While they were busy arguing about who had the best way to get rid of this evil thing, those snakes with their great power would be devouring people by the hundreds. That is what is happening all over the country now.

These two snakes are the United States and Great Britain or Canada, and they have disrupted our life, our dreams, our vision. They have suppressed us in such a way that most Indians cannot find comfort in their own being anymore. It leaves our people restless and without direction, unable to focus on what our ancestors did and what we are supposed to do, our duties on this earth, who we are supposed to be. We can't focus on this any more, and so it has created panic, confusion, struggle and unclear vision.

Most Indians, all over the country, are now in that state. We don't know how to make a judgment or an informed choice as authentic indigenous people. The choices that ninety-nine percent of all Indians in this country make today are based on second-hand information and second-hand spirit. Second-hand manufactured Indians are the product of United States. Indians are not Indians anymore, most of them. They think based on the value of the institutions, Carlisle Indian School, Spanish Indian School, Thomas Indian School. There are Indians all over the country who are choosing a second-class system of values. Their values are not really Indian anymore. Their decisions are not informed based on their Indianness, but based on their American education, Christianity and greed.

I fear for the people from the little that I know. I spent a good thirty years of my life, in my youth, studying from the elders, not only from the Iroquois, but from elders all across the country, who still understand the old ancient ways. The Iroquois were told not to touch five things which the White Brother was going to bring from across the salt water, five things that he would use to defeat, suppress and manipulate the Indian. The Creator said not to touch these five things or otherwise they would lead to our destruction and dismay.

We were told not to touch the black book of the white brother, I guess that's the Bible, meaning the religions of the white man; the fiddle, for that will take you away from your sacred drums and your sacred rattles, and it will cause men and women to break up the sacredness of marriages and families; playing cards and gambling, for the white man will take all our land from us with it; mind changers, any substance that alters the natural state of your mind and your thinking—alcohol, whisky, wine, marijuana, cocaine, anything that changes your natural state of mind; and the last one was a bag of decayed leg bones—that means European witchcraft and disease. We were told that these were the things that he would use to conquer us. Don't touch those things and you will survive.

The traditional Iroquois try to follow this, so that we can remain Iroquois, and remain free from these things. That is what our longhouses are about. That is why we don't mix our spiritual ways if we follow the Longhouse Indian Way. We are not Catholic or Baptist or anything else because we are told not to do that. We are already mixed up enough as it is.

I see Indians all over the country today bringing bingo and casinos onto their reservations. That will destroy our Indian lands, and bring municipal laws, and create municipalities out of all the Indian lands. Casinos are not a morally good thing, I don't care how you cut it. They may bring temporary fast income, but they are evil.

Indians all over the country are heralding the great economic boom of casinos and this is what will destroy us once and for all. The American doesn't have to clobber us—we will clobber each other. We will lose the support that we have had these past years. How do you rally and support casinos, which are not morally good? It is not like somebody flooding your land.

The fifth thing that we were told to stay away from is the sickness that came from the white man. I have been thinking that this also applies to nuclear waste. There is a spiritual prayer which says that long ago, there was a strong power of a monster, which was placed under the ground. The teaching said that it should remain beneath the ground, because it is so powerful. Thunder with its arrows of lighting suppresses the power of this monster and keeps it under the ground. If ever that monstrous thing were to come out of the ground, just to see it for a moment would kill you, that's how powerful it is. I believe they were talking about how nuclear radiation is supposed to stay under the ground, not come out, because it would destroy thousands of people. This is in the prayers of the ancient ones.

At any rate, this is going on all over the country now and it's a very sad thing. I don't know if there's any good coming out of it except to make Indians into good little white people. I think it is sad. We do have to make a living but to me, that is no justification for gambling.

For the first time, Indians are signing compacts which open the door to the state and federal governments to control our affairs, and so our sovereignty is gone, given away, signed away. These compacts give them permission to tax us a percentage of the revenue from these bingo halls and casinos. Eventually the states will make it legal to have casinos. When that happens, nobody is going to come to Indian reservations. And the state and federal governments now have a paper with our leaders' signatures on it, saying that they can collect taxes. They are really doing it nice. Our leaders are so blind to put our sacred land in such jeopardy. They are so nearsighted, it's pitiful. Well anyway, you can't dwell on the negative, no matter how negative it is. You have to try to find positive things, so you can survive. Otherwise you will get sick and die. This brings us to what the move to the Mohawk Valley is about.

"WE WILL BECOME YANKEE-DOODLE-WENT-TO-TOWN KIND OF PEOPLE."

In the meantime, our language is dying. A lot of Indians across the United States have already lost their languages. Some Indian Nations have only two fluent speakers and when they are gone, the language will be gone forever. Some have ten years left before they lose theirs. Some linguists say that one's language represents fifty to sixty percent of traditions, culture, values, and spiritualism. These things are inherent in the language. Once the language is lost you lose fifty to sixty percent of who you are. Whole nations have lost their languages. The Iroquois have less than 20 years and then we will be extinct too.

That is not to say that there won't be Iroquois who are fluent. I'll be an old man and I'll be fluent yet. What will be gone is the ability of my generation to transmit fluency in our language to the next generations—that's what will be dead. It's just a matter of time until individuals who are fluent and old will die, one after another. The number of able-bodied people who will be fluent will have gone below the level where the language can naturally flow to the next generation. Even if everybody became awakened to and conscious of this fact, it's almost too late, and there are a lot of doubts as to whether it can be revived. Nobody knows because this has never happened before. It is going to be a hard job. These are some of the decisions that are not even being addressed, except in a very superficial kind of way.

Without the language, there will be no more ceremonies, they will close the longhouse down. Old people told us, once the language is gone, you can't run your ceremony anymore. Got to put away the drums, put away the sacred things, and because they don't understand any other language, our spirit will be dead. Then we will just become a Yankee-Doodle-went to-town kind of a people. We'll just do whatever other people do in any small town in the United States. Worry about how we are going to pay the taxes, worry about policemen and whatever is out there. So, no more stories, no more history, no more spirit, we just become Sunday churchgoers like everybody else.

When the thunder comes we don't know anything about thunder except that it's a nuisance and it makes a miserable-looking day, just like Americans say when it rains, "Oh, it's an awful day today." Indians will be saying that too. In the past, when it rained, we always prayed and we thanked the Creator for the wonderful rainy day, for everything that will grow. That will be no more.

There will be no more Sun Dance. The sun is going to kill us with its ultraviolet radiation because of the depletion of the ozone layer. Instead of saying to the sun, "Thank you, sun, for brightening the day and warming the earth, so that all life will grow," now you have to put your shield up and think, "Oh sun, don't kill me, don't give me cancer." That's what Indians are going to have to do, like Americans are doing. Unless we can stop.

Our people say that when you put away your sacred things, like your rattles, drums and the things you use to thank the Creator, then the earth doesn't recognize you anymore, Mother Earth doesn't recognize you as her child anymore. The rivers don't recognize you and the wind doesn't know you either, and the thunder and the lightning don't know you anymore, the stars and the moon and the sun don't know you. The birds don't know who you are because you no longer sing to them, you no longer praise them, you no longer thank them individually with song and prayer and dance. They will not help you anymore either. You'll be in a bad way. When the thunder comes it may hit you, when the earthquake comes it may knock your house down, when the tornado comes it may blow you far away and hurt you, and when the sun shines it may burn you. All the things that were our friends—they won't know us anymore and we will die.

The songs we use in ceremonies are what recharges the world in friendship. The ceremonies we do, the tree hears them and they feel good and they grow. When they don't hear that anymore, everything will die. The world will die because the spirit of life is dying, that's what it means. In the meantime, casinos are being built by the Paiute, Omaha, Winnebago, Lakota and even the Iroquois are trying now. What's the priority? Oh my God, what's the priority? It's so sad. That's why there are people who still believe in the old traditions. Universal truth knows no time, and it doesn't get old or lose its fashion.

"OUR PEOPLE SAY THAT WHEN YOU PUT AWAY YOUR SACRED THINGS, THE EARTH DOESN'T RECOGNIZE YOU ANYMORE."

The Mohawk Valley is an attempt by Iroquois, particularly Mohawk people, to remove ourselves from the pettiness, foolishness, and the misjudgment of today and return to making real decisions. To go back to our homelands where we can refocus on our traditions, language, and ceremonies, to learn to work hard and to have an honest life based as close to Mother Earth as we can get without being too foolish. So we can have visions and dreams again like our grandmothers and grandfathers did when the world was new. They had great visions, and that is what the new place in the Mohawk Valley is. It is a chance to take the goodness of our people and give it space where it can grow.

That's what we're going to try to do. We are not saying that this will result in success because there is no blueprint, no formula that says you do this and it will work for you. So we go there only with a desire and hope that what we do will be beneficial to our children, that our unique identity as Mohawk people will become stronger, and we will make our people happy as they live on this earth. That is what we are about. That is going to be our attempt. We may fail but at least we will have done it with the intent of benefit to our people. If we fail we will have at least given it our best shot. That is our hope.

We have learned over the years that the human being is not accustomed to rapid, radical change. If you want to change, you have to do it in a manageable time frame if you're going to be successful. We'll have to set our goals from where our reality is right now and begin the changes where it is manageable and comfortable, so that we don't defeat our own purpose or suppress or kill our energy or our hope. We are not going there like a hippie movement, to renounce this and defy that. What we're going to do is start right from our reality today, the way we are accustomed to right now.

The first couple of years we are going to review all of our teachings. What do we remember about what our religious leaders told us, what do we remember of our elders, of our ways? We will accustom ourselves to the teachings, what they say and what they mean. This will create the possibility that together we can pull the big load at the same exact moment, so that we carry the load easily.

It is going to take a couple of years to get ourselves refocused, so that we can begin to dream and see clearly again that which most people cannot see today. Then we will identify goals that will enhance our uniqueness. We are not going to have instant traditional community. Our goal is to get there at some point. We don't know how long it's going to take us and we don't know if we're going to be successful. We are going to try to be very realistic about it, so at least we will enjoy and be satisfied doing it. If we rush then anger begins to develop and we defeat what we are trying to do. So it means a lot of meetings and a lot of healthy arguments. We are not used to that, so it's frightening. I might get scared, I might even run away for a little while, but I know that it's needed, so I'll return. If I get scared I'll run away for as long as it takes to get enough nerve to go back, but I know that's what has to happen. I hope others will know it too.

The four sacred rituals of the Iroquois are the basic principles which will form the foundation of our community. The same as it is in the longhouse now, except that there will be no alcohol or drugs allowed anywhere on the new land. If anybody has a problem, we will work with them, but they can't live here. They will have to rehabilitate themselves and once they do that they can come back to us. Right now we are not equipped to deal with alcoholics or people with drug addictions. We are not trained in that.

So, the Great Law, the four sacred rituals, and the Gaiwio will be the principles, the value systems and the ceremonial practices of our people. Christian Mohawks are welcome because they are our relatives. They are welcome but we have agreed they can't build a church here. There is already a church here. There is no need to build one because our community is trying to return to the way the Creator made us, not the way the Europeans made us or the way we made ourselves. The Creator gave us ceremonies all year long according to the stars, the moon and the different things that grow. These are thanksgivings to all of the life forces.

The one rule of the universe is that everything has life. Human beings, animals and birds really appreciate it when you say, you are important and thought of with compassion and love. Everybody appreciates that and it makes them feel good. If you are compassionate to a dog, the dog will wag its tail and follow you to the end of the world. If you talk and sing to the corn, it grows healthy and strong.

When the Sun Dance is done, the sun feels strong and committed and will continue to give you the things you need to live. The Indian way is a whole series of songs, dances, and speeches that say, "You are important and we say thank you." You give us the important things we need to live and so we say thank you in a special way by singing, dancing, and saluting you, the corn, trees, wind, thunder, sun, moon, ocean, grass, birds, deer and all the other animals, everything that's life. That is what the Indian way is, saying thank you to all of them. They are important, so that we and our children may live.

That is what it is, a series of songs, speeches and dances of expressing thankfulness to those powers and their combined powers, which is what we call the Creator. The Creator is that of many faces, beings and powers. You could say that all of those things of power and life are what we call "Creator" and it's as simple as that. No big institution, no big technicality, no need for universities. It is so simple, but yet people don't know anything about it. We are attempting to understand that again.

We are studying viable alternative economic ideas, so that we can physically survive. We are going to work with the State University of New York at Albany. The professors and the vice-president have offered us any help we many need in terms of economic programs, lawyers, engineering, or alternative energies. We want to incorporate technology that is harmonious to nature and the earth as much as we possibly can.

We need the combined effort of good minds, wherever they may be found. We are not going there as isolationists. We are going there so we can have a chance to focus. We want privacy, but we don't want to isolate ourselves. We want to be open and talk to Asian, black, or white people, or whomever has good ideas about life; but we don't want to lose who we are in the process, either. We are always willing to exchange ideas, even spiritual thoughts with others.

In the third or fourth year, we hope to open up a center where we will give classes to people about history according to our viewpoint, Mohawk philosophy, Iroquois spirituality–without mimicking something and without selling it.

"WE NEED THE COMBINED EFFORTS OF GOOD MINDS WHEREVER THEY MAY BE FOUND."

Right now the land is held by a corporation called the Viola Whitewater Memorial Foundation, which is based in Harrisburg. Viola Whitewater was a Shawnee woman who used to help the Indians all over the country by taking clothes to them. Her son began this foundation in her memory and continues to help traditional people, especially in the areas of education, tradition and culture. We put the land in the name of the foundation for the time being. We don't want to put the land in trust because none of the Iroquois lands are held in trust. They are our lands. Out west, all the reservations are held in trust, which means the land is not really theirs. Eventually this land will be the same as all Six Nations lands.

Another reason we are going there is because of the pollution from toxins at Akwesasne. You can't eat the fish anymore. Fluoride was emitted from the aluminum factory on the grasslands that our animals eat, it destroyed the whole cattle industry that we had there. When treaties were made, the United States government was supposed to watch out for anything dangerous to the Indian people. They were supposed to protect the Indian people, so they could live in peace. There is the basis of a legal grievance, which will help us to re-establish this land as Six Nations land. The only way we will be able to do that is if we befriend the people in the area, as well as in Congress, and explain to them the justification in moral, as well as legal grounds. If you use a positive mind and a compassionate heart, many things can get done, if you are not side-tracked.

"MOHAWK VALLEY TOOK TWENTY-FIVE YEARS TO MATURE INTO REALITY."

I've been wanting to do this for twenty-five years. It's like an apple that starts to grow on the tree in the spring. You have to wait for the apple, wait until it grows, turns red, and falls to the ground, before you can eat it. That is when it tastes the best, that's when it's good to eat. If you pick it prematurely it can make you sick. Mohawk Valley took all these years to mature into reality. It is just the beginning, because I don't know how strong we are. I don't know how much the Indian way of living and understanding of Indianness is within our comprehension. Then, when it is within our comprehension, how strong are we to make it a reality, so that we walk our talk instead of just calling it from the pulpit? That's what the young need if they are going to have good teachers. This is frightening, because we will be living in the fishbowl like they say. People will be looking at us from all over the world.

There were a lot of things that led up to this. Our White Roots of Peace group met with the people before they went to Alcatraz. White Roots traveled all over the country in the 1960s and 1970s. The Freedom School, alcohol programs, Partridge House with the rehabilitation of drug and alcohol abusers, all of these elements together caused this to reach fruition. It took many years. It is important for young people to realize that sometimes things that you need or ask for may not happen next week or next month. It may not even occur in your life, but it may, if your belief is strong, occur in your grandchildren's lives. This is what I feel has happened here. The seed was planted when they left the Mohawk Valley. They said that one day, the grandchildren will return. That was two hundred and twenty years ago, and now it has happened.

My message for the young people is this: leave the alcohol and the drugs alone, you've got enough damn problems just to live with life itself. Our teachings and the Creator told us not to touch that. Alcohol and drugs make you forget who you are, forget your responsibility to your brother, sister, mother, grandma, uncle. They make you forget your responsibility to your community, they terrorize your family, your community, and they even terrorize your own self. It is a negative power that does not need to be part of your life.

The other thing is, go back to the traditions of your ceremonies. In Iroquois, it says, "Leave the black book to the man across the ocean who needs to carry it every day." Indian young people, go back to your traditions and put them in your heart and in your mind. Carry them so they live and don't accumulate dust but are protected by the power and the strength of your body and your life.

The next one is, never abuse women, never hit women, emotionally or physically. Honor the woman. Woman is like the Earth Mother, she has to give birth and she has to give compassion. She can't become scarred because her job is too big and important. You can't abuse the woman, because if you do, you abuse your children and grandchildren. This is why you must always respect the woman, because she is like the Mother Earth. She gives the next life to come, so she must be wholesome, respected and dignified to be able to pass the same on to her kids.

Every time the ceremony is going, I encourage the young people and their families to get their children all together and go to that ceremony. This is where they can hear the words of our Creator and the intent for human beings, the way we are supposed to live on this earth, so they will have a spiritual knowledge and guidance. Know who you are, and if you don't know who you are, then hurry up and start searching. Find out who you are because once you become fathers and mothers, your responsibility is to transmit all that knowledge to your kids. People have no business making a baby if they are not prepared to help that baby develop into a real human being.

Find out the truth of the history, too; what really happened. Look at it with an open mind and don't let resentment warp your vision. Take it, look at what happened, study it and know it inside and out. Learn from it, but don't let it cause resentment and sour your thinking. Use it in the proper way so that our ancestors have not suffered for nothing. Use that suffering, so that it will help us as a people. If you have resentment, if you scold and yell at your kids, they aren't going to listen to you. They will get mad and resent you because you are yelling at them. Whatever you're trying to say as you're yelling isn't worth two cents. If you talk with compassion and peace then people will listen.

If you are going to plant anything good, you've got do it with love and compassion. If you're going to talk to the white people about history, you can say that what has happened is beyond your control and mine. It happened. We can't do anything to stop it, but we can do something to keep it from repeating, if we can understand what happened and why it happened. If you stand up there with a gun, wave your fist and defy this and that, you're going to get a fight. Do you want to fight? It is not energy efficient. It's a waste of time and doesn't help anything.

Find the truth and share your feelings of that truth. If that truth involves pain, share it in a compassionate way, and from that good things will grow.

Once You Walk With Your Spirit Again,

It is Easier to Find The Way

CHAPTER FOUR

An interview with Juanita Perly

(Maliseet)

Juanita Perley is a Turtle Clan Mother of the Maliseet Nation, an Algonquin-speaking people of southeastern Canada. She lives in Tobique, one of seven Maliseet reserves. At one time, twenty-seven Algonquin Nations were joined together in a vast confederacy which encompassed Ontario, Quebec, New Brunswick, Nova Scotia, Prince Edward Island, Labrador, Maine, Massachusetts, New Hampshire, Connecticut, New Jersey, and part of New York. Several Alquonquin nations remain on the east coast, while others migrated west in fulfillment of a prophecy, and some were forcibly removed to places as far away from their original homelands as Oklahoma.

As an East Coast nation, the Maliseet were among the first people to feel the impact of the European invasion of North America. They have been exposed to European influences for most of the last 500 years.

Juanita has been working actively to bring back Maliseet cultural traditions, practices, teachings, and ceremonies; strengthen the clan system of her nation; and revitalize the Wabanaki Alliance. She and her son, Perry, chief of the Turtle Clan, are reintroducing traditional Maliseet principles into tribal government. She is a grandmother and provides traditional guidance to many Native people of the eastern Algonquin nations.

A woman came to interview me when New Brunswick had its bicentennial and invited me to speak in a town nearby. I declined but she kept insisting. She asked, could she interview me on the Bicentennial about the good that Canada has brought to the Indian people? I told her, "What you are going to hear is not going to be something you want to hear. In this short two hundred years, you've turned our Mother Earth into a huge garbage dump. Our rivers are nothing but sewers. We lived the way the Creator placed us here. Nothing was disturbed. Just think, in the short time that you have been here, this is what has become of our Mother."

Photograph in this chapter by JJ FOXX/NYC.

"You believed in your small minds that we did not have a government when you got here. You couldn't comprehend our complex governmental structure. You were so used to the ways of the old country where you had kings, queens and peasants who owned nothing. When your people got here it was like walking into a paradise, but only the peasants recognized the paradise. All your leaders saw when you walked onto our land was dollar signs."

"THE SPIRITUAL WAYS WERE THE FIRST THINGS THEY TRIED TO TAKE."

The culture, the spiritual ways were the first things they tried to take. All the spiritual instruments were taken and destroyed. When priests began infiltrating our reserves, it seemed like they had made a deal with the government. Wherever Indians settled around a church, you never heard of a massacre. When the scalp bounty started here in Canada in 1756, most of the traditional people headed up river. Some settled here in Tobique and the ones that chose to be baptized remained back in King's Clear. Baptism is like an exorcism to Indian people. All my children were baptized except for one. I find their road is harder.

It takes a long time to remove the cross they burn on your forehead. Once it does come off and your spirit walks with you as one again, it is easier to find the old ways. After they stripped us of our spiritual ways and our medicines, a lot of people began dying. What they did not kill off with their scalp bounties and wars, they killed through their education. They built schools wherever the Indians settled and started massive brainwashing in our communities with the white man's religion, culture, history, and language.

I fought real hard when my children were going to be integrated into the white school. As time went on, I really began wondering how much deep damage had been done. I speak only Maliseet at home. When forced integration came and they had to move to the white schools nearby, they began to suffer because they could not speak the white man's language. For the last five younger ones, when I could not win the battle, I switched them over to all English. I regret today that I did because language is the heart of our people. Our language is what opens the doors to the past, to the knowledge of our ancient grandfathers and grandmothers.

When you look at a culture and see it dying, a great sorrow hangs on you. I wished so many good things for my people. I knew that no matter what came to distract me, I had to keep firm on this road, the same way as my sister. The gentle and diplomatic one, my sister, took a kinder and more lenient view of the corruption that the white man brought. She began teaching dancers way back in the 1960s and had a troupe traveling around. She put together a language program and had it in the school.

"WHEN I WENT TO FAST FOR THE FIRST TIME, I BEGAN TO SEE THE MISSING PIECES."

We had the first traditional gathering in the 1970s shortly after Wounded Knee. My sister brought elders from all over. The Iroquois traditional travelers were called the White Roots of Peace. I had the privilege of talking to the elders that came. They read the wampum belts, talked of the prophecies and left us teachings, gave us a foundation we could start building on.

Our Iroquois brothers had opened a door for us. I used to envy them when they spoke of their clans because I did not have a clan. I used to wish I had one too. I wished I could look back and see how much we had. I began reading books, old interviews, but there were always parts of the books missing. They were like puzzles. When I went too fast the first time, I came back and started reading again. I began to see the missing pieces of those interviews where the grandfathers had left messages. Those blanks began filling in. The more I fasted, the more blanks filled in. I always knew we had to have language. The language had to come back because only in your own language can you talk from your heart, not your mind. The teachings that the elders bring you, the grandmothers and grandfathers, are in our language. Although I am pretty good in our language, there are words that they speak that I can't understand. But they will point to something, so that you will know what they are trying to tell you in the real old language.

One day my sister told me, "You are wasting too much energy on hating the white man. Concentrate your efforts on finding the old ways." But I never listened. I joined every militant movement there was floating by. I joined Red Power and then when AIM came along I joined that. Though I could not get to where they were, I supported them. I thought, somewhere along the line there has got to be a beginning for us.

When people told me our culture was dead, I never believed it. I knew it had to be there somewhere. I thought that instead of wondering what happened to our culture, I should focus on trying to find a way to bring it back. Our ancestors would not leave without a clue on how to get it going again. There had to be a way. I would sit and cry sometimes, thinking about when the pipes, the drums, the rattles were taken, when our longhouses and sweat lodges were burned. I thought, well, why not build them again? Anything that is burned can be rebuilt again. We will make new pipes, we will make new lodges, and we will rebuild our longhouses. We will rebuild our nation and we will look to our ancestors and seek the Great Law that we had put to sleep for a while. The teachings started coming. They started coming back. It was not easy. Twenty years and I still have to say today, we know so little.

Culture and tradition to me are just like getting up in the morning, opening your eyes and being happy that you were born an Indian. This is how I have always felt. I would not want to have been born anything else.

When I arrived on the Tobique Reserve in 1947, I was eight years old. No one spoke English on this reserve, not even the children. I had been raised in a white community and my training had all been white but I understood Maliseet because it was all my family spoke. No one would talk to me in English, so I had to make up my mind real fast to talk Indian. I began making replies in Indian. I always noticed how droning, how songlike the Maliseet language is. In school, where the white man talks English, it is like you are talking in your throat. When you talk Maliseet, it comes from deeper within.

I always did very well in school except for going to church. We were lucky here, the school was right on the reservation. The nuns did not have us twenty-four hours a day, just eight hours a day. But in areas when children were transported to residential schools, they lived under vile and inhumane conditions. You were not allowed to speak your language. There was physical, mental and sexual abuse. These places were run by nuns and priests, people you were supposed to be able to trust. The language was pounded out.

So we began fighting, my sister and me, to have our language in the school. She taught for three years until the program ran out and they did not continue it. We started fighting again to have language teaching in this school and even today, only kindergarten has it. The government knew. They knew how to bring down the Indian nation. For them it is all physical things, material ways. One thing that you can never take from an Indian is the spirit, unless the Indian surrenders it. So despite all this hardship, all the wars and disease, scalp bounties, forced integration and religious teachings, we stood up one day and we said, that's it. It is time to find our own way. And we began our search.

We planned a survival camp at first. We wanted a structure that would be visible to the younger people and we built the longhouse. We held the gathering there every year. In the meantime, my sister was still working and researching. She found all our wampum belts. She traveled all over this country and corresponded overseas. One day she came and said, "I found a place in New York where they make wampum beads. We need money. We have to raise money, so that we can buy some beads and rebuild our belts." So we raised money. She drove down, picked up the wampum beads and brought them back, and showed us how to rebuild our belts.

The belts are recorded history of the Great Law. They are sacred to our people. They record the great peace, the alliance of our people. This is contrary to what the white man tells us, that we were constantly at each other's throats. There was a great peace of the Algonquin nations here at one time. The twenty-seven different tribes that were joined together had these belts of peace, unity and alliance. The Algonquin Nation was vast. It took all of Ontario, Quebec, New Brunswick, Nova Scotia, Prince Edward Island, Labrador, Maine, Massachusetts, New Hampshire, Connecticut, New Jersey, and part of New York. That is how vast that confederacy was. That peace had been established hundreds of years before the white man came. That was how he was able to walk ashore and be taken in as a brother, nursed through sickness, and nurtured like a child. He was helped to survive and asked to live alongside us as a brother and share this land. It did not work out that way.

"IT TOOK ME FIFTY YEARS TO LET GO OF THE HATE THAT I CARRIED IN MY HEART."

I'm fifty-four years old now and it took me fifty years to let go of the hate that I carried in my heart for that nation of white people. I had a vision once of how this land was before they came and how we lived. Nothing you could imagine could show you the beauty of what we had before the white man came. That grudge stayed inside my heart and never left. For fifty years, I carried that hate. It has only been over the last four years that I let that hate go. It is not for me to judge and condemn anyone. That is not my place. I am not the Creator. I felt that if I wanted to be forgiven by the Creator, I also had to learn to forgive those that had done me wrong.

A few years back, I used to work with the Fishermen's Committee. We had countless meetings with fishery officers. We were attacked with guns, the fishermen would be attacked while they were fishing. The argument we always put up was that there is one law that supersedes all man's laws, and that is God's law. Our aboriginal rights descended from our Creator. The Creator's law gives you a way of life, so that you can live in harmony with everything that is around you. Once a year we light the pipes and talk of these great laws. They are so simple, so undemanding. All you really have to do in your life is to get up and acknowledge the presence of our Creator, our Mother the earth, and the spirits will guide you through everyday tasks.

No two days of your life are ever the same. The gifts that our grandmothers from the past bring us are things that you can hold onto in your heart and teach your children and grandchildren. They are simple things. They are not things that require a huge library or large amounts of money. Everything that we were ever given by the Creator is still there and free; not everyone will grasp it, and that is the sad part. It is sad watching people stumbling around, looking and searching in all the wrong places. All you can do is wait until they decide to acknowledge that without the Creator man is nothing. Without Mother Earth, man is nothing. You can't survive without the Creator and Mother Earth. That is the simplest law there is. A lot of people have tried to survive without them. Though we can't record the Great Law, all you have to do is look around you and see how it was so badly ignored and broken. Everything now is polluted. We even have to be careful where we swim because the rivers aren't clean. The air is not clean. There are huge holes in the sky. Radiation is ruining the people. They are destroying everything, everything around us. Everybody suffers along with the people that are destroying the earth, the universe. They choose to live by man's law and not by God's law.

When we started walking this way, it was hard for us because we were stumbling around, looking, grasping but always in the wrong way. I know now it was the wrong way. When you look to humans for teaching, there is always a flaw. When you look to spirits, then the teachings are true and straight. They are good spirits.

"DRUGS AND ALCOHOL KILL THE SPIRIT THAT IS INSIDE OF YOU."

To walk the true tradition you have to stay away from alcohol and drugs. There are some that believe that they can use these things and still be traditional. Drugs and alcohol kill the Indian spirit. The drugs are shortcuts to the visions you would normally seek through fasting. The alcohol kills the spirit that is inside you. Gradually it will shrink and shrink until it steps aside. If you do not bring that spirit back, then you are with the walking dead. It is never too late. Anytime you turn to the Creator he will come. But suppose you should die before you decide to look. You will not have fulfilled your purpose on earth.

My sister brought medicine conferences here. She tried to get the people interested. She said, "Even if you never get a hundred percent of the audience, out of those fifty people, if just three choose to look for the medicines, then it will never die." She was right. There are people picking up the old ways of the medicine now, learning how to prepare them. The seeds she planted with us are still growing. Every day we find new things, new ways to deal with this and to deal with that. We have a good elder who lives north of us and he is helping us too. He is Micmac of our nation. He has brought us a lot of good teachings, just enough to make us get up and help ourselves.

"THE SPIRITS OF THE YOUNGER GENERATION ARE NOT BEING FED."

Traditionally, you made sure that everybody was cared for. You made sure that they had the food and the basic things in life that they needed. Today, some are better taken care of than others. I don't know how else to explain it. It is not that I am knocking what people are doing. I think they mean well but most of the needs they fulfill are material and nothing is done for the spirit. They ask, "Why is this generation of young people like this? Why are they so destructive? We build them big gyms, ball diamonds, we do all this and still they are destructive." The spirits of the younger generation are not being fed. They don't have a culture and can't identify with their own people. They are brought up like white men and they are expected to be Indian. They do not know what an Indian is.

You watch the children and there is no respect for the elders, they have no respect for anything. How do you really begin teaching them? Is it by example? Will they follow if you set an example? Will they listen to the elders if you teach them when they are young? Culturally these children need an identity. If you don't know what was in your past, you are never going to know what is in your future. You have to look back to learn. The spirits don't necessarily want you to live in teepees or go out and skin animals and make skin clothes. The spirits will compromise but you have to teach the young the old ways. One basic thing, first, before you teach them anything else, they must have the language. These children, they have been forced to be integrated, integration upon integration, until the language is gone. This band council and the one before it places no value on culture. Sure, they will have beading or leather classes. We did not even have beads before the Europeans came. All of a sudden this is the "in" thing. The government says, "Oh, let those Indians make their beading and baskets." How much money have they put into bringing back our language?

I wrote our band a proposal for Maliseet immersion. Everything that the white man brought has a parallel in the Maliseet way. The young can grow up with both languages and cultures. When they stand up, they know what is good and what isn't. They will have respect for their people, but they have to know who they are first. You have to generate pride in the fact that we are Maliseet and that we aren't useless, no-account, drunken savages. We are rich in our culture and we had a way that joined the needs of the people with the ways of the Creator so well that you couldn't tell where the government started and the religion stopped.

Every time you plant something, you pray. When you open up the earth, you pray. Everything was done through prayer. Where did the agriculture start and the religion stop? It was all interwoven. There were ceremonies for water spirits, for the air spirits that bring us fresh air, everything that we take for granted today. The wind will blow in and bring us fresh air. But will it really, if you don't acknowledge it? This is what our children must know for them to know who they are, for that calm to take place in their lives so that they can look out and say, "Look, this is what my ancestors were. They were a group of people who looked seven generations ahead to make certain that everything they had then would still be here for me." It is not going to be here for long because our generation, the sixth generation, could not carry out our duties; the white man would not let us.

"YOU RECOVER BY WALKING THE WAY THE ANCESTORS TELL YOU TO WALK."

You recover by walking the way the ancestors tell you to walk. We can live in these houses, as long as we don't forget what is out there. We have to remember that our spirit needs to be fed. We have to remember to teach the children the ways of our people. All these things were not left way back but are ahead of us. They are waiting. All you have to do is find the key and unlock that door. Everything will be right there waiting for you. The key that opens the door is language. It always comes back through your language.

The spirits will make allowances for you on certain things, but they expect you to learn as you are going along. It is up to the individual when the teachings come. But the younger people must know this also. Long after that building crumbles, the Maliseet will still be here. The Native people of Turtle Island will still be here, long after all these material things are gone. That is why they have to learn how to open their hearts, learn their language. Even if you stumble through it and don't sound very good, try it anyway. It will come back.

You don't blame the young. The young are the way they are because we did not do a good job. We did not stand firm enough in our teaching. We always point to the younger generation because they are unruly or drug-addicted. You have to help these people to bring them back to the good way. It is not their fault. Just like my parents. If I had to live through what they had to live through and raise a family, I probably would have been an alcoholic too.

Sometimes you'll meet an Indian who is so Indian-like—black hair, nice copper skin—who doesn't even want to be Indian. Then you will meet this blond, blue-eyed Indian with long hair headband Indian stuff. That was in the prophecies too. That the light-colored Indians would stand up and walk the darker ones back. The search is in the heart, it is not in the color. The spirit is strong. When the spirit tells you to stand up, you listen and stand up. The dark Indian has been beaten down so many times and discriminated against so much that he figures, "If I turn toward the white man's ways, I can survive." This one counselor told me, "I even contemplated dyeing my hair, having it permed, just because I didn't want to be Indian. It never got me anything but a lot of discrimination."

That is what those children face when they are integrated into white schools: discrimination, racism—constantly, day after day. You know who they blame that on? My generation. They say, "Why did you let this happen?" That is why there is no respect for elders. The same generation that the elders find unruly, I have talked with them and found they are respectful and that they listen. But they do not do the same for their families. I think that they hold that grudge inside because they were forced to be white people and not given a chance to be Indian. When you talk with them, there are endless questions. "Why do we learn of another race when we don't even know our own? Where is our history? Why aren't we taught those ways?"

In the old days, there were what the white man calls subchiefs. They were clan chiefs that represented each clan. These clan chiefs were spokesmen for the whole clan. When there was an issue or dilemma, the clan chiefs would sit together and talk about their concerns and solutions. When they sat together in this council, each clan chief held a staff, a talking stick. On each staff was a record of the history of his clan, who had married whom, how many clans were intermarried. This was to make sure that you did not marry into a clan that you were related to. When they sat in this council, each one would be heard as long as he held a talking stick. All the concerns he voiced came from the people who stood behind him, his clan. Nothing was ever left unsettled. They did not leave until everyone had been heard. Unanimous decisions were reached that were in the best interests of everybody.

Today, the mock government of the Indian people is more like a puppet of the white man's government. The white government places obstacles in front of these elected chiefs

"WHEN THEY SAT IN THIS COUNCIL, EACH ONE WOULD BE HEARD."

and counselors. Even though they start out with the intention of helping their people, they become preoccupied with material things, and the real needs of the people are neglected. The elected system on a reservation is like the white man's system. It is politics. You will get a house if you are a favorite or if the council wants to pay back a favor, not because you need it. Years ago everything was based on need. The needs of the people came first. The elected system is more white-oriented. You see some people receiving the help they need, while others are totally ignored.

They have no pride in being Indian. I would say about ninety percent of the band council can't speak their own language. They can't conduct their meetings in Indian. They never fight based on aboriginal rights, they fight with the Indian Act. The Indian Act is just a piece of paper that the government slapped together to get rid of the Indian quicker. Today, you have some people on the council that go home for lunch and have a marijuana joint or a bottle of beer. Then they go to a council meeting and make decisions with a mind that has been polluted by mind-altering things.

All traditional council meetings were opened with a pipe ceremony and closed with a pipe ceremony. Your mind was clear. You did not pass that pipe around because you needed to smoke tobacco—you were conversing with the Creator. Each one of those clan chiefs—including the clan elder, the head chief—were pipe carriers and they were all elders in the village. You did not get a title like clan chief when you were young, like we have today. Today, we don't have the elders we had then. Any decision that is made by young people is not going to be the same kind of decision.

The band council is scared. They see everything slipping away. There was money pouring in from this and that way, up ahead of you, above your head, stacks of money. Now all of a sudden, there is only a little pile of money. So now, you take care of your Indian people. Didn't you ever wonder why the money is getting smaller and smaller? They are developing the Indian until he reaches a certain level, then the government is going to step out and let you sink or swim on your own. All you have to do is look at this reservation. All the modern homes. There is not a house here that does not have one or two cars, trailers, or skidoos. The government is not going to stand for that. Eventually they will cut back.

It is important to start working for a traditional government. We will revive whatever we had. They don't want the strict rules that go with traditional government—no drinking, partying, or toking. But they will consult with us. They will call my son Perry, the clan chief, or they will ask me to go down and talk to Perry. And they just go on their merry old way. It is because no tobacco was ever exchanged and nothing sank in with my own people. Now they are beginning to look. They called us in when they had trouble with the Fisheries Department. They asked Perry to conduct a pipe ceremony before the meeting began, and he did that. We sat and we talked with the Fisheries officers. One of the councilors had signed an agreement with Fisheries, guaranteeing a quota of eight or nine hundred salmon for the men that net here. They had not caught that much salmon. They caught about twenty-five from June first until the end of July. Something was wrong.

Right off the Fisheries Department came and said they wanted us to stop fishing. If we refused to sign the permits that went along with the agreement that the councilor had signed, then we could not fish at all. They told us that if we did not agree to sign the permits, then the contract would be null and void. My son told them, "If you do not live up to the contract that you signed with our band council, you can be sued. We will take you to court and we will make you honor the contract that you signed with our people. It is time that you learned that your word has to be kept. You are not dealing with our ancestors who signed those treaties. Your time for pulling these fast ones is over."

I said, "The only reason why these two Fisheries officers want you to sign those licenses is to further compromise your aboriginal right to fish. You have the right to fish in any manner that you want, in any water that you want. The waters were never ceded. There are no land surrenders here. The only kind of treaties we ever signed were peace treaties to live side by side with these people. There is not one document anywhere in Canada that proves that we surrendered the land or the waters. All of the waters within the Maliseet territories are ours. We can fish; we can hunt anywhere we want."

I said, "Now, you sit here with your documents and you are telling us if we do not sign, nobody can go fish. We are telling you that those licenses were brought in after the agreement was signed. You added that on after the agreement had been signed. You are famous for doing that. But now, if we pull out of the waters like you want, you better pull out every angler that is left. There better not be one angler anywhere in New Brunswick fishing."

He said "Well, we can't do that. That is a hundred and twenty million dollar income for New Brunswick." I said, "Well, that is how it is." He said, "If you don't stop fishing, we are going to close the rivers through conservation. We supercede aboriginal rights." I told him, "You seem to be overlooking another law. That is God's law and that is where our aboriginal rights come from. His law supersedes your conservation laws. You want to make this an issue, you can sit here and argue all day. These fishermen have already told you that they are not pulling out of those waters. I demand that you bring those nine hundred salmon to Tobique and dump them right in the middle of the reserve so that we can go get them. You want us out of the water, go get those nine hundred salmon."

The spirits of the people, their spiritual grandmothers, bring the people to this house. It is a matter of waiting for them. There are those that are more comfortable with my son because he is in their generation. They are a little bit scared of me. He can see more of their ways because he has walked that same path and knows where they are coming from. I feel for them, but I never really know where they are coming from. He works well with those people. They have been coming around to him a lot.

In the East, we have come a long way. We lost a lot, but we have regained almost everything. That was always my thought. I am not done with what I set out to do, and we are coming along well. Our tradition here is strong and will survive whatever is coming. If it can survive these past five hundred years of persecution, it can survive anything. I guess I still have a little of that war spirit in me. I will be old and gray with my cane and I will still be out there fighting.

I have always had a strong belief in my heart that no matter what Native nation you are from, I will always feel a bond with you. We were one people at one time and we will be again. I do not see Cherokee or Sioux or Mohawk or Micmac when I look at people. What I see are Native people, my brothers and my sisters. I know that maybe it is a hard thing for

"I WILL BE OLD AND GRAY, WITH MY CANE, AND I WILL STILL BE OUT THERE FIGHTING."

some people to swallow, because they want a pride in a nation. It is good to have this pride for your nation, but the first thing you must acknowledge is that all the people of Turtle Island have the same mother and father, that is Mother Earth and our Creator. We all came from the same mother and we are all one people. We have to drop this animosity over who's better than who and who has hung on to their traditions the best. I believe that if I have something to share with another Nation that they don't have and come seeking, I will share it. I don't care if they don't speak my language. This one Sioux who came to visit and help build the nation house, he told me his Indian name was Wobun and I asked what that meant. He said that it means dawn. That is the same thing in our language. So why would a Sioux and Maliseet, one who lives off west and the other one who lives way east, have this one word in common?

I found something out when we were in a sweat one day that I will share with all of the people. I was singing one of the sacred songs in my language and there was a young Micmac man there. He understood every word because he listened from his heart and not with his ears. He was so amazed. That only reinforces my theory that at the beginning of time we all spoke the same language. It only changed a little bit as we spread out over Turtle Island and began taking care of different parts of the land.

One day we will stand as one speaker, and our people will understand this one person, because we are all one. I hope I will live long enough to stand up and truly say, we are brothers and sisters. They will know that the names of the nations are descriptions of where they were or how they lived, but basically we are all one. We can feel the same connection from one Native to another. Sometimes there will be a long silence in a gathering, yet you will feel what was said in that silence, more than words could say. You feel what this person has seen during the silence. That is the one bond that Indian people have. One mother, one umbilical cord, and one afterbirth nurtured us all. All four brothers and sisters, red, yellow, black and white, are all connected. We were all created from Mother Earth.

You Need to Prepare Yourself

CHAPTER FIVE

An interview with Vivienne Caron Jake

(Kaibab Paiute)

The Kaibab Paiute, a part of the Southern Paiute Nation, are located on the Colorado Plateau in Northern Arizona. Vivienne Jake, a member of this tribe, has been active in protecting the Grand Canyon for the future generations of her people, who continue to use the canyon for gathering food and medicines and for ceremonial purposes. Vivienne is working with the National Park Service to incorporate the Paiute perspective into the Grand Canyon Management Plan. She helped defeat a proposal to build a toxic waste incinerator on a sacred site on Kaibab tribal land, and received an award from the Indigenous Women's Network for this work. She is active with environmentalists on a variety of issues related to protection of the Canyon and surrounding lands. Vivienne and her mother Lucille have taught the children of their Nation about the plants indigenous to their area as well as their people's language, ceremonies, and traditional teachings.

My mother has told me many stories of encampments around the Grand Canyon, or down inside the Canyon during the wintertime when it was cold and snowing up here. In the summertime, some of them would go down inside to farm or gather plants. She tells me of incidents that happened a long time ago. She told how the Paiute people would make ropes out of yucca fiber, which is very strong. They would braid, weave and make ropes out of it. Every year they would pick the agave. They would tie a man around one end of the rope, while the rest held onto the other end of the rope. They would lower him down the cliff of the canyon with a basket and he would pick the fruits off the agave plant. When you look down from the top of the canyon rim, it makes you think that our people were strong and brave. When you look down the Canyon from that height, it takes your breath away. And to think that this person would dangle from a yucca rope to pick the fruit for the purpose of helping his people. He would then send back the basket, the people would take care of it and lower the basket back down again and again, for as long as it took.

My grandfather and a distant relative once showed me how to fix and prepare agave. These two old men and I picked the agave near the Grand Canyon and brought back a pickup load. They showed me how to roast it under the ground, treat it, make cakes and then dry it. We dried it and made it into little patties. You could either cook them in water and make a hot cereal or chew them like cookies. That is one thing I learned from my grandfather.

When I go to the Canyon, or anywhere that is really special, I am always aware of the plants that are in that area. I have great respect for the plants. I talk to them. I think it is probably because of what I have been taught and told. I have an awareness of natural things. I take great care in making sure that I pay respect to them.

One day, not too long ago, Mother was talking about things that make you fearful. She asked me, "What is it that brings you great fear?" I told her, "There have been three things that happened to me in my lifetime that made me fearful or spiritually aware of the power and the magnitude of the Creator and creation. One time was when I was standing before a redwood tree. You know how large they are. You look up and keep bending your head and bending your head. They are so huge, you can feel the power of the tree. I was such a small little thing compared to that tree. If it were to fall, it would crush you. Imagine what you would feel trying to climb that tree."

The second time was when I had to cross the Mississippi River. I was going to school back in the Midwest at that time, and would drive back and forth. It was after I was able to get a car. Crossing that Mississippi in a car with some friends, I said, "That river is so huge. It is so powerful." Again I felt so small, just a tiny little seed among a lot of other things.

The third time was when we were going to Montana. I was so afraid. We were in a little Volkswagen and Mom wanted to go and see her Crow friends. I was driving and we started up this mountain. I did not think that we were ever going to start coming back down. We kept going up the mountain. The snow got deeper and things around us started to disappear, hills and groves of trees and the rivers got smaller. They were not at eye level anymore and we knew that we were going up higher and higher. I was so afraid. My mother told me, "Don't be afraid, just keep on driving. We are going to get back down to the bottom eventually, in time." I wanted to get down to the bottom very fast because of experiencing how huge that mountain was. It amazes me that sometimes people do not experience that power of the universe.

When I am in the Grand Canyon, I have such appreciation for it. It imbalances my spirit when I am in the Canyon and I hear helicopters, airplanes, and the noise of the motorboats that go by. There is so much traffic down there that you can't enjoy just being with the Canyon. Our people lived down in the Grand Canyon, too. There are sights down there that are so awesome. There are these huge, huge black rocks, that look like granite. They are immense rocks where the people used to grind seeds or pulp. There are holes in this granite rock. We took some scientists on a trip down there. One of the Shivwits Paiute guys who was down there with us said, "Here, Vivienne, this is the way they used it." I said, "Yes. You get up there and do that. I will sing you a song. This is the way they really did it." So there he was with this huge old stick going around and around, and I started singing for him. We were just fooling around but the scientists took notes on what we were doing. I said, "Now, this is the way that they did it. When women used these tools, they had a song for it and all the things that they did. They don't just do it to be doing it. If they are grinding corn, they have a corn-grinding song."

Seeing these sites, going to where the farming areas were, the petroglyphs, the hematite cave, the salt cave—it made me feel good, spiritually. It made me respect what is there. My cousin was with us. When they took us to the petroglyph wall, where all of these writings are, he was crying. I said, "Tim, what is the matter, Tim?" He said, "It makes me feel good and yet it makes me feel bad because the people aren't here any more. Those people aren't here to tell me what these writings mean." I said, "It is not hard to get the meaning of the rock writings." I have this little rubber stamp of this petroglyph human form. I always put that on my writing because it shows that it is from me. There was a group of young Paiute men with me. They particularly had interests in those petroglyph sites. I told them, "If you want to know about these things, you are now starting to feel for the natural surroundings in which you live. You are just now barely experiencing and there is more. You need to be preparing yourselves if you want to learn more."

So I explained to them that my great uncle, an elder, was in a nursing home down in St. George. He told my mother he was going to come see her and knock on her door two times. (It was this house—my mother and I exchanged houses.) He said, "I am going to knock two times and you are going to come to the door. You will not be able to see me. I will be there but you will not be able to see me. I don't want you to become frightened, I've just come to check to see how you are doing." That was my great uncle.

I was telling Tim, because that was Tim's uncle too, "You need to stop drinking your beer. You need to stop spending so much time in front of the television. You need to stop that horrible smoking. Then you need to become prayerful and prepare yourself for receiving. You can't receive when you are contaminated by all of these other things. You have to be pure. You have to work yourself up to where you can meditate or communicate with the Great Spirit. You will not ever be able to do that if you continue on."

"It is good that you appreciate the petroglyph figures. You look at each one and you wonder, what does it mean, and why did they do it this way? Our people made contact with these beings many, many generations ago. They met these beings and the white culture has not. So, they wonder what this is all about. Our people were able to travel in space and meet with these beings. This is where this comes from." They couldn't believe that because they had never been introduced to that kind of teaching and learning. Tim was sobbing. He is an artist, and half Hopi and Paiute. He was really taken by these drawings. I told him, "There is so much here in the Canyon that our people have left here for us to learn, but you have to prepare yourself. You have to learn what the plants are down here. In our stories and legends, we are told about how these plants saved mankind or how they saved the animals. You need to go back and learn. Unless you take the time to do it, you are always going to wonder. You are not going to have direction."

One of our prophecies talks about this mountain, *Túngwavahant*, which in our language means Thunder Mountain, because every now and then it rumbles. It used to rumble more than it does now. When I start to feel that little tremor, I think *Túngwavahant* must be moving around. The prophecy has it that now the mountain is sitting upright, but it is going to turn over when Mother Earth starts to cleanse herself. *Túngwavahant* is going to turn inwards. The prophecy says, "Don't value your new house or your new building." My great uncle, the one that was in the nursing home, told me about the prophecy. He told five people, and I am the only one remaining. He told my brother, my uncle (who was chairman at the time), an elder man named Georgie George, a neighbor named Dan Bullets, and myself.

I tell these young men what Uncle Robert said. "Don't value the new house that you are living in. Don't flaunt it and say, oh, this beautiful house. You need to start preparing yourself spiritually. When Mother Earth starts cleansing herself, you are going to have to know and follow your directions. You need to be guided by the spirits. They will help you. There will be great suffering among the Indian people. On the other hand, those who are ready and have their ears and eyes open spiritually will be guided."

There is a plain down on the flats as you leave. No trees grow there. It is a lot of rocks and sagebrush and looks desolate, like nothing would live there. In the prophecy, that is an area where we are instructed to take the elders and the children. It really does not say too much about those in between. That was the area where they wanted to dump the toxic waste incinerator trash, that is the area where they wanted to dig up the earth and bury the ash that would come out of the incinerator. The toxic waste incinerator was proposed to the tribe by Waste-Tech of Golden, Colorado. That is why I put up such a big fight. People could not understand my reasons for protecting that site. It is so different from what they were thinking. I was standing in the way of progress. The Kaibab Paiute would have made a lot of money off that. It is just my way, against my belief, to destroy what is there or to put toxins and radioactive wastes into Mother Earth. When she starts to cleanse herself, then we would not have survived. That is the area where we were supposed to take the children, and it would have been contaminated.

When earthquakes hit an area, sometimes they will open up new natural springs or close old ones. A couple of years ago, there was an earthquake in our area. The town of Hurricane was hit hard and people lost their homes because the earth started shifting. There are some natural hot springs down in Hurricane with small circular grottoes. After the earthquake, they were no longer used because the earth shifted and turned off some of the hot water. However, there is still some hot water that comes through the river area. You have these kinds of things happen when there is a natural disaster or a shift in the way the natural things are. Think of the ash being buried where we are supposed to take the children and the elders. Maybe earthquakes would open up a way for water or a spring to come out of the earth, where you see nothing today. The water would not have been drinkable because it would have been contaminated by the ash that is buried there. I am very conscious of the dangers.

Uncle Robert says in this prophecy there will be a lot of cold winters; the ice is going to be thick. When you are spiritually aware and awakened, you will know where to get the wood to make the fire for the elders and the children. You will recognize the plants to feed them, and you will know how to hunt for animals. You will know how to help them heal with the plants that come up. They will reveal themselves to you. You will know without a doubt which plants are to be used for what purpose. You now need to prepare yourself spiritually. You can have a lot of nice things, but let them be secondary. Your priority is to learn all that you can about the old ways. Go back to the original teachings and hold on to them as much as you possibly can.

Don't be ashamed of who you are. Don't be concentrating on how attractive you are or how ugly you might think you are. Don't spend a lot of time in your grooming. You have your own natural beauty. Others look at you as being attractive in your own way. You don't need to mask yourself up with the white man's paint. When you get old, accept the fact that you are old. Don't do anything to try and hold onto youth. Appreciate the age that you are. Appreciate that the Creator has given you many years of life on this earth and make others aware that they cannot take their lives for granted. Think of yourself as a person created to be here in this lifetime; find your purpose and help others.

Last year I was asked to speak in Des Moines to environmental groups. They were mainly focusing on opposition to military activity. They wanted to hear a message from the downwinders about what we have experienced here in northern Arizona and southern Utah from the Nevada test site. I had a radio interview with a guy pretty much like Rush Limbaugh. A young German man and I were there for this interview. The interviewer was so rude. He was making fun of the Native Americans saying, "What are you here for? Why aren't you back where you are supposed to be? What kind of message do you have to bring to us?" I told him, "I was invited by this organization and I am here to talk to them about what has happened to the people in the southwest from the Nevada testing." He said, "Oh, I am aware of that. So what is it that you have to tell us? What is it that you want to say over the radio? Are you going to try and convince them that they need to start worshipping Mother Earth like you people do?" I told him, "You are obviously not ready to listen to what I have to say. I am

"MY PURPOSE IS TO SPEAK TO MY PEOPLE AND WARN THEM."

obviously in the wrong place at the wrong time. You are not ready to receive." He said, "If you are talking about worshipping mamma, of course we are not ready to hear that. We are people of a different type and we do not worship mamma and you are not going to convince us." I said, "That is not my purpose." Then the young German man got very angry. The radio man swore at him and said, "You kraut, why don't you go and give that message to your kraut people? You don't have to be over here in America telling us how to run our lives." He was very rude. So I told him, "I'm finished."

People were calling in who were for Native Americans and there were some people who weren't. One of the callers said, "Why is it that when you come and speak to us, you always try to put the guilt trip on us?" I said, "What guilt trip? You decide if you want to feel guilty. I am not going to make you feel guilty." So anyway, that was one caller. My friend was watching the telephone. He could read on the computer that there was someone who wanted to talk in favor of the Native American way of life. They had that person on hold and would not let that telephone call come through.

I had just spoken to them about the natural powers of the world and told them not to be abusive. Shortly after that, they had all that rainfall and the Mississippi overflowed. I wonder what that guy is thinking and what is going through his mind. The people who invited me were wonderful. One of them had been elected into the House of Representatives for Iowa. He took me to the Capitol Building and introduced me to this group. I got

a standing ovation from the Iowa legislature which made it all worthwhile. If the general population did not want to listen to my message, at least their legislature knew why I had come to Iowa.

Those kinds of experiences make me more determined, more aware of the work that we have to do in defense of our environment. The work that I am doing in the Grand Canyon is meaningful to me in my life. That experience urges me on and strengthens me from within. My purpose is to speak to my people about that and to try and warn them. That is my message and my work.

I try to teach as much as I can to the children about plants and the language. We thought that by now we would be into the legends and stories. Soon, we cannot tell stories until next winter, until the next first snowfall and then we start telling stories again. This is our oral history. In each one of the stories there is a message, a lesson to be learned, and I want the children to know what they are. We have not done that yet because I have been busy with family issues. We had our own family crisis that I have had to attend to.

Ceremony, and retaining as much of the tradition as we can, is very important. When we say we are Paiute, then we have to live that. We can't just say that we are Paiute because we were told we were Paiute. We have to know something of what it means to be a Paiute. If you can't speak the language, then maybe you know the songs. If you don't know the songs, then maybe you know the stories, maybe you know plants, medicine, or how to teach the children to go out and give thanks to the plants, water, land, animals, creation, the air that we breathe, Father Sky and Mother Earth, all the directions—from where the snow comes and from where the wind comes. To be aware of where the natural things are.

There is a cave in Utah, near Hurricane. A lot of people say that Hurricane is named for hurricanes that come from the ocean. My mother and grandfather told me that there is a cave in Hurricane. In Paiute, those caves are called *túngkan* which means, "the home of the wind." An elder told my grandmother not to ever go near that cave because that is the home of the wind. Some days you can see the wind coming out of that cave. Other times when you are near there, deep within that cave you can hear the rumbling and the humming of the wind. Every now and then it comes out. The name of the place is *Núahtúngkan* which means "the home of the wind" which is far removed from the hurricane.

The other town is called La Verkin. I asked some people there why it was called La Verkin. This person told me that in the Paiute language it means beautiful valley. So then I came back to my mom and I asked her the same question. She said, "No, there are hot springs there and our people have gone there for healing purposes. In Paiute when you bathe, you say *nahvaqúún* which means a place for bathing. The people that live there think the word was La Verkin when it really is *nahvaqúún*, an area for bathing. See how these names have changed. You need to be aware of these things."

A hurricane destroys a lot of things, that is not what this place is named for. There is the place where our medicine people went to receive messages from the Great Spirit. It is a medicine rock. People who are going down the Canyon leave things on top of the rock for good luck. Maybe they will leave a cigarette lighter, a hair clip, or another stone there. People are abusing the power of that rock, they are not respecting it for its significance to the Hualapai and Paiute people. Our medicine men went to this rock for fasting or vision quests. I went there. They took me by boat and left me on the beach. I said some prayers and put down some tobacco. I went by the rock and started picking up some of those things and threw them into the river. I gave thanks to the rock. I asked her to forgive those who did not understand and who left this trash on it. I asked for forgiveness for us, the children of this Mother Earth, if we have failed to visit that rock, to help and nourish it through fasting and prayer. I told the rock to forgive us.

We are all brothers in the nation of Southern Paiutes. All of us have had some activity that took place within the Canyon. All of us at one time had special sites down there. Very few, most of them are men, now make that journey down to the salt cave or the hematite cave. They walk for a long, long ways to get to those caves. Paiutes are still using those sacred areas.

The National Park Service cannot say it does not matter how high or fast the water flows, or how deep the water will be, because it is important to us. Every person that has been down there has recommended that the water flows be lessened. Water rushing through there will destroy a lot of sites. Our people still use these places. The Paiute people have already lost one salt cave. When Lake Meade was being developed, it covered the cave. That was where Paiute people gathered salt. Those are the sacred places. These are natural resources we use for ceremonies which are very important to our people. We have to keep doing the ceremonies because this is our way. We still need to have the salt, hematite, clay, and rock sitting in the river.

These are special places to our people. They are not just rocks, or holes in the side of a cliff, or obscure remnants of salt hanging from the cliffside. We don't see it like that. Our eyes, hearts and spirits tell us that these are things the Creator gave us, things we have to continue to use and pay respect to. That is why it is very important to me to speak out about the use of plants. There are so many different types of teas, several varieties of tobacco, and different types of sage. I think that our study will probably show at least five different varieties of sage. There are healing clays, rocks that have power which are used for healing purposes or for meditation. Rocks that most people would look upon as just pebbles.

"YOU AND THAT TREE ARE BOTH CREATIONS OF THE GREAT SPIRIT."

There is a tree down in the Canyon that is older than the time when John Wesley Powell was there. It is an old, old tree where Paiute people had their picnics. Babies in their cradle-boards hung from that tree. One of the anthropologists or ethnologists that was with us took a picture of me in front of it. I look upon that tree and I say to that tree, "Tree, you have been here for so many years. Despite all of the cutting away on your branches, all the ropes that have been tied to your trunk by the boatmen, and despite the way people have abused you, you are still standing. You are still standing erect and you have been here for hundreds of years. Tree, I want to say thank you for allowing me to see you, to look upon you for the beauty that you are." Those kinds of things that you experience and appreciate—you know yourself that you and that tree become one. You and that tree are both creations of the Great Spirit. He created me, he created that tree. We are both creations of that Great Spirit.

I look upon that tree and the beauty it has, the age it must be; still, it is so beautiful—the texture of the bark, and the design that it shows you. It is standing right there at the edge of the river. I think about all the people who have been there. I tell that tree, "So many of our people have visited you, maybe they slept underneath you by this river. Maybe they were sick, hungry, or just passing through. Maybe there was an encampment here. Tree, you have seen so many people. I appreciate that I am one of those people that you have seen. I want you to know that I am not going to forget you." You have that kind of communication with the tree. It is there. The tree just brings it out.

You have to be ready to receive. When you see a grove of trees, it makes you feel strong because those trees are there and they have life, they have spirit. When you go to a grove of trees, when you are on the river, or when you go into a canyon, you always give thanks. You give thanks to the Creator and you feed that place. You might want to give it tobacco. If you go into a canyon and you go into that grove of trees, you give it food and give it thanks. "Thank you for allowing me to be here in your midst. Thank you for letting me lie down and rest for a few minutes, to cool off from the heat of the sun. Thank you for being here for me." You talk to the chief of those trees. Where there are trees, there is always a chief, always a leader. And the animals, too, there is always a chief.

An anthropologist friend of mine, who has now become a lawyer, told my mother that he and his wife went for a hike near the Cedar City Mountains. They were walking up the road and coming to a little valley. Just as they were coming on top of the hill, they started looking down into the valley. The site they saw was awesome to both him and his wife. He did not quite understand it but he told my mother about it. He said that there was a circle of bald eagles and other kinds of eagles. He said there was one bald eagle sitting right in the center on a rock. It was like they were having a meeting. My mother told him they *were* having a meeting. She said there is always a leader and he was the chief. He was sitting there having a discussion with his eagles. He said that they stepped back very softly, very quietly, moved back away from that site and left. My mother said, "Thank you, thank you."

There are different experiences people have which they don't always understand. These are very special times, very meaningful, if you know what might be behind them. I have another friend and she lives down in La Verkin. One time she had a vision. She had to go to Cedar City and she did not know what for. As she was going on the freeway, she was receiving this message which told her to go off on another road toward the place called Burrow, New-castle. She did not understand why she was getting this message. While she was on the road, she just stopped and had this feeling that she needed to go to this grove of old cottonwood trees. It was quite a ways from road, maybe a mile or so. She said she kept walking and trying to meditate on the message she was receiving. She came to the cottonwood trees and there were a lot of eagles on top. She said one of them was a white eagle. He dropped about four feathers and those were for her. Everybody has been wanting to get a hold of her feathers.

We are who we say we are. We are the people of this land and we are not going to leave it. We are going to continue to reside in this place that was selected for us. In doing so, we have to become familiar with it again. We need to be in harmony with all things and in balance. We need to know that one day these destructive acts of mankind have to stop because Mother Earth is going to cleanse herself. We need to value who we say we are. We are the people of the Americas. We need to be responsible in a way that is going to prolong the lives of the generations that follow us.

"WE ARE THE TEACHING GENERATION."

We are the teaching generation. Once we are gone, that is going to be it. There is not going to be another chance. We need to appreciate who we are, ourselves. We need to know that we have self-empowerment. We have power from within, but we have to recognize these powers. We need to know where to go to be shown direction, we need to know who to speak to for guidance. We need to make people aware that the ceremonies that we do are ours. They are not to be abused or used by other people and done in the wrong way. We need to tell people not to use sage or cedar commercially. I see sage being sold in stores. I tell people sage is not sold. It can be traded for something but don't let money cross hands. Our ceremonies should not be paid for with money. There are other ways of paying a leader that conducts a ceremony—with food, tobacco, medicine, or tea.

People have to become environmentally aware. Those of European stock can't go back to Europe. They are here on our land. They have to help us to take care of the earth. This land was meant for the Native Americans. Now we are sharing it with the Japanese, the Chinese, and all the other cultures. While they are here, they should take care of it, like we were instructed to take care. Otherwise, these things are going to be destroyed.

There are enough archaeological artifacts in the Smithsonian Institution. Why should there be any more digging of our ancestors' graves? Every time one is dug up, we have to go and do ceremonies all over again because that is an endangerment to us. What if there is a medicine person's skeletal remains that are uncovered? The non-Indian does not understand the powers that go with the remains of one who was here. The spirit of the deceased is very powerful. So those kinds of activities have to stop. They have enough in the Smithsonian. I have been there. I have seen the drawers and drawers of skeletal remains. I see tables in the Smithsonian which are laden with huge, large pots that were made by our people just sitting, gathering dust.

This generation has to teach as much as we can remember of the language, the songs, the dances and all of our original teachings. We need to teach the generations that are coming up. When Mother Earth starts to cleanse herself, they have to have some idea what to do, where to go, and how to survive. We are the teaching generation, we are the last of our people who know the language and the songs.

All around Indian Country, you will find that a lot of the language is gone. You see people out there for show. Our ceremonies are no longer being conducted. Flashy dances of show and contest have replaced them. We have to start teaching the ceremonies that we were given. Our songs have to continue, so we need to make time for that. We need to get away from the television, which takes up a lot of time. It works like a computer—whatever television gives you is fed into your mind. When your mind is so full of all that other stuff, how can you know how to make fire when there are no matches? Those things need to be learned. Ours is a teaching generation. Once we are gone, there will be even fewer teachers than there are today. Our numbers are getting smaller.

BOOK TWO

WHOWEAREASAPEOPLEISWITHIN
USWAITINGTOBEAWAKENED

T his book contains interviews with individuals who have returned to the lifeways of their peoples. Some were raised traditionally and left their communities for a time to gain experience in the ways of the Western world; others have been active in the revitalization of traditional lifeways in contemporary Native life and the resurgence of their nations. Through the practical reality of their experience, they demonstrate that we as Native peoples can awaken that which has been asleep within ourselves and our communities.

Through the voices of those interviewed we hear that all things have spiritual and physical reality. They speak to the fact that our ways of life as Native peoples originated spiritually. They add that understanding of spirituality comes through the practice of a natural way of life which is harmonious with all of creation. This understanding is revealed in small steps along the way of life. Jim Dumont says, "The way of life is the path the spirit takes through life." As Native people, we have patterned ourselves to survive in the Western technological world which emphasizes the physical and mental aspects of being human. A natural way of life also includes the heart and spirit. As Jeanette Armstrong describes, "The spirit of love is what keeps us together as a people. It is the most important part of us. The closest Okanagan word for spirituality means 'how we do things.' How we do things expresses our spirituality toward each other."

Those interviewed emphasize that for many of us as individuals and nations, our ways of life are dormant and waiting within us to be awakened. Floyd Flores states, "You just need one person to pick up that word, or ceremony, or knowledge, dust it off, say a prayer over it, and begin to use it again." The speakers are clear that if we do not perpetuate our ways of life, there will be very little to pass on, just the form and not the substance of who we are.

Bridging the Gap Between Two Worlds,

But Walking the Red Road

CHAPTER SIX

An interview with Henrietta Massey

(Sauk and Mesquakie)

Henrietta Massey is a Sauk speaker and traditionalist, secretary of the Sac and Fox Nation's Repatriation Committee, and one of the founders and leaders of the Working Group on Sauk Language and Culture. She is a former tribal council member; served on the Title IV Parent Advisory Committee for the Sac and Fox Nation and Town of Drumright; founded Sac and Fox People Inc. Voice of the People; and is a founding board member of the Thakîwaki Foundation. She has served on many tribal committees, including Election, Budget, Powwow, Business, Grievance and Law and Order. She attended Draughons School of Business, Drumright Vo-Tech, and Oklahoma State University. Henrietta is the mother of two children. Her daughter Sandra assisted with this interview.

At my stage in life, I can review and see clearly the lessons life taught me. My parents practiced both the traditional and Native American Church ways. My maternal grandfather, Edward Butler, introduced the Native American Church to the Sac and Fox people. My maternal grandmother, Ida Mansur Butler, lived with us after her death. She couldn't speak English but we could understand her.

In my early years, my parents, Henry Scott and Mamie Butler Scott, sponsored four Native American Church birthday meetings for me. With assistance, I was the water carrier in those meetings where elders said prayers for me. For that I am fortunate. I believe that my parents, grandparents, and all of those elders who prayed for me are watching over me even today.

I thought my home environment was restrictive, but later I learned that the restrictions were, in fact, teachings. Both my parents were disciplinarians, and I just knew they "had it in" for me. Today I see the love in that discipline, and that discipline as guidance.

I believe in destiny. I believe that when good or bad occurs a lesson is involved. If I could learn how to listen to my first instinct, I would be better off because that is God talking. In mainstream society, we question and analyze too much. It then becomes only human and confused.

I graduated from a small rural elementary school. My two children graduated from that same school. I excelled at basketball, which I loved to play, but at first I was forced to do it. My coach was the principal's wife, and the principal had been my mom's coach, so they knew I could play.

Basketball figured largely in high school as well. When I entered high school as a freshman, the basketball coach knew of my athletic ability and put me on the "A" team, or varsity, as a substitute. My teammates were juniors and seniors. That year our team won our way to the state tournament in Oklahoma City.

Despite my success in basketball, high school holds some bad memories for me. Because I was an Indian, students taunted me. The worst experience was when my teacher called me a "squaw" in front of the whole freshman Oklahoma History class. That was demeaning and humiliating. I recognize it now as racial discrimination and a violation of my civil rights. Even when my children attended, that high school has never had many Indian students. I understand that the other two Indian students who were there with me were not affected by the prejudice, which leads me to ask, "Why me?" That was for me to learn.

I attended business college after high school and moved away from home. I developed a different lifestyle and had many new experiences. My first best friend was Caucasian, and I began to flow with the mainstream society. During my first few months of school, I lived in a private home where my job was to care for a six-week-old baby. I couldn't concentrate on my studies and my grades began to fall. I was then placed in another private home where my job was to clean house and prepare some meals. My room there, next to a garage, was very quiet, but I wasn't happy there. I was treated like a household servant, and by then my self-esteem had grown enough that I resented it; so I left.

I was hired by the Tulsa Junior Chamber of Commerce and worked there until I was hired by the Norvelle Marcum Wholesale Jewelry Company, owned by two Jewish gentlemen, who played a major part in helping me to overcome my shyness. They made me see that I was an individual with a place in this world. They understood prejudice. They taught me to stand up for myself. Once, I walked into the office with a big box that held a cocktail dress I had just bought. They asked me what I had bought and told me to remember that if I didn't like it, I could take it back.

I worked there for six and a half years. Because of their confidence in me, I began to excel in my position as a billing clerk. When they purchased a billing machine, I learned how to use it and did the work of two people. I made my job a challenge. When orders came through just prior to quitting time, I strove to finish them to avoid staying late. The company's clients from New York and New Orleans said I could have a job with them should I ever move to either city. Due to the beneficial influence of my two Jewish employers, my self-esteem had blossomed into self-confidence. I believe they were meant to be in my life.

As a result of my newfound self-confidence, I got very brave and incurred my first big debt, for a combination record player, television set, and radio. I had dreamed of such an item, and it was a proud moment for me when I showed it to my dad. Recalling it now, I believe that Dad used his psychology on me. I was stepping on the edge of something that could get out of control, so he commented, "Well, when you get hungry, you can make soup out of it." He was telling me to be cautious and think ahead before any major decision. Today, I try to stay within my limits on everything.

I don't smoke today because of his psychology. While we lived at home he didn't allow my three brothers or me to smoke. He always told us, "When you can afford to buy your own cigarettes, you can smoke." Smoking was an "in" thing with my peers. Once, on a visit home, I reached into my purse, pulled out my cigarettes, and calmly asked Dad for a light. I wanted to shock him, but, instead, he obliged. I never developed the smoking habit.

As I swam in the mainstream, I felt something was missing. I was hungry for more than the frybread, corn, and meat gravy—I was hungry for my traditional home life. When you grow up in a traditional Indian home, what you were taught is always there. That spirit is inside you.

I didn't immediately recognize it that way and began to search for a way to pray. I attended Methodist and Baptist Indian churches with my Creek girlfriends, a Baptist church with my roommate, and a Catholic church with a Spanish girlfriend. The Catholic Church seemed more attuned to my Sac and Fox beliefs, but didn't satisfy me. I realize now that I wasn't seeking a way to pray to God, but, rather, was seeking the way I had been taught from infancy. It was like trying to fit a square peg into a round hole.

Destiny took me away from my Sac and Fox home and destiny brought me back. My lesson was to learn to survive in the white mainstream. I can now recognize the line between the red and white societies.

I married and returned home with a little daughter. Her father, Ray, a Choctaw, did not wish to raise his family in a large city and decided to make our home where I grew up. I was sorry because I loved all the conveniences of Tulsa, where our baby was born, but in time I saw that this was the right decision.

My son and daughter were the only grandchildren, niece and nephew, born to my parents and my three brothers. They were showered with the love given only by grandparents and uncles. As the first grandchild, my daughter was pampered. When she whimpered, two grandparents and three uncles were ready to pick her up. An elder once told me to let babies cry, because that's how they exercise their lungs. However, when I let my daughter exercise her lungs, her youngest uncle picked her up at the ready urgings of her grandparents.

As a young mother, I relied upon my parents' spirituality. My children needed Indian names. Since their father was not a Sac and Fox, they belonged to my clan, my father's clan, the Wolf clan. Ray not only gave his blessings but participated in the name-giving held in a Native American Church ceremony with Dad conducting the services. Until his death, Ray always knew the meanings of the kids' Indian names.

"DESTINY TOOK ME AWAY FROM MY SAC AND FOX HOME AND DESTINY BROUGHT ME BACK."

69

My family's beliefs guided my children. My dad, lovingly called the "Lobo Wolf," talked to my children about Sac and Fox ways. I didn't know this until after he died. My family held birthday meetings for my children as well. During one ceremony when my son was still very young, my dad fanned him with cedar and an eagle feather. My son said nothing until Dad completed his prayer and then said, "Again, Papa!" Dad chuckled—and fanned him again.

My brother Thomas, the eldest of the three, taught my children to respect Grandmother Earth. One day they were in their grandparents' backyard, hitting tree branches with a long stick. Instead of telling them not to hit the tree, he asked, "Do you believe in God?" They replied that they did. "Where is He?" Thomas asked, and they said, "Everywhere." "Is He in that tree?" he asked, and they said, of course He was. Then Thomas asked, "If God is in that tree, why are you hitting it like that?"

As long as my parents lived, I relied on their spiritual efforts and continued my life in the mainstream. I worked to provide for the educational needs of my children. I was determined that they wouldn't have to endure the prejudices I did. Although still married, I was a single mother because Ray was a traveling pipefitter.

An elder once told me to always listen to my children's problems, because to them, their problems were big. I tried to do this. I also played with my children, and I still do things with them today. A few years ago we even attended U2 concerts together in Dallas and Ft. Worth. They had restrictions and curfews, but I didn't have any problems with them.

I've learned that dreams have a very significant purpose: they show you things. My first vision dream was about my dad's strength and his demise. It occurred several years before his death and showed me that he would die, but before doing so, he would give me his strength. In the dream Dad gave me a blue shirt. I had once been told that blue is the color of strength. At that time he was very active, but he developed cancer of the kidney. The tumor was as large as a football and surgery was inevitable. Doctors said his chances were fifty-fifty. He survived the surgery, but it revealed nodules on his lungs. He became weak, but his stamina kept him going. My mom took care of him at home. Together, we all fought the battle with his cancer. During his illness, Dad believed that I could get him whatever he needed. Our roles were reversed; Dad now depended on me. I was with Dad the morning he died in 1979. It had begun to snow when Dad and I came home.

In 1981, two years after Dad's death, Thomas passed away. Absolutely beside herself, my mother had to be placed in the hospital. She didn't want me to leave her, so I stayed nearby. The void in her heart upon Dad's death had never healed, and losing her son was almost more than she could endure. She had already buried her youngest son in 1968.

Mom died in 1984, and with her death, I felt that good times were gone forever. We would not celebrate Thanksgiving or Christmas ever again. I used to call Mom "our matriarch" because she was our guide and control. I carried this feeling of hopelessness until I remembered I had children of my own. My middle brother and I are the last survivors of my family. He suffered most with the loss of our parents because he'd been very close to them, and after Mom died he was lost.

Mom used to tell her first cousin, Pearl, a sister in the Indian way, how greatly concerned she was for my brother and me. Pearl's son, Earl Dee, heard her, and when she died he promised her that he would take care of my brother and me. This was the beginning of a beautiful and strong relationship. Earl Dee was blessed by God and had good insight. He passed away in 1988, but he still takes care of us through his teachings.

I've shared a small part of my life to show where I crossed over the mainstream's society threshold. Many years were involved with this process but I made it with the perseverance and encouragement of my parents and maternal grandmother, who had the foresight to recognize the changes of time and the realization that I had to learn to walk in the path of the dominant society to survive. It is through their teaching that I was able to recognize the distinction between the Red road and the White road. Today, I am grateful for that. For a short time, I tried to suppress my Indian beliefs because of the prejudice. The effects of prejudice had placed me in a shell, but I know that destiny put that hurdle there for me to learn, cope with it, and go on.

Following my mother's passing, my brother Earl played a big part in bringing me back to the traditional Sac and Fox way of life. He reminded me that my mental and moral power comes from my Sac and Fox traditions, customs, and beliefs. Earl's life experiences dealt with the good and the bad. The bad had to exist for him to learn the difference. He began to seek spiritual guidance and knowledge through fasting. After many fasts, he was blessed with the knowledge for the Sac and Fox sweat.

Our spirituality served as a very close bond between Earl and my family. Our first prayer together was to heal my brother's grief over the loss of our mother. One day he invited me to a sweat, but I refused. I had been in someone else's sweat once before and suffered claustrophobia, and I thought that I would never go back into another sweat. When I did sweat with him, I went in with a skeptical frame of mind.

I had an experience that I will never forget. The rocks were a glowing red and I saw the poles turn white. I believed that the light came from the glowing rocks and I waved my hands over the rocks to see if it would show a shadow. I tried to bring this to the attention of the others. Finally, Pearl told me that those were really spirits who were showing me how powerful they could be. My skepticism no longer existed. After that, when I went in sweats, I had good feelings. The prayers touched my inner being and gave me the opportunity to remember my family, relatives, friends, people and world.

I feel a great satisfaction in practicing our traditional ways. The sweat was instrumental in helping me to understand. Earl began to teach me the knowledge he learned from fasting. I told him that there was no way I would remember everything he taught me. He told me I would remember when I needed the knowledge. He was right. He was my guidance in my first fast, and his last words to me were, "You have to fast for knowledge."

The sweat is like the womb of our Grandma Earth. We enter and exit left to right because that's the way the world turns. When you bend to enter you're humbling yourself. The sweat involves the fire, wood, rock, water and cedar, who are all a part of the twelve spirits called upon to help us. Our Grandmother Earth revitalizes and renews us.

"I FEEL A GREAT SATISFACTION IN PRACTICING OUR TRADITIONAL WAYS."

I believe that all of God's creations have spirits and belong to families. That's why we were taught not to cut a tree down unless you have a purpose for it. It is the same with flowers and plants. People today refer to some plants as weeds, but some of these so-called "weeds" have medicinal purposes.

"WE MUST LEARN TO LISTEN TO THAT FIRST INSTINCT."

My personal traditional practices regarding my care of our sacred fire brought criticism from some people. I told a one-hundred-and-twelve-year-old elder, my father in the Indian way, about this. He told me to ignore the talk, to continue on, and to trust in what I was doing. Being human, I used to let criticism or talk interfere with my thinking and I would end up in a quandary. While going through a time like this I spoke to one of my relatives, a Mesquakie elder in Iowa. She pointed to some woods and instructed me to go into them and think about it. She said, "There is a spirit within us that belongs to God. We live forever through that spirit, and when we die, only our body dies. You go there and listen. Whatever you are told first is God talking to your spirit." I didn't understand at first, but when I came home something happened that made it clear, and I understood what I had been told.

We must learn to listen to that first instinct. We, as human beings, tend to doubt our first instinct. We will question, analyze, and finally ignore what we are told. After analysis, we choose a different path and it won't be the right one. Human nature, especially in today's society, will question everything because logic enters in.

I believe that once we learn to live within the Creator's spirituality we open ourselves to becoming a part of the whole universe. We begin to recognize all of our grandfathers and

grandmothers and realize that they are there to listen to us. They hear us as we acknowledge them in our sacred ceremonies. They have the power to help us.

Any time we are in our sacred place talking to God, we must be mindful of what we say and think. Lies and insincerity are not welcome in God's universal temple. He is our witness and when a lie is told, the one who speaks the lie is the only one fooled.

In this day and time, how many of us sit down and give thanks to Grandma Earth for providing the material composite of our houses? She has furnished the wood, metal and rubber. We should acknowledge that spirit in our homes through a prayer offering. I was told that when the spirit of the home is happy, then all things will be good. In our homes we rest our bodies, minds, and souls from the stresses of the day. Sometimes stress is brought home with us, and, if everything is okay, we will have a peaceful rest and can meet the challenges of the next day.

I have attended the Native American Church. I find this religion very beautiful because it includes members of the Feathered World, like the eagle, waterbird, scissortail; members under the care of Grandmother Earth, like cedar, sage, wood, rock, and water; members of the Animal World, like the drum; members of the Heavens, like the Morning Star, Moon, Sun, and the Four Directions. The prayer temple is a teepee, which is a circle, and in this circle we pray about life. The leaders are the peyote, sacred fire, and tobacco. The important connection is you, your spirit and the spirit of the religion. Many other beautiful things are associated with the Native American Church religion.

As a youth, I can remember my dad's concern for the United States government's intrusion on the Native American Church. When something is not understood, it is feared. The best policy would be to learn and understand why there is fear. It's hard for me to understand why the first American's religion and beliefs are always scrutinized. I learned in my history class that one of the reasons the Europeans came to the homeland of the First American was to have freedom of religion. Today the Euro-Americans enjoy their freedom of religion in a variety of ways, but they adopt laws that require the First American to obtain licenses and permits to obtain and hold our religious items. This is sad, but I remind myself that God is the boss.

My one-hundred-and-twelve-year-old father told me to go into the Native American Church ceremony to help yourself, to become revived and strong. I also attended because the Native American Church was my dad's religion. Dad composed many touching songs for the church which are still heard today, and as I hear his songs they give me strength by his voice, the words, the song, and the sound of the drum.

A few years ago, a Canadian gentleman joined our Christmas services. He said how grateful and honored he was to be sitting on the ground where my dad had prayed. I was deeply touched by his expressions and remember that feeling like it was yesterday. My dad died in 1979.

Miracles can happen. My brother is a severe diabetic and has had several complications of his disease. Over the years he's been in and out of hospitals. Once the doctors thought he had cancer. He was scheduled for major surgery that could have taken his life. This scheduled

"WE WERE BLESSED BY A MIRACLE"

73

surgery was to follow two other surgeries that had been only a week apart. The family was called in and told to prepare for the worst. I thought I had nowhere to turn. As I prepared to sit with my brother, Earl urged me to go home and pray. The next morning my daughter and I went to the hospital waiting room where we waited and waited. After some time, I asked the receptionist about my brother and was told that the surgery had been postponed until my brother was better able to recoup. The doctor explained that he had had reservations because my brother's symptoms didn't respond as cancer. After meeting with his colleagues, he decided to wait. My brother had already been anaesthetized. That is how close he came to the surgery. I was glad that I had listened to my brother Earl. I had asked God and His helpers to guide the surgeon. My brother did eventually have the surgery and came through fine. We were blessed by a miracle.

"ALL ANIMALS AND BIRDS ARE WELCOME ON MY HOME SITE, AND THEY ARE ALWAYS SAFE THERE."

Lessons occur in my life. Several years ago, I had a dream about an old lady sitting near a fire and telling me a story about the animals in our native tongue. I understood everything she said, and it made me very sad. When I awoke I didn't remember the story but remembered the sadness. Hunting season is a bad time for me. I don't believe in killing animals for sport. Once we were behind a trailer carrying three stags, and I cried because they had been killed just for their heads to hang on a wall. I had to pray for their spirits because I felt so bad. I prayed for all the animals killed on the highways. They are unaware of man's "progressive" highways. That week, different animals, the ones you usually find on the road, came into our yard and close to the house. I believe the visits were an acknowledgment from them.

The birds, through their actions, can have a connection with you. I see the mockingbird as a warrior who will warn you. The cardinal is good luck, goodness, and joy. He has different tunes which he will sing to his heart's content. He lets you know that you're on the right track. For several weeks a red bird woke me up every morning at six. He'll zip across your path and has a color that reaches deep inside you.

As I began to return to my traditional ways, a scissortail came to me in an experience I won't forget. One day, as I was reading, I heard an unusual noise outside and I went to investigate. Outside, a tree full of chirping scissortails had alighted on a big old elm tree by the house. I called my brother and he told me to give them an offering. I did. Now the scissortails let me know when they're around, like in the spring when they return from the south. When I'm down in the dumps they come around.

A turtle ambles across my yard every year both to and from his winter home. He seems to stay around until I can see him and then he continues on his way. Sometimes I wonder if he's the same turtle I had such great pity for once because he had been deformed. I had prayed that turtle would be taken care of. All animals and birds are welcome on my home site, and they are always safe there.

I wanted to share some of my experiences because there was once a time in my life when I wanted to remain in the city. Today, we as Indian people have two roads to follow. We can stay assimilated into the dominant society or we can come home to our traditions. My dad once told me a story about a roadway that came to a fork. One road was easy and smooth. The other was full of barriers and uneven. I had a choice, he said. The rocky road was the good road. Life would not be easy because it is full of barriers. At that time, I didn't understand, but today I can see what he was telling me. To be successful, we must overcome the fallacies brought about by deceit, anger, jealousy and hatred. We as a people are in sync with our own beliefs, legends, and customs; we will become strong as a people. We must defy acculturation and come back to our *own* God-given way of thinking. That can be our goal. The strength for that goal will come from prayer. Prayers are powerful. That's how to maintain in both the Red and White worlds.

"THE ROCKY ROAD WAS THE GOOD ROAD."

Life is nothing without our Creator. We are now working on a project to save our language. Our first step was to ask the Creator for help, and He complied. Laying the foundation hasn't been easy, but nothing is easy for something different. We have barriers of criticism, disapproval, judgment, jealousy, and misinterpretation of our method. But we also have those people who know our language fluently or semi-fluently, those who understand and those who want to learn who have volunteered to participate with the language project. Our goal is to *save our language*, and we will be providing one method as an option. We believe that language, traditional customs and beliefs, and land are synonymous to the Sac and Fox people who follow our ways.

We have much to teach the next generation. We must show them how and why we respect all the things God gave us. We must tell them why we have life and death, explain about the spirits who gave themselves for humanity's sake, familiarize them with the rules of respect for our ceremonies, and teach them to see the beauty of why we do what we do. We must all combine our knowledge to strengthen our circle. If we don't, we could lose it forever.

CHAPTER SEVEN

An interview with Jim Dumont
(Anishinaabe of the Ojibwe Nation)

Jim Dumont is a member of the Fish Clan, the Three Fires Midewiwin Lodge and the Shawanaga First Nation of Eastern Georgian Bay in Ontario, Canada. Since 1970, Jim has pursued the cultural and spiritual roots of traditional indigenous North American ways. Jim has been raised up as Ogimah (chief) at the Eastern Doorway of the Three Fires Midewiwin Lodge and, as such, is the keeper of the sacred Water Drum and leader of the eastern part of Anishinaabe Midewiwin territory.

Since 1974, he has been a professor of Native studies at the University of Sudbury at Laurentian University of Ontario, Canada. He is one of the founders of the department and served as its chair for four years. Jim is a founder of the Centre of Indigenous Knowledge, Research, and Process. The Centre will provide a place in which indigenous research and learning can be interpreted into contemporary Native practice. The Centre is based on the philosophy that the revitalization of indigenous communities is not simply a revival of "old ways" but a renewal of the vitality of "lifeways." The spiritual foundation of indigenous values, traditional knowledge and culture form the source of inspiration for contemporary paradigms of indigenous learning, development, healing, and creative expression.

In our understanding—the Anishinaabe way of understanding—when the Creator created this world and lowered the human being into it, everything was made as the finest, most beautiful expression of his desire to create life. In that beginning time, it is said that the original human being was given instructions on how to live; he was to live in harmony and balance with all of life, and to contribute to it as a sharing member of the family of creation.

The human being was also given a path to follow. That was his own path and his responsibility. In order to follow that path, he was given instructions. Those instructions are what we call the lifeway, the way that life is. In those instructions are what we call the teachings of life. They tell us how life is and how we are supposed to live. Each succeeding generation

then passes on that lifeway. It becomes the responsibility of each generation to pass those teachings on to the generation that is coming into the world. When we get to future eras of human beings' participation in the earth's experience, in every generation, those instructions and that knowledge will be renewed through the teaching. Our way of life—what was given in the beginning—is what has always been.

When you go all the way back to the beginning, the Creator gave us the way of life and that is the way he intended us to live. We are supposed to keep that going. There isn't any other way of life that will come along and replace it. It was given for all time and he did that for all the colors of human beings. They all have their original instructions. They all have their way of living on the earth and respecting creation and living in harmony with it. Ours is particular to our way of being. We depend on the other colors of man to keep their ways of life going. Our responsibility is to keep ours going.

"THE SPIRIT IS STILL THERE WITHIN THE PEOPLE."

People say these days that if we are to go on into the future, it is necessary for us to go back to the old ways and revise them. What should be said is that we have to return to, revive and renew that which has always been—the lifeway. The Creator gave us our lifeway and as long as we follow that we will always have life.

What we are looking for now is that lifeway. Not just our survival, but our ability to live, to have life. And our quality of life depends on us being able to renew and revive the lifeway itself. That is the true understanding of the revival that is taking place in this time.

In the last two to five hundred years, we have experienced a whole new people coming here and a whole new way of life that has been foisted on us. We have been forced and persuaded to accept their new way of life and the whole, apparently spiritual way that they brought with them. We were told that their way is the only way. We have set aside, abandoned, or have been forced to let go of our own way of life. And rather than receiving new life, it has almost destroyed us as people. We have almost totally lost our language, our culture, our tradition, our knowledge of how to live in this world, our relationship to the environment and to the relatives of this creation. We have almost totally lost our ability to take care of ourselves and our families, our own healing, and the rebuilding of our communities and our nation. But what has been given in the beginning and what has always been is still there. It is said it is scattered along the trail of the last five hundred years. Here and there is our language, our culture, our spirituality.

The most critical thing we have lost touch with is the spirits, our own spirit and the spirit of our ways. That is our spirituality. A lot of people, even at one point the majority of people, have accepted or adopted a whole other way that is not our own. It has not really done anything for us. In fact it has crippled us as a people and it continues to do that. This other religion depends on our being dominated and controlled by the people who own it. We can only be adopted into it if we accept that. Actually, it is a tool of colonialism. The only way that we can find ourselves, reclaim ourselves, is to go back to that way which has always been through the revival and renewal of our lifeway. It is still there. It is still within ourselves. We can go back along the path and reclaim it. The spirit is still there within the people. It has been hidden, it has been pushed aside, but it is still there and is the Anishinaabe spirit.

Our ways are still there, our way of life. Here we are in the dying moments of the twentieth century, almost into the twenty-first century, and we say the reality that we live within is totally different from anything we ever knew. It is just a different environment, a different context. Not a very good one, not a very harmonious or balanced one, not a very healthy one, but this is the environment that we live in today. The lifeway that spoke to our people before, and gave our people life in all the generations before us, is still the way of life that will give us life today. How it will manifest itself and find expression in this new time comes as part of the responsibility of how we go about the revival and the renewal.

There are ceremonies, teachings, and songs that have always been and will always be. They cannot and should not be changed, but there will be new ceremonies. There will be new songs. There will be a new way of speaking but it will be a way that comes from the foundation of what has always been. It will find a new expression that speaks to the people of this time. But it will still be that which has always been. That is the very core of our lifeway, our teaching, the knowledge of our way of life. It is the heart and essence of our spirituality. That does not change and will not change. It will find an expression that in appearance may be new because this is a different time. It is not going back and reviving the old way we lived five hundred years ago. It is not time to go back to the teepee, not time to travel by canoe instead of driving cars, not time to dress the way that we dressed five hundred years ago. That is not what it means, but when you say, we go back to the old ways, that is the impression that it gives.

What is at the heart of the way that we are, the way that we dress, the way that we live life, and the way that we surround ourselves with shelter and with those things to which we are entitled in life? The environment in which we live is an expression of what we believe and what we trust in, what we depend on. If it emerges from out of the lifeway, out of the teachings that carry them, then it should create an environment around us that is an expression of that. Is living in square buildings piled one on top of another, where you never are able to touch the earth or feel the environment, the highest and best expression of our belief and lifeway? Does that allow the spirit of who we are to give the finest expression of our being? The answer to that is no. How do we find and experience that in this life we live today? It probably isn't getting out of where we live right now and setting up a traditional wigwam out in the bush somewhere.

For us, we are part of the Anishinaabe people. When we use the word, Anishinaabe, it means all indigenous people of Turtle Island. But Anishinaabe also means all those who are of the same culture and language, so it includes the Ojibwe, Cree, Saukee, Mesquakie, Kickapoo, Shawnee–all those people are Anishinaabe. The people of the Ojibwe Nation were entrusted with the teachings, knowledge, and preservation of that way of life. The Midewin, which is our sacred and spiritual way of life, houses all that knowledge, the ways and understanding of life. It houses the healing and healing practices. All that is held within the Midewin was entrusted to the Ojibwe people. This does not mean it was given only to the Ojibwe people. But they were the ones who were told to hold onto that and keep it going, which is why the Midewin is still among us. It almost disappeared even among the Ojibwe people by the end of the 1960s.

"WHAT IS THE HIGHEST AND BEST EXPRESSION OF OUR LIFEWAY?"

79

I became involved around the time the revival occurred. That revival was part of a prophecy that was given and a realization that we now had entered the time that the prophet had spoken of. It was a prophecy of the seventh fire, that the time would come when the people who had almost lost everything would begin to retrace their steps to reclaim those things that were left scattered along the trail, and bring them into this new time to revive, rebuild and renew them, and hand them to the next generation. We would be the children of the seventh fire, the ones to live fully and completely within this again. We are the generation of the seventh fire, the children of the injured ones who have experienced the loss of all these things. We are the ones upon whom future generations depend.

The revival, the spiritually centered renewal, started in the early 1970s. As that spiritual revival takes place, it brings us back to the very heart, the very core, the very spirit of who we are. In order to get back to the spirit of who we are, we have to know the teachings, the prophecies—we have to understand what life is all about. Spiritual renewal is the renewal of everything. Everything depends on it. The spirit is at the core, the center. We cannot rebuild our nation politically without coming back to the core and the spirit of who we really are. Within our teachings we must learn to find our own spirituality. It is based right in our culture, our own knowledge, our own way of life.

We have never experienced physical and sexual abuse, as we have in this generation. Abuse is rampant in our communities. That is new to our time. The process of healing, the very heart of our way, has to be able to speak to the disease of abuse which is everywhere around us. How that is passed on, from one generation to another, perpetuating itself, is new. The total degradation and abuse of the environment, all the chemicals that have been put into it, weakens the food that we eat, weakens the natural medicines that are there. These are all factors in the reality in which we live which were never there before. We have to work in a context and environment oppressive in ways that we have never experienced before.

We know that the answer to all of this is in our way of life. It is in our teachings, it is in our spirituality, it is in our relationship to the environment, to the earth and to one another as human beings. In knowing that, we know that is the answer even with the critical state of this environment, the context in which we live today. We have to be able to translate from what has always been and will always be. We have to translate those principles of nationhood, government, healing, and education in all areas and make them speak to the situation today.

It can work today, but we have to recognize the situation in which we live. We may have to create a school in which we can educate a number of people rather than doing it as mentor to novice, teaching one-on-one. We may have to create a more formalized system of learning, where we can teach and learn in an environment that is very different from what we have been used to. We have to do that on a traditional foundation. It may take a different shape, it may have a different appearance, but the base will be in tradition. The healing practices that we engage in today may not involve the healing lodge, the traditional context of healing. We have to help them and lead them to that time when they can become a part of those ceremonies that do contain those traditional elements.

The nature of things now is that the whole knowledge of our life and way of being is operating in a context which is not traditional. We are not familiar with those things. We are in the process of learning all those things. We would have the tendency to dream about something that comes from television programs or some rhythms that we had to learn in school. Then we would dream our dreams within those images we have learned rather than from a traditional context. We have to learn our concept of life again and begin to come into touch with the tree life, the animal life, the spirits that are around us. Then we will begin to have within our imagery and our minds greater ways of conceiving of and perceiving life, and the patterns and images that will allow us to dream in a way our spirit can work with.

Right now, our spirit has to work with giving us understanding through dreams and images that we can relate to. It is the same when you go through a healing process. You might have to write on a piece of paper instead of drawing on a traditional scroll. You might have to give people something to read, or tell them to keep a journal. That is what people are used to. They are not used to bringing all of these things together in a holistic way, the way a ceremony does. As people go through their own personal healing process, they should be learning their own ways. As they evolve through the process and reach higher and higher stages of healing, then they merge into the higher forms of healing and spiritual strengthening. Fasting, the sweat lodge, healing sweat, the spirit sweat, and the healing dance are all stages of healing. By the time you go through the midewin ceremony itself for initiation, or by the time you go to the Sun Dance lodge, you can participate totally within that context and experience the wholeness of it. You can actually be in touch with all of the levels of your own body, mind, feeling and spirit.

The Sun Dance is actually one of the greatest healing ceremonies there is. Why do people go to Sun Dances today? Some of them because it is Indian, and because it is supposed to be an expression of our spirituality, and not for much reason beyond that. But it is one of the highest forms of healing that there is. To be initiated into the midewin is not only a spiritual quest, it is a total healing in every sense of the word.

By the time we fully revive those greater ceremonies, our people should be going through all these processes of their own healing, of their own education, of their own way of relating to one another. But to do that, we have to know ourselves at the most fundamental level.

CHAPTER EIGHT

An Interview With Jeanette Armstrong

(Okanagan)

Jeanette Armstrong is a fluent speaker of the Okanagan language and has studied and practiced traditional ways for many years under the direction of Okanagan elders. She is a writer, sculptor, artist, teacher, and an outspoken aboriginal rights activist. After studying creative writing and receiving a degree in fine arts from the University of Victoria, Jeanette focused her work on the development of First Nations educational institutions. She is founder and former director of the Enow'kin Centre and is currently the Director of their International Writing School. The Centre is a postsecondary institution, dedicated to Indian control of Indian education, which provides programs in fine arts and first- and second-year university courses.

Jeanette has written a number of books including *Slash*, a novel, and *Breathtracks*, a collection of poetry. She recently co-authored, with architect Douglas Cardinal, *The Native Creative Process*, and has also written children's books and film scripts produced for television.

She is a founder of the Indigenous University of the Americas, which will encompass an international network of Native scholars in North, Central and South America. The philosophy of this university defines education as a healing process of mind, body, feeling and spirit, focused on restoring the whole person and whole community. She lives in Penticton, British Columbia.

I think about education in the way that we have been developing it in the Okanagan community and Okanagan nation. Over the past hundred years, there has been a slow internal disintegration of the survival principles developed over thousands of years. There are a number of ways of speaking about education in the Okanagan tradition. These ways have little to do with schooling, which is not even counted as education in Okanagan.

I grew up in a family that practiced traditional education. In high school, I started to question the contemporary situation we found ourselves in. The society that colonized this country and surrounds us dictates to our community a kind of education that is destructive to our people and their people as well. One of the things I could see, but could not articulate, was that this form of education was not oriented toward how human beings need to interact with one another to be healthy—spiritually and emotionally—as people, families, and communities. Studying sociology, psychology, or political science was like looking through a telescope at something far removed, something external to yourself. Public mass education has to do with that separation from yourself as a human being and as a part of family, of the land, and the community.

When I decided to go to the university, I wanted to be able to find my own answers about education. If the answers made sense to me, then they should help make a change happen in my community. I guess the question that always entered my mind was, why is it such a hard thing to convince ourselves to be happy? When I completed high school and started college in the early seventies, I could see the breakdown in our community, the factionalism between various groups of people, and the breakdown in the family. I could see the abandonment of principles which were central to our being as Okanagan people and as caretakers of the land.

Our conduct displays our change in values and our lack of good education. I could say in my own language what we needed to be educated in as individuals, family and community, and in terms of human interaction with the land. I could not see in the contemporary world how to make that possible without stepping back into history and living in the old way. This is the work that I have been involved in—finding answers to those questions about how it is possible, how it can happen. That has led to the development of a number of things which have become a widespread movement in the Okanagan. I can't say that I am responsible, because I did not have the answers or the solutions either. All I had were questions, and I thought they were good questions.

I also had some understanding, from my own upbringing and family, that these principles were solid and could outlast anything. Through them, we could overcome whatever challenges there might be as individuals, family, community and interface with the land. It is how you apply those principles, given different circumstances, and how you reinterpret and reintegrate them every time new circumstances happen. The key is in the process of how to reintegrate and reinterpret these principles continuously.

"WHAT DO I REALLY KNOW ABOUT THE OKANAGAN TRADITIONAL LIFESTYLE?"

When I completed my program at the university, I decided that if I wanted to begin my Okanagan education, I had to come home. I had to educate myself, with the help of other people, in history, tradition, ceremonial ways, language, social and political structures. I also had to educate myself every time new learning came along, as to what that means in today's world. I spent two years looking at beliefs, ceremonies, and political movements in relation to our history and understanding of our land, ecology and our society itself. How does that integrate itself into the kinds of actions, activities and decisions we make every day? My thinking flip-flopped between the externalized form of decisions that can be documented (the political) and the everyday things that we do in order to express that in community (the sociological).

In the 1970s, there was a movement across the country of political thought in resistance to colonialism. At the same time, there was a resurgence of awareness about what being Native might be and a revival of ceremony and tradition. In the Okanagan we questioned how these things become expressed in our world, how we work at our jobs, and how we socialize in the community at functions. Those questions fascinated me. That is where change takes place. Change takes place around the table, at your work place, and the places you socialize.

So I started asking, how do we socialize, how do we approach our work, how do approach each other in our families? What are the things that have changed from the way they were to what we are doing now? Are there things we need to relearn in order to make healthy change happen where disintegration has taken place? Questions like that were occurring to me.

Right off, I thought, what do I really truly know about the Okanagan traditional lifestyle? What do I really know about family organization, family interface with community, how each individual fits in terms of work, responsibility, roles, and their own freedoms and liberties to express themselves? How did that traditionally happen? How does the land tie in with that?

There were many missing gaps, even for me, and I am a traditional person. I was brought up in a family that does ceremony, that goes out every year and brings in the four main foods, and we feast on those four main foods. And every winter, we have the medicine dance, and we have sweats ongoing. Yet, I had no understanding of these things.

So I started talking to the elected leaders in the Okanagan. I speak Okanagan fluently and have been an interpreter of Okanagan. I was always interpreting for the elders into English, or from English back to Okanagan, so I could go to any reserve and be welcomed and accepted. I could speak about things and people would listen to me. I would ask a lot of questions and we would get discussions going. In the early seventies, there were discussions from one reserve to the other for about three years. Some people who could not express those issues in words expressed them in frustration, and in feelings and emotions of anger and grief.

We closed the Okanagan for two years. The chiefs and the people met in every reserve they could, and we finally had a huge meeting. Out of that series of discussions emerged an understanding that, number one, we were Okanagan and we had valuable things to reintegrate into our lives—but we couldn't just tell people to do that. It had to make everyday sense. We all came to the understanding that we had to pursue it in a way that was people-based.

We decided that education would be made a priority. The whole nation decided that. The elders, chiefs, councils, the young people, and the mothers and fathers who attended. I am not saying that everybody attended these meetings, but they were the biggest meetings that I have seen in the Okanagan. We have videos of them. They were spectacular because we had no agenda. I don't remember there ever being a day when there was an agenda.

We developed a group of people to act as facilitators. Synthesizers, I guess, is the best word. We would sit and talk and talk and then they would go into the community and talk to the people in the community. These weren't older people. Most of them were in their twen-

"THE PROCESS ITSELF WAS PUTTING TRUST, HOPE AND A LOT OF STRENGTH INTO THE MOVEMENT."

ties, very good facilitators and hard workers. They went house to house in the community explaining that there was going to be a meeting; explaining what we were concerning ourselves with; telling people that we needed their input, thinking, and comments about jobs, tradition, and politics. People would come because we made that contact.

The meetings themselves demonstrated that this was a natural process for our people. We had, I guess you could call it, democratic consensus-making, which people depend on to give them voice and a feeling of strength. Even if we don't know how this is going to come together, we are all in it together. It took us a year to realize that the process itself, in how we were gathering and talking with everyone, was putting trust, hope and strength into the movement. The process was the backbone of the movement.

We looked at that process and said, we need to recognize and reinstitute it in all of our decision making in the Okanagan, wherever we can. We need to articulate it as a way of carrying out one of the main principles of our people—respect. We respect difference and the need for everyone to be included and for no one to be left out, no matter how small a minority. Everyone has the ability to participate and to say, "No, that is something I do not like, and here is why," and be listened to and not be argued with.

This is known as the *enow'kin* process. This process does not presume an agenda, outcome, or direction. It presumes we all have minds, that we all have good thinking, that we all have the best intentions but we do not know what everybody else is thinking. If we know what everybody else is thinking, that can help us make the best decisions because we care about each other. The underlying thing is that we care about how the other person feels. We are in community. We care how we make decisions. If we can make decisions that feel good to everyone, then that is the best that we can do. If we do that together, we are more likely to be healthy and stronger. The underlying principle is respect for each other and caring for one another. That means taking responsibility for listening to the other, hearing the other from their perspective, and understanding why it is important for them and then seeing how it comes up against your perspective. Where those two things come into conflict, you take the responsibility to find a way to make it more comfortable for the other person.

If everybody in a room or everybody in a nation does that, it creates solidarity. It does not mean that everybody gets what they want, but it means that everyone understands clearly why they must make compromises. You can't do that by insisting that your thinking is the only right way. This became one of the underlying principles of the movement. That is why *enow'kin* to us is the central spirit, the spirituality of our people.

With that, we began to look at the traditions of our people. So that began for me the process of finding all those people who were interested in looking at the ceremonies and spiritual practice of our people and how that interprets into an everyday sense.

From all of our research, we know that, historically, the people were very spiritual. They did not even eat food without it being a spiritual act. The gathering, the blessing and the feasting of the foods were spiritual acts. They did not make any kind of clothing or implements without recognition of where those things came from and how they were gathered. All of those things were incorporated into their ceremonial process, which they recognized in how they treated each other. All of this was incorporated into the social customs that we have and the ceremonies that underlie those customs. If you are a community developer, you need to engage the community in looking for that—understanding the tradition, how those traditions are reinterpreted, and then understanding how to strengthen them, so that they reintegrate back into people's lives in a natural way.

I found many things. I thought there had been a big loss, and there has, but actually many things have evolved, been reinterpreted and displayed themselves in a very different way. I found that we, as Okanagans, find any excuse to get together. If somebody says that we are going to do something, then all of a sudden everybody will start showing up and participating. That is an Okanagan thing. If somebody said, these people over here need furniture or something built, so we are going to have this flea market or this supper or this rifle shoot, people who do not even engage in those things will show up. If everybody knows that people are raising money and half of the jackpot is going to go for nails or whatever for the longhouse, people will show up who do not even shoot rifles, who are not part of the hunter families. They will show up and they will pay their five dollars and get their three targets and they will hire somebody to shoot or whatever.

Inside of us as Okanagans, we want to help people to do things. We want to do it in a way that is enjoyable to us, so that is not like welfare or something like that. There is an understood principle that those people are putting time and effort into organizing themselves, so we need to assist with that. We will enjoy one another and will commune with one another. We will all take part in that good feeling.

In simple words, it is the good feeling more than the obligation to give that is the underlying motivation. We know that we do not have to say it, but we can all feel it together.

That is a communing to me, in a real community sense. It is not so much dwelling on the responsibility, which is where the emphasis is placed in some other religions, but on the fun, the communal aspect. We all feel that. You can see it in everyone's eyes. So things like flea markets, bake sales, potluck suppers, rifle shoots or walk-a-thons—people will drop everything to go to them and they'll really look forward to them, put them on their calendars. That is amazing to me. That is totally amazing.

We need to look at ways to reintegrate this aspect of our lives into education; not in a regimented, institutionalized sense, but as a way to expand and enrich our community. This does a number of things that politics and formal meetings can't do. It accomplishes things among people who are progressive and positive about community and economics and the material things that we need from each other.

In addition to the *enow'kin*, a democratic process where everyone is listening and engaging and which gives strength to each other, there is the internal spiritual need we are born with as humans. That is the creative need we have to feel part of others—the community, family, and nation—and the need to have that reinforced by our actions. While that is easily implemented because it is a natural process already there, it needs someone to give more permission and focus to it. So our educational process looked at teaching people about finding ways that families and whole communities can engage in that process. We talked about this with our leaders, the people in our communities, and with our elders especially. They said yes, that is the spirit of love of our people, that is the spirit of the Okanagan. That is the most important part of us; it holds us together as a people. Otherwise, we could be anything else, and we will be anything else, unless we can, as a community, recognize how to keep that going.

The spiritual leaders, the medicine people who had done ceremonies during this process told us that we had their permission to go out as spiritual leaders, understanding that the spirituality of our people has to do with the internal spirit of our people. So, wherever there is a communing of our people, that is a celebration of our spirit as Okanagan. It does not have to be in the traditional sense, like we used to have big powwows and festivals. There can be a powwow once a year but that is only once a year. You can have a festival maybe two or three times a year to feast different kinds of foods, but only some of the people get to that. The awakening of the communal spirit is done maybe once or twice a year, where it needs to be awakened all the time. So, they said, this may not be appear to be spiritual processes or awakening because it is not recognized as ceremony, but any time people can pull together to do something, make or build something, to pool together to make something happen, in other words to be able to work together and give of each other, that is a spiritual practice. This is what pulls our people together spiritually. It does not have to be a ceremony; it can be a flea market. Anything we do together, anything that pulls everybody together for a common purpose, is a spiritual act.

The second principle that we learned in our educational process in terms of health, community, and tradition, is that spirituality needs to make real sense, needs to make sense on a day-to-day basis. Spirituality belongs to every Okanagan person and it belongs in an everyday sense, everywhere, in everything that we do.

The *enow'kin* process takes the view that there is no conflict. What appears to be conflict is a fear of hurting each other or being hurt. That is what conflict resonates as, and, actually, it is not conflict. It is really people who are afraid to come any closer—in order not to injure one another—because there has been a history of injury. If people start with the understanding that we have different views and we need to come to a point where we each understand our different views, then we can adjust our behavior towards one another in a better way which is not hurtful. I want to know about your different view. I am responsible for knowing about it because I do not want to hurt you. I do not want to do anything painful to you because we have to be in this community together. I solicit your different view; I ask for it. I want to know, I need to understand, and I need you to tell me even if you think it is going to hurt me. I need to know, because otherwise it is going to go on hurting us. It is not going away if I don't know. That person then feels safe enough to say what they need to say. If they give you permission to do the same thing, then it usually resolves in a really good way. Conflict is not conflict, it is simply not communicating.

Communication then becomes the third principle that we looked at. Traditionally, we used to have runners who went to every community to explain current news and issues. They went from one end of the valley to the other, which is no different from sending a bulletin from here to there, or sending an emissary, somebody who acts as a spokesperson. We said we need to put together a weekly bulletin in every community. The bulletins are real

straightforward: the meetings that are happening, political issues that are being debated, recreational things that are happening, fundraising events, family gatherings and ceremonies that are going on. Each community has one. So every week, everyone is informed and looks forward to that little bulletin. It is not a newspaper with a journalist's view. It is important communication because people write in to those bulletins and will express a view about it. You will inevitably see a view about something that is being planned or ignored or overlooked. The views will come up like that and soon as a view comes up there is usually a meeting. If someone disagrees with something or is mad about something, it will come up and then everyone will have a meeting about it. So people are not left with their anger.

Communication also extends outward through the publishing program that we have developed at the Enow'kin Centre and the development of a number of other programs for communication internally in our families. In the last three years, we have been re-instituting traditional family meetings. Every week, extended families will get together and they have a spokesperson from every household. Sometimes just the household heads get together to discuss all the issues in the family. Sometimes the whole extended family will get together, if it is something that everybody wants to talk about. There can be a wide range of subjects. This was something that was slow in bringing back into our community. We talked about it and wrote about it. Different families who were still having family meetings opened them up to other families to come and observe. In the last three years, that has been the thrust of our communication efforts.

What happens at the family meetings is really important and it is something I am really excited about in terms of community development. In the family meetings, all the issues that people want to talk about are brought up and everybody talks about their views on those issues. They can be talking about our rights, employment, administration, religion, recreation or any topic. They also talk about internal family problems like alcohol or drug abuse, marriage problems or conflicts between family members. These are brought to the family meeting and everyone helps with finding ways to help bring about understanding, so that they can be resolved. Sometimes there are even smaller meetings in which one household group will have a family meeting. There are some real problems with children and the disassociation that is created by the town people. In a family meeting, parents come to understand their young people and their feelings; and the young will be able to talk to their parents. There are a lot of people being trained in how to facilitate that kind of group meeting. People can learn to speak with honesty and without shame, without the fear of rejection or of someone being angry at them, putting them down or denying what they are saying.

In the Okanagan, whenever you call a circle, it is understood that there are rules to the game. The first understanding is that what is said is to be kept in that group. The second is that every person who speaks can say everything they want to say, however they want to say it. They need to do that to fully express themselves and make themselves understood at an emotional level. They need not be fearful of doing that because of other people's reactions or feelings. Another rule is not to debate, argue, or put down what someone else is saying. It is really a process of understanding how we communicate emotionally, understanding that emotions are often the greatest obstacles between us and making good and sane decisions and interacting with one another in a good way. It moves people away from fear and denial to being honest, open and emotionally healthy.

One of the things that happens is the relearning of sensitivity, care, and respect for the emotions of another person. It bonds people in a real trust of one another. Bonding at that level is one of the community development mechanisms that creates the cohesiveness that keeps community together. Being able to trust and care enough for one another, to hear one another's real complaints, anger, or grief is what we understand in the Okanagan tradition as essential before any decisions can be made.

One of our spiritual elders said that no one can make good decisions if their emotions are standing in the way of their understanding of how other people are affected. They should not be in a position of making decisions out of their own emotional corner. In order for good clear thinking to happen, we have to be able to be compassionate and loving enough to know that we are human, we care about each other, we all have feelings, we all can get angry, and therefore, we need to understand each other at that level. That is absolutely essential.

This is one of the really hard pieces of work we have because we have learned from the European how to suppress emotion. Everyone is fearful of expressing their emotions. If you cry or get angry in front of somebody, you have disgraced yourself, created something sinful. You do not bring your emotions, you leave your feelings at home. To us, that is the most ridiculous thing to tell anybody. We say, bring your emotions here, otherwise we are going to come back to this question over and over again. We are not going to get anywhere until we deal with these emotions. You are going to get people taking separate corners from now until doomsday.

If those things come into place in our community, we can do anything. The economics are not a problem. The social net is not a problem. The violence and abuse are not, those are symptoms. If we fix the economics or if we fix the social violence and abuse by finding ways to cope, we have still not dealt with the real underlying community issues and those symptoms will continue to occur. Poor economics, decision-making, political functioning and all those things are symptoms of what is not happening at those levels that I am talking about.

Community development is a multi-layered and complex process. The fourth level is the intellectual, analytical, or logical part of community development. The heart of the community is the need to bond at an emotional level. One of the overriding and aggressive parts of our beings as individuals is our intellect, our mental process. Traditionally, logic was given a different place in our world than the emotional place—what we call the spirit of the people or the physical place. The mind needs to be able to bridge those connections logically and analytically. It needs to be able to see where those two things come together and make sense. In other words, the sense making of. That is one of the parts of relearning how our common Okanagan mind and spirit can survive in the contemporary world. The hardest part when we talk about education is the mind and the intellect.

The scientific concept of the world is that you can only prove the existence of something if it is quantifiable, measurable, or definable. It emerges for the Okanagan as a real center of contention. In terms of community, what does that mean? What does that mean in terms of what we think about, what we concern our minds with? What are the things that are at issue in our minds, when we are thinking about religion versus Native philosophical tradition? What is the philosophical expression of that as a whole, as Okanagans?

That is a question that is really exciting in education and community development. What is the philosophy of the Okanagan and how has it been changed? What are the things that have been integrated from the non-Native community? How does that affect our every-day lifestyle? How does that make us decide to do this and not that? How does that make me decide to go to university rather than stay home and just have kids? How does that make me decide to become a Christian or not a Christian or become involved in the Native tradition? Those are intellectual choices. They are tied to the heart, but they are intellectual choices.

"YOU BEGIN TO SEE WHERE THE ANGER COMES FROM." Part of my work is finding the commonalities in communities. Say everybody gets mad at certain things, what are those things? If I were to go to any community and ask a real honest, no-name kind of opinion, they would say, "The band office sucks." I would say, okay, what is it about the band office? You could go into any Indian country and hear that. So if it sucks, why does it suck? The regular everyday person does not want to have anything to do with the band office. Even though they work in the band office, they will say, "Yeah, we are doing our best here, but we are in turmoil." One of the things that I am led to ask is, why? What underlies that level of emotion and intellectual thought toward the band office? What is creating that?

Overlying everything is the thought and mind of the people. The word for it in our language is hard to describe in English because there is no equivalent word for it. The closest I can come to is our communal tribal mind consciousness. It is not one person's mind that creates that consciousness, it is many minds that create that consciousness. All those many minds have the same kind of logic processing equipment. If you feed their processing equipment certain input, they are all going to come up with the same answer, the same conclusion at the end. So what are those things that get fed into that logic-making communal mind that says "the band office stinks," at the other end?

In the Okanagan, it is not the band office that stinks. There are other things that are happening that are not in the best interests of the people, and they know that. It ends up equating with "the band office stinks." You begin to see things like the dependence on the Department of Indian Affairs program, and then you begin to see where the anger comes from. Not the band office, but how those programs don't work. What they do achieve is dependence but what they don't achieve is a way to utilize them in a way which brings forth the self-sufficiency, usefulness, and creativity of the people and the empowerment that comes with that. Federal programs don't engage the people in terms of their contribution to the community or to the family. They negate that. So the program is something that you take and don't feel good about. You use those programs, but they are not fulfilling in terms of your contribution as a person who has certain gifts, skills or qualities.

Intellectually, people can point to all the different problems, but the underlying issue is that the programs do not supply what the people need. The things that are necessary for community are not thought about in how these programs are designed. People have all kinds of reactions because there is the underlying awareness that the programs are not meeting the needs of individuals, families, or communities in a healthy way. In fact, they create ill health, dysfunction, and dependence. So the people end up with the conclusion that the band office

stinks. I use the band office as an example, but this applies to all the programs, housing, welfare, and employment—that flow out of that process.

The work of the Center has always been the *enow'kin* process of having the liberty to reach out with those questions and presume that not one person has the answers. That a lot of people through their minds, hearts and intellect can find and build those solutions every time new circumstances come. That the four underlying principles just described are teachable, functional, realistic and usable. The process does not talk about how economics should be done, or how tradition should be carried out, or how society or politics should function. It talks about what the underlying principles are that are meaningful to us as humans, in terms of us as individuals, family, and as spiritual beings on the land. The Centre refers to those as the underlying principles that define what politics, economics, or social functions should be, so that there is continuous openness for change.

Being an Indian Is Like The

Frosting on a Cake. It Is The Sweet,

Juicy Part of Being Human

C H A P T E R   N I N E

An Interview With Floyd Flores

(Hia-Ced O'odham)

Floyd Flores is a leader of, and former coordinator for, the Hia-Ced O'odham Alliance, which seeks to reacquire and establish a homeland on their tribe's aboriginal territories. Prior to European contact, the Hia-Ced O'odham (Sand Papago) lived in the southwestern part of the present state of Arizona, east into the existing Tahona O'odham Nation, north beyond the Gila River, west of the Colorado River, and south, extending into Central Mexico.

The Hia-Ced O'odham and their territories were subject to the Spanish government until 1820, when the Mexican government was established. In 1854, the settlement for the Gadsden Purchase separated the O'odham by the establishment of an international boundary. The Papago Reservation, established in 1916 by American presidential decree, excluded the Hia-Ced O'odham and their territories were seized by the federal government. Since that time, they have been deprived of access to their aboriginal territories, resulting in great loss of language, customs, ceremonies, and pride.

In 1975, the descendants of the Hia-Ced O'odham initiated an effort to reacquire a home base for their future generations. In the past eight years, they have registered over 1,500 members of a people declared extinct by noted historians and researchers. In 1994, the Hia-Ced O'odham Alliance was formally organized and work to recover their lands begun.

The Alliance is researching and documenting the current and historical subsistence, cultural, and religious uses of their aboriginal lands for tribal records, archives, oral history, reservation-based elementary school curricula, and university-level courses, and as evidence to be used in the court fight to reacquire a landbase for the Hia-Ced O'odham citizenship.

It is difficult to live in this society and retain indigenous cultural values but if you retain the spirit, I think it can be done. I think if you really have the spirit, nothing will interrupt or stop you.

Photograph in this chapter by JJ FOXX/NYC.

Our philosophy is based on holistic thinking. Most projects have become specific and do not integrate the other aspects of our philosophy as Native Americans. You get these experts who have specialized in a field for a number of years, and then they go out and give conferences, workshops, and speeches and get paid very well for it. In the meantime, that universal thinking, that holistic philosophy of the Indian people, is put on the back shelf. I see this universal thinking as both a necessity and a choice that one makes. You can always put that philosophy on the back burner and go out and make a decent living being an expert. In some regards, it is a necessity because a guy has to eat, provide for his family and make ends meet. Sacrificing this philosophy is a personal choice that one makes.

"WE ARE PART OF THE HUMAN FAMILY ON THIS PLANET."

Native seed production is becoming a specialized field that is geared only towards the reproduction of Native crops. But do they have the spirit? What about the land the crops are planted on? Where is the prayer for that? Is the plant strategically located to incorporate the natural forces that contribute to the overall health and well-being of that particular crop? A lot of people do not understand the interaction of plants with insects of various sorts. There is often a certain bug that only pollinates a certain plant. People begin to view that plant as being endangered because there are very few of them. They neglect to observe that this plant's particular insect has been trampled on, or his food source has been depleted because of cattle grazing, for example. So, because the insect is being trampled on, the plants are not being pollinated. All of a sudden the plant becomes an endangered species. So you have to look beyond the plant and at the whole environment.

In our projects, we try to integrate all factors. Our project is a land acquisition and a community and nation-building project. Israel is a good example of nation-building. They took that land, settled it, and they began to build. They had to incorporate a lot of elements in order to get to the point where they are now. Our project is very similar. But rather than leaving out the prayer for our land, we do it first. We begin to tap the economic, political, and educational resources of the region. We begin to examine the regulatory aspects. We begin to scrutinize the biodiversity of that region and the interaction between plant and animal or man and environment. Many people look at the impact of man on the environment, but they do not examine the interaction between man and environment.

We looked at all the established institutions—the National Parks Service, the U.S. Air Force, the various agencies of the federal government. We began to scrutinize their policies, regulations, and management styles. We began to question why the Bureau of Land Management has a set of policies in their area, which is adjacent to the National Park Service, which has a different set of polices and regulations for their areas. Why is it different? If you look on one side of the fence from the other, one looks real nice and the other looks really bad. How come we can't get these two agencies to sit down at the same table and figure out a policy that would benefit the whole environment? Each one of them has a mission statement that is not compatible with the other's, although they live right next to each other.

In order for our project to work and for people to understand where we are coming from, we had to examine all of these various factors and simultaneously look at our human factor, our children, our future generations. We look at them and ask ourselves what type of education they really need. What type of direction can we provide for them? We began to try to incorporate projects in the school curricula that would exercise their minds, make them aware of the interactions around them.

We began looking at this whole region and developing plans so that we would have a say in everything that goes on. We would tap everybody, from the youngest to the oldest, with regard to what is going on in this region. For example, Ophelia Rivas runs this environmental education project with the National Park Service called Juntas. The project goes into the elementary schools on the reservation in the towns of Ajo, Rocky Point, and Puerto Panesco and the community of Sonora across the border in Mexico. It provides a curriculum that teaches the young kids to respect, protect, and preserve the environment. Everybody looks at it as a very good, environmentally-oriented project. The whole environmental movement is based on an Indian way of thinking. You are right in line when you begin to teach environmental education.

At the same time, this particular project can get our people's voices into the school system. In our land acquisition project, we decided that rather than focusing all of our energies on that, we wanted to encompass everybody in the whole region. We wanted to create the belief that Hia-Ced O'odham exists; that we can be self-sufficient; that we have a philosophy, goal and mission. We are a part of this whole human family that is on this planet.

The Mexicans on the other side of the border say the only reason that we are having these projects is because we want to take land in this area. They are absolutely right, except that we are not taking it from anybody–this is God's land and it does not really belong to anybody. We have a right to be on this land, as much as anybody else, whether we pay taxes or not. So, in that regard, we are here to be a part of the land, but we are not taking it in the way they think we are.

Our project encompasses economic, environmental, educational, social, and political aspects. We organized a town hall meeting, before they were popular or trendy. In that meeting, we managed to get all of the agencies, all the prominent and political people to come and address some local concerns. We orchestrated that to the point where we were up on the stage saying, "We are the Hia-Ced O'odham, we are in this area, we have an intent, and we want you to know about it." We told the people of the town of Ajo, "Hey, you guys have some economic concerns. Let's get them out in the open, so your neighbors know about it and can discuss it." Everybody contributed and everybody benefited.

From that town hall meeting sprang an organization which they now call the Sonoran Desert Alliance. It is made up of people from all the little towns in the area, on the Mexican side of the border, and Indians from the reservation. These guys meet on a monthly basis. This provides a forum for the Hia-Ced O'odham effort to address land acquisition. We have the border patrol, the INS, U.S. Customs, the mayors of all those towns, and council members sitting in one room. We are telling them what we see and what we want to see. At the same time, we are taking the time to listen to what they see as their needs and how they would like to fulfill them. When Indian people want land, they sometimes take this militaristic type of approach–guns, barricades, protest marches, and so on. Rather than being

"RATHER THAN BEING RADICAL OR MILITANT, WE HAVE A PRAYER ON THE LAND."

radical or militant, we have a prayer done on the land. When we arrive at that day when we stand and say, "This land is ours," we will be able to say to God that we have it in a good way, so that he will bless our future generations. That is our approach.

We frown on this militant attitude. In real life, you don't treat people that way. You don't expect people to treat you that way, although sometimes it happens. So I told my fellow workers, "I can't hold nothing against nobody, no matter how bad they treat us, no matter how bad they talk about me. I have a goal of my own. I am going to this place, and along the way, I can't hold nothing against these people, no matter how bad they treat my people, me, my mother, my father, child, family or anybody else. This place I am going is everlasting life; I am going to be with God. In order for me to get there, I can't hold nothing against these people. All I can try to do is forgive and pray for them, and hope that they will be all right. I hope that they can see the way we look at things."

Our project encompasses all of this whenever we deal with the phone company, power company, or board of supervisors. The state senator came down and provided some money for us to start this educational project. People began to look and listen to what we were saying. We began to look at housing and health needs. We began to seek out ways for our homes to become energy efficient, and our families to become self-sufficient.

I brought Bill Mollison, who is the founder of Permaculture, over here to see what we are doing and to help us. He stayed for a couple of weeks and did a workshop. A lot of people missed the point that you can integrate all of these various aspects into one holistic project that takes care of your health, food, shelter and everything else that you need to sustain a livelihood. All of these principles are also based on Native American concepts.

We did an assessment of community members in Ajo to determine their health, financial, educational, and youth needs. It took about three months just to compile the data. We have not been able to get all the data together into a report. It was very important to identify the real needs. And then we started to establish people to act as communicators, people we can call to deliver messages, people in the community who have access to resources, be it a food box or energy assistance, so they don't shut off your electricity. We started establishing these people in the communities, so that people have someone they can call for a ride to the store, or to pick up their food stamps, or in case of an emergency.

So we started organizing the people in the communities and it has become visible. Sometimes you don't see these things but they are there. When you go into a community, you don't see or recognize this network of people doing things until you have been there a while, and then it becomes obvious that there is a person you can call if you need some help.

"WE ASKED GOD TO HELP US BE BACK IN THIS PLACE."

We are not far off from upholding and practicing our traditional culture, values and principles. It has been there and it will always be there. This is our foundation and it is where we get the strength to go on, no matter how bad the political or economic scene gets. And it is pretty bad out there, when you live right next to the border between the United States and Mexico. You have unscrupulous dealings going on with the drug trade. The drugs are coming across both sides now but nobody wants to do anything about it. Some customs people got very, very wealthy off the drug trade. They have made some significant arrests, but it is not anywhere near what could be happening.

One of our men complained about the street dealings and the effect on our high school kids. He got threatened. One group said they were going to beat him up. Another group said they were going to take him to court for slander and libel. I told the man we would come over and pray for him. He said okay. He is the kind of person who wants to believe the Indian philosophy, but he was not living it. We came to his house early one morning last summer and burned cedar for him, fanned him down real good with cedar, prayed in the four directions, and asked the eagles to help and protect him. A week and a half later, all of the local drug dealers got arrested. Those people who were making the threats could not come out and say that what he was saying wasn't true. Today, this man is doing all right. He doesn't have the fear of being sued or beaten up. The people who were doing or selling the drugs eventually got back out, but now they have respect for this man.

This was another way of using our traditional culture to keep our project alive and help our fellow workers. We are not only thinking, believing, and carrying the philosophy—we are keeping our project alive by practicing it.

I think the situation at Quitovak in the state of Sonora, Mexico is another example. It is a ceremonial site, we call it a sacred place. There is a mine being built and operated on the reserve. The only way we can get the mining company to listen is to tell them, "This is an Indian community and we have a ceremony here. It is sacred and our spiritual foundations are based on this place. So before you blast any dynamite, we want to say a prayer." They shut down their whole operations for a couple minutes, so we could go in there and say a prayer. We talked to the plants and the animals and told them, "They are going to blast you fellows, so all the animals scoot and get away." All the spirits of the plants were real sad. They knew that their time was up.

Based on our cultural philosophy and practice, the mining companies had to begin to take us seriously as a group of people who had an interest in that area. We began to re-negotiate the contract they had with that community. It was for four thousand dollars a year for two years. We investigated, researched that project, and determined that they were going to get some six hundred and sixty-six million dollars over a two-year span. The Indian community was only going to get eight thousand dollars because it was a two-year contract. We asked, what is this, who do these guys think they are? So we contacted Global Response Network and asked them to send letters. The State of Sonora Governor's office was swamped with over two thousand letters in three weeks. The mining company was swamped with a thousand letters in about two. All these people and environmental organizations from around the world wrote letters to their offices. Now they are starting to take a back seat role and ask, what do you want to do, how do you want to talk this out? We said, "We want to organize ourselves and bring forth a Native American traditional philosophy so that you can hear what we are saying."

Another example is the establishment of the Biosphere Reserve in Mexico. President Salinas signed a decree and declared the Pinacate Mountains a national reserve. According to our creation story, we emerged out of those mountains. There is a cave there which they call the Creator's home. So for thousands of years, our people would go there and leave offerings. We went there to read a prayer. We asked God to help us get back to this place and to have a say in what happens here. This was all prior to the signing of the decree. So the Mexican government had to include me and Fernando Valentine in the negotiation process to develop a management plan for that place. They acknowledged the Hia-Ced O'odham in the decree as being the original inhabitants of that sacred place. We are now participants in designing the management plan for that area.

Community people are beginning to realize that there is hope for them to one day go back home. There is hope that the Indian people will reassert their dignity, pride and integrity when they walk among the American people or the Mexican people. Hope that people will know the Hia-Ced O'odham have been here and are here to stay. They had written us off the books, but now people are listening to what we say. We are getting a lot of support from the Mexicans, the Americans, and the Indian people, as well. All this stuff started happening real fast in a short time. The reason we have come such a long way is that we started with a prayer for this project. The faith that we had in that prayer has taken us a long way. Now we are in the position where we are in charge. We will make sure that the Indian people's livelihood is enhanced, not run over, sidestepped, or ignored. I am enjoying the recognition that our people are receiving. I don't take credit for any of this. We all said that prayer. This is God's way of answering that prayer. So, it really is his work.

When we began, there was a lot of dissension because people did not have that prayer, they did not have that spirit in their work. It was more of an approach that a research scientist or a politician would take. A lot of stuff they tried to do did not happen. There were obstacles and roadblocks. A lot of people ignored what they were saying and took them for granted. So I told them, "Let's change all of that. Let's create a myth." In the short time that I was in that program, you could hear people complaining about "Hia-Ced O'odham this, Hia-Ced O'odham that." Hia-Ced O'odham became a household word on the reservation and that myth had started. They said "There is such a thing as Hia-Ced O'odham and they are alive and doing something." They called me the "Sand Man" because *Hia-Ced* means sand and *o'odham* means people. So they started making fun of me, calling me the "Sand Man." But I said, "Hey, I am proud to be called the Sand Man."

Even then, I told them, "You know, I do not buy this Hia-Ced O'odham stuff. I am the kind of person who looks beyond that. When the Creator had us emerge from that mountain in the earth we were O'odham, the people. Somewhere along the way, they began to label us. They said that you were Tahona O'odham, or I was Hia-Ced O'odham. They said those guys in Gila were Ackhim O'odham because those people lived along the river, and *ackhim* means river, so they called them the river people. We all have a common language and common cultural traits. We all live in the same geographical area, so we are O'odham. That is what we are. One man was upset that I said that. He told me, "You young educated people go off to school and come back and use these words and labels here on the reservation." I said, "I don't buy that, that Hia-Ced O'odham. Me, I am just an O'odham. When I was a kid growing up, that is what people said I was."

But I said, "There is one thing that I will tell you, sir," because he is an older man and an elder. "One thing for certain is that you are going to have to acknowledge the fact that my people, whether you call us Hia-Ced O'odham or Sand Papagos, have a medicine bundle, a ceremony, and a prayer. My people proclaim that mountain over there as their sacred mountain. You are going to have to acknowledge that because that is a God-given right. It is not like we made it up. It is not like we took it from somebody and proclaimed it ours. This has been handed down from generation, to generation, to generation. It was given at the time of the Creation, when it was given to my family.

"Call me what you will, but we are carrying the medicine bundle, the sacred ceremonies, and the prayer for all O'odham, for this whole world, this whole universe. We said we are carrying that on behalf of mankind. You can acknowledge it today, next week, in ten years, or in however many years it takes. If you don't acknowledge it in your lifetime, then after you have died, you will acknowledge it in the spirit world. And that is not me, that is God's way.

"I did not ask for that medicine bundle, I was just born with it. It is like the rich people are born with a silver spoon in their mouths. Our people are born with the prayer in our mouth and the medicine bundle in our hands. That is what happened to us. People like me did not ask for this. We were just born with it. One thing for sure, I'm an O'odham, you are an O'odham, we are all O'odham. My people are special because we have a medicine bundle. You guys had one, too, but you dropped yours. I do not know what you did with it. My advice is to go back and find it and help us carry this prayer for all mankind, the earth, and everything on it. We need all the help that we can get." So that man, he could not say anything more after that. But that is how it is for us because we are Hia-Ced O'odham.

Whether we want to or not, we have to go ahead and say those prayers. We have to do that ceremony. They say we have to keep the universe in order. If we stop doing that, then the universe will come apart.

You are born with a spirit. God gave you a spirit. The spirit that is in you, *that* is what it is about. You could be any color, but if you have that spirit, all of these culturally related values and traits will come back to you in due time. It is not like you have to practice a ritual and proclaim yourself to be an Indian. It is the way the spirit moves, how it feels, and how you use it. A lot of people abuse the spirit, so it becomes easy to not recognize the Indianness in the person. People do not recognize the fact that it does not matter if you are Indian or black or white—the spirit is what counts. If the spirit is nurtured well, taken care of, and used in the appropriate way, you begin to understand the sacredness of the earth, and the plants and the animals and everything else.

John Mohawk has said that spirituality is the highest form of political consciousness. In each spirit there is an answer for any question, but it is a matter of attaining that spirituality in order to perceive the answers. I always liked Gandhi because he was considered a real humble man. He was devious, if you think about it. Gandhi single-handedly took the whole empire of England and flipped it upside down. He did not raise a fist. Gandhi attained a certain level of spirituality and he had an answer for everything England did, said, believed, and thought. I have always used Gandhi as an example of how one can move nations or move the world. Gandhi is recent within history, and we recognize that he was a real human. Jesus

Christ lived two thousand years ago. Never having seen him, people don't really know that he did what they said he did. Some people just have faith that it really happened. Gandhi is closer. You can see the practicality of how he lived and what he did in our lifetime.

The way you nurture and strengthen the spirit is in the way you live. Using that example, I don't hold anything against anybody. There are some basic principles that Indian people have always had, that I think all people had at one time, and still have, to a certain degree. Those principles are love, faith, hope, charity, honor and respect. If you understand and practice them in an everyday way, then you begin to attain that feeling of spirit. Things happen that you would probably call miracles. People have this tendency to make miracles out to be something foreign that hardly ever happens. If you look at all the goodness and blessings on an everyday level, they are all miracles; because you tried to be a good person, a good thing happened to you. You try to think good thoughts always, so new revelations come to mind and your mind grows. When you begin to practice those principles, good things start to happen. When good things start to happen, people recognize that and are drawn to you. You become like a magnet and people realize that there is something special about you. They can't quite put their finger on it, but they know there is something special and unique in you.

When you attain a certain amount of spirituality, it is self-evident. You don't need to dress, look, or act a certain way, or try to profess the joy of being a spiritual leader. This man came to me and said, "I am the spiritual leader for this tribe over here." And I said, "Okay, whatever." He quickly walked away. If he were a spiritual leader, he would not have to proclaim it. I guess that he was what he said he was. To me, that is not real spirituality. Spirituality is just being who you are, and if you are spiritual, you are spiritual. If you practice those principles, you will become spiritual. Your social or economic status doesn't matter—it is how you live your life. The paths you choose let spiritual growth take place.

You can function in any kind of place, among any kind of people, if you have this spirituality. You can look or be any kind of way and function in any setting or environmental condition. If you have those principles, people learn to respect you. If you come off kind of rude or obnoxious like I do, then you might not be able to. If you practice love, faith, hope, charity, honor and respect, then it becomes self-evident. If Indian people have that sense of loss, despair, or hopelessness because they feel they are not Indian any longer, or they don't know their language any longer, it is because they are looking superficially at how Indians really are.

Indian is a spirit. The spirit of Indian people is what we have to look at—not at whether we know our language or not, whether we practice our traditional ceremonies or not. If a person lives with that spirit, who knows, a ceremony may come back. It may come back to where the whole tribe begins to practice it and it is revived. They say that this stuff is not really lost, it is just laying there, it is not being used. You just need one person to go over there and pick it back up and begin to use it again, and practice it again, and then other people will come and join in, and that is how it goes on.

This ceremonial tradition is not dead. This Indianness, the Indian language, knowledge and culture are not dead. They are just lying there dormant, like seeds. The seed is just lying there dormant, until the rain comes. When the rain comes, the seed sprouts and life starts all over again. The same thing with the culture, language, and Indian spirit. They are dormant. That person who takes the initiative to go pick them up is like the rain. I did not understand that concept but now I do.

I was told this about ten or fifteen years ago because I asked some people about the round house, the ceremonial house. They said, "Oh, that is where it used to stand, over there." And, of course, there was nothing there except a mount of dirt. And I asked what happened to it. "Nobody took care of it, so it just went back into the earth." And I said, well, what if I go pick it back up? They said, "Yeah, go ahead and pick it up. If you pick it up, say a prayer for it, and it will be all right again." I had a hard time understanding that concept then, but now I understand what they were saying. Those people who have that despair, all they need to do is pick their culture back up and use it. Practice it. Believe it. It is real important to believe it.

Being an Indian is like icing on the cake to me. It is the beauty part of it. It is like all the pretty things on top. Deep down, we are all human beings. We all put our pants on the same way, we all comb our hair and brush our teeth the same way. We do everything the same as human beings. Our blood is red, our heart is beating, and we have the spirit that God gave us. I can look however I want to look and still be okay. I can function in any society, in any environment and still be all right. But being Indian is frosting on the cake. It is the nectar, it is the honey, it is the sweetness and the good things. I encourage young people to believe that because, all in all, we are the same. We are no different from the next guy. Tribes are no different from other tribes, the way I see it. We all have a spirit that God gave us. But being an Indian is just a little bit extra. That extra is frosting, the sweet stuff about it. If you know you are an Indian, you know it. You don't have to try and act like or profess it. There is no real way to act like it.

I see people who braid their hair, put feathers in their hat, wear chokers around their necks, and they do all this funny stuff. They put stickers on their bumpers, all over their cars. It's like, "Hey, I'm Indian." It is okay, if that is how they want to get along in life. The way I see it, I don't have to go out and advertise being an Indian. I just am. I don't have to jump and yell and say, "Hey, look at me, I'm an Indian." I don't have to do that. That is how I feel, how I think, how I believe, how I live, how I walk, or whatever. I just am. The best part about being human, is being an Indian.

"THE BEST PART ABOUT BEING HUMAN IS BEING AN INDIAN."

In Order To Be Helpers And Healers,

We Have To Heal Ourselves First

CHAPTER TEN

An interview with Tessie Williams

(Cayuse, Paluse and Nez Perce)

essie Williams is a member of the Confederated Tribes of the Umatilla reservation. She has been a Community Health Representative (CHR) for the Confederated Tribes for twenty-seven years and is now a supervisor. She began working as a CHR when the program was begun to help elders who were not receiving adequate medical attention. At the time, they had no interpreters and did not understand what their medication was for or what the doctors were doing. The Native health movement has since expanded to include better health care, wellness and environmental health, and recovery programs for alcohol and drug abuse. Tessie is a First Aid Instructor who believes in self-healing and has worked within that belief to restore health and wellness to her community. She serves as an important resource to the Health Promotions Program of the University of Oklahoma, directed by Billy Rodgers (Kiowa), which has inspired the Native American wellness movement. She is the grandmother of seven and has one great-grandchild.

About a week ago, I was talking to people who are working as healers to try and give them strength and encouragement. We want to focus on ways to help each other to heal, be well, feel good, and be comfortable. I try first of all to focus on the foundation of our people and give thanks to the ancestors and their way of life. Our ancestors had a very beautiful life because everything was free. They could wander and go anyplace in this country and be free and comfortable. There were no barbed wires or signs that said, "Do Not Enter." The water was open and the mountains were free. You could feel and smell everything beautiful.

Our ancestors gave us a great deal. They have tried to pass their gifts down to us for the next generation. Today, our foundation is in the grassroots people who were born and grew up on the reservations, people that were born in the mountains, near the river, in the deserts. Their parents and grandparents were put on reservations after the freedom of knowing everything that was open to them.

When we were young, we were nourished by gentle people. Seeds were planted within us to remind us of who we were. They nourished us by talking in Indian, teaching us our culture, reminding us to be strong, to understand the songs and the ceremonies. That is the foundation we built ourselves on. How do we nourish the next generation and build them to be stronger? How are we setting an example for our children to be free of alcoholism and AIDS? How much do we sing to them, tell them stories to help them believe and understand who we were, why we are here, and what they have to do in order to continue with this Indian life? The foundation is planting the seeds of who they are, who they come from, and what they will become. We look seven generations into the future when we nourish our people.

I talk to people about yesterday, today and tomorrow. You can focus on what happened yesterday, what you see today, and what you hope for tomorrow. In making your path that of the helper and the healer, you have to believe there were powerful people who were gifted with medicine. They had a special gift for healing and caring for people. Few had a real strong power but there were many helpers. You see specialists today in the modern world—so were there yesterday medicine men to heal the eyes, to heal children, to use the gifts they had to take care of everything.

Our tribes were told by the government that they could not do that, so they did not. Some of the Indians had to go to the mountains and hide to sing their songs. Today our traditions are coming back, we are making that circle. Our songs and prayers are being answered. Our generation is nourishing that seed again and it is giving us strength.

Yesterday, there were few diseases because the Indians were nourished by traditional foods. In the Pacific Northwest we were nourished by salmon, deer, elk, roots, chokecherries and huckleberries. We were given that food to eat and to take care of. When we take care of that food, it takes care of us. That is the way we were taught by our elders. Today's diseases are complicated because sometimes Indian people do not want to take care of themselves. They feel that this is my life, leave me alone, don't touch me. So we have to just be part of them and watch as they deteriorate or be there when they die.

Today, we look to television for entertainment. You see all that competition on TV and in the games that the kids play. Yesterday, we had storytelling, root digging, quiet time and just being part of the extended family. We learned what things were for, what this tree was for, what this herb was for. Today, our people go to the clinic and are treated by many different doctors. Sometimes they help and sometimes they don't. Tomorrow it is going to be more technology. Drive up to a store and put in fifty cents and get a pill. That is the way that we are going. You can order anything from that drive-up box.

When I talk about building a foundation, I talk about going back and saying, I am Indian, I believe in what my ancestors taught me. I am who I am. If I plan to be a physician, I can be a physician. If I plan to be somebody with a bachelor's or a master's degree, I can be that, too. We encourage that. We build that foundation for them to grow upon. We don't know what the answers are, but we keep encouraging them.

We talk to young people about the choices they have. "You have three choices. You have a choice of letting your family life stay the way it is. You have a choice of raising hell and going in the direction where you are always going to be in trouble. Or, you have a choice of remembering who you are, the self-respect that was taught to you, and the pride you have in yourself as an Indian." Those are the choices that young people have today.

I talk about being a role model. That is difficult because you have to grow into it. You don't become the person you would like to be overnight. People have to support and encourage you in becoming the kind of person who can be a role model. When you become that person, you have to face the consequences of being disliked and not respected because people think you are showing off or that you want to be in the limelight. That is how some people think. When you become the kind of model that people want to see, they admire you. The Creator already knows your path. He puts you on that path.

There are many traditional ways of learning the life of an Indian. There is bringing out the drums. When somebody gets a new drum, there is respect for the drum and singing. There are the ways someone rejoins the people when the period of mourning after a death is over. There are many ways of respecting the elders. There are many feasts, feasts of thanksgiving and springtime, when everything starts coming out—the new roots, the new fish, the fresh water after the snow, and all of the new things that we are glad and happy to have. We learn about all of these things because we are Indian. That is the way our life was meant to be.

When we talk about our youth today, we look at what they have to go through in order to become role models. Sometimes they come from very abusive homes. We talk about the lack of responsibility, abandonment of children, sexual abuse, and incest. These things were never talked about, but today, they are brought out. It is helping some of the Indian people. We can't be judgmental, but for some reason, this happens in families, and now their children have to suffer for it. They continue to abuse people because that is the way they were taught.

There was a medicine man who said, "In order to help people, you have to help yourself first." If you are a helper and healer who has been hurt, you must heal your own wounds first, your mind, your body, your own spirituality, and then you are able to help others. That was his teaching and that is true. In order to be a helper you have to be clean, you have to be able to see why people suffer, and love and understand them.

You have to love yourself first and then you can learn to love other people. You have to learn to understand yourself and then you can understand other people. You have to have a great deal of self-respect, in order to respect other people. I guess the hardest to learn is how to forgive yourself in order to forgive other people. Sometimes this is very difficult, because we have been abused by many people for a long time, and it is difficult to forgive. In order to be helpers or healers, we have to heal ourselves first.

When I talk to people, I talk to them about how powerful words are. Some words that you hear can be very good, gentle, and understanding. Sometimes words can be abusive. Generally, in councils, people get up and they say very strong words. Sometimes people go home hurt. In families, sometimes mothers and fathers have strong words for their children. They do not realize what they are saying. A child can hold onto something very simple, but it is words that hurt them. Sometimes words just come from the lips, cold, not meaning a thing. But when you speak from the heart, that is very sacred and beautiful.

"IN ORDER TO BE HELPERS OR HEALERS, WE HAVE TO HEAL OURSELVES FIRST."

I talk to young people about their bodies. Our grandmother said, "You have a beautiful body and there is a purpose for that body. Someday, you are going to be a mother and your breasts are going to feed your babies. You are going to have a baby that comes from this canal. Someday, you are going to be a mother and a wife that a man will hold. That is why you keep your body clean and pure. The Creator gave us this beautiful body for a purpose. We use it to make love and we enjoy that love because it comes from the Creator. People today look at sex as something that can happen in a minute and be forgotten the next. When we were growing up, it was something precious and beautiful. We were taught to make love to make our companion feel good and ourselves feel good. It was a beautiful time for a man and a woman when they got married for love. They made love and enjoyed it because it was pure, beautiful. Man has made making love dirty. There is no respect for anyone's body. The way they feel and think is reflected when they use children to make the films they make today. The body was meant to be beautiful, but today it is abused. What will it be tomorrow? We worry about what the children are going to become.

We talk to children about keeping their thoughts clean and happy. If we are a good role model in the home, then they will have that good feeling of being happy and clean. If we take a sweat bath with our children, we explain what the sweat house is all about. To some people, it is just a place to go and cleanse their bodies. To some people, it is a place to sing songs and to talk to the Creator, *Pusha*, as they call it in our language—we talk to grandfather.

We talk to our children about the importance of the four directions. We talk to them about the east, where the sun comes up, and in the morning you get up and sing your song or say your prayers. Some say them to the west, because that is where their power comes from. Power comes from any direction for anybody who can understand what that power is. There are many kinds of powers. We call it *chukwat* spirits, the holy spirits that are part of everything around here. Spirits come out all the time. They try to find places to stay. As my grandmother would say, "Always be careful of the kind of spirit that you respond to because there are good and bad spirits, just as there is good and bad in everybody."

We talk to young people about everything that is Indian, so that they can understand who and what they are. That is their foundation. I feel it is important to have some understanding of the people you take care of. It makes it easier for you to be that helper or that caring individual.

Wellness means trying to keep your body well by eating the proper foods, exercising, keeping your mind clear and clean of all of the bad things. There are good thoughts and bad thoughts. There are good foods and bad foods. Some of the young parents dash through fast food places instead of cooking meals. Our children are not nourished properly. Sometimes they don't care how they look. They deteriorate as a family. They feel that it is okay because it is their life. They get to the point where their children become sick and they just don't care.

On the other hand, many Indian people do believe in wellness. They balance everything they eat. They fulfill their spiritual needs by going to ceremonies or to church. What you put into your mind is what you become. When you are working with your body, mind and spirituality, you can achieve a balance. It depends on the families and on how well they want their next generation to be. If the children are going to be smokers or drinkers, they are going to have problems eventually. As long as people are pushing drugs and things that mess up the mind, we will have sickly people. Wellness depends on parents. They have the choice of good nourishment for the body, mind and spirit.

Healing young people who have grown up abused takes a good length of time because they do not know that they were abused—they just lived the way they were brought up. So it starts from the beginning. My grandmother was a very gentle lady. She talked soft and she told us in Indian what to do. She was always making us feel good. When she corrected us, she would always tell us, "It is because I care for you. *Atow nanwa*—you are precious, you are important to us, you are special." Some parents don't do this with their children, they naturally get into an abusive stage. A child will act out and ask for help. Children do not understand that this is not the right way to live. They will go to somebody and say, "I hurt." They do not know why they hurt. They do not understand why they are the way they are, until you can listen to their feelings and help them understand.

A couple of times, I took children to a medicine man and he explained to them and prayed over them three times. He took away a lot of things that were wished on them by their parents because their parents were so unhappy with themselves and with each other. They did not know how to be anything but unhappy. As the children began to understand all of these things about the parents, they could see hope for themselves. They did not have to be like the parents. They had that choice of being different. They learned how to handle situations which sometimes became pretty rough. The more they tried to behave in a normal pattern, the more the parents abused them.

Anything and everything—love, sex, tenderness, forgiveness, anger—is taught in the home. Alcoholism is taught in the home. Abuse is taught in the home. We have to admit that this is actually where everything is taught.

You have to show the child that you really care and that there is a lot of good in them. What is happening is not their fault. You have to make them understand that it is something that happened to their parents. Once we talk about the parents, we move them aside and look at the child as an individual. The majority have a lot of good qualities. We start bringing those out, instead of the things that made them angry. If a child is sexually abused, it is the most difficult thing for them to ever forget because they remember that hurt. They don't know how to let go and become angry because of the pain they had to tolerate. This requires long-term healing. Each time, you tell them to bring out something different to focus on, instead of that pain. You try to get them away from the pain and hurt that is always there.

When children are about sixteen or seventeen, you can ask, "Are you still angry with so-and-so? Are you still hurting? What is bothering you today?" They might come out with twenty issues that you could deal with but you choose one to focus on. "What is the worst right now?" So you try to focus on one thing each session so that they can feel and understand it a little bit more. With all of the pains they have, they can't figure out which one they want to deal with. You have to help them find whatever hurts the most and then deal with it. Maybe two or three times you go over the same issue until they say, "I feel okay, I don't want to talk

"YOU PULL AWAY THEIR PROBLEMS ONE BY ONE IN ORDER TO HEAL THEM."

about that anymore." And then you say, "All right, what is the next problem that makes you feel angry or hurt or makes you want to cry?" It is time-consuming counseling. It takes about a year, because you are pulling away their problems individually, one by one. Then, they gradually start seeing in a different way. "I don't worry about that anymore. I think that is gone now. I am not mad anymore because I don't want to feel that way all the time."

The whole purpose of working with them is to have them get rid of that sad suicidal feeling. "I want to kill myself." "Well, give me one reason why?" "I don't like myself." Then we talk about what they don't like about themselves. Then we talk about why that thought came into their minds. Where does it hurt the most? And they talk about it and they bring it out. After a while, "Are you afraid to go home because you might kill yourself?" "Well, not so much right now." Some people have a caring talent for dealing with an abused child and taking away their pain, little by little, each time. When the child gets tired of it, he or she will figure, "Well, I don't need to talk about that anymore. It is gone." They decide when it is gone, you don't decide.

Inside, there is good and bad in everybody. When you feel good, you say so. "Oh, I feel so good. I just ate a good lunch and I feel so good. I feel so relaxed." Or, "My heart, it just feels so light." I try to give them examples of what feeling good is, and show them that feeling good is something that is normal. I tell them that feeling bad is normal, too, but when you feel bad, it is heavy, you feel blah and it hurts. But when you start feeling light, that means you are getting rid of that hurt. Children go by feeling. Feeling is important in people's lives.

The majority of people are never taught how to feel. My grandmother said that there is a certain age when you don't sit on grandpa's lap anymore, you don't hug your dad anymore. There is a certain age that they feel different and you feel different. When your body goes into that maturity, you feel good, things make you feel good. There was a doctor who worked with us one time and she said that her little son got into the tub and he was playing with himself. And she said, "Oh, does that make you feel good?" He said, "Yeah, that feels good, Mom." She said, "Well, that is your penis and when you get older that will always make you feel good. But you don't feel too good right now because you have to wash your penis." She talked to him, using terms he understood. That is the way it is when you talk to children. You have to be frank with them, so that they really understand what makes them feel good or bad.

There is always going to be that balance of the unwell Indian or the really well Indian. That is the way the Creator made it. We have to balance everything. We can never have everything too perfect because that would unbalance everything else. We have to have people to take care of.

There was a young person who was mentally ill and this one boy asked, "Why are people like that, why do we have to have people like that?" I told him, "Because maybe the Creator wanted you to go and take care of somebody like that, so that you can learn from him, or teach him how to drink, or teach him how to walk, or just be his good friend and visit him." "Oh!" He stood there and I said, "Well, come on, be honest." He said, "I don't know if I want to be his friend." I said, "That is true, there are a lot of people who don't like people like that. You have the choice of liking him and being his helper and noticing him; or you have the choice of ignoring him like everybody else does because he is sick and he wasn't meant to be that way." But he was meant to be that way, because we have to have people to take care of, people like him.

With all of the new technology, with our people having advanced degrees and getting more into the teaching field, they are getting to practice more wellness. There are a lot of reservations that see that they have people with diabetes and work on helping them. They have several different trainers, they have people that go out and check patients' feet and do their toenails. We have people that go out and transfer dialysis patients. We have people that are doing a great deal. So if we want our next generation to be better then we have be working on it today. When we talk about wellness we want people to understand that there is a great deal they have to do for themselves, their people, and their reservation.

Each tribe and each reservation has different ways of interpreting what and how they were taught. All of the teachings of body, mind and spirit should be interpreted in the way they were taught in their area. To balance the mind, body, and spirit is to be in harmony with the Creator.

I am in mourning. Sometimes it is very lonely. I remember the good times I had with my husband and that keeps me going. I remember his aches and pains and I think about how now he does not have to suffer any more. I think about all the good things we shared and even the bad things and how we balanced our thirty-five years together. The Creator gave us a good life. We were meant to be together. I share with people that, when you lose a mate, the Creator always has a new path to add to that path you had together. I pray that he lightens up my path a little bit more and that he will guide me. I open my heart to him all the time.

I can't remember when I gave myself to the Creator, but I open my heart every day, and I ask him to come into my heart every day. I open my mind every day and I ask him to come into my mind. I ask him to give me the strength to help people who are sick. I ask him to be there to guide me when I need him. At the end of this day, I will thank him for the making of a new friend and for letting me be there to help the people who needed help. I thank him for all of the things that I have because he made me. He gave me this life and every day I try to offer a little bit of my life to give thanks. That is the way people should be—we should remember that the Creator gave us this life, and we should try to give some of it back and be thankful. That is the way I feel now.

I always try to start with that foundation when I talk about parenting. I ask the father and mother about the values of traditional life. The majority of the time, the men focus on the things they were taught by their fathers, like hunting, fishing, going on walks together, putting up fence together, or going to powwows. That is their values, that is what they are taught. Women usually talk about food digging, housekeeping and sometimes just talking with their parents. I go into the value of a good relationship. I ask them, "What do you like best about your companion?" I make them write down three things that they like about their companion. Usually the husband will say, "I like the way she looks, the way she talks and the way she keeps the baby." The woman will say, "I like the way he takes care of us, takes us everyplace together, and helps in the kitchen." Then I ask them for three things they dislike about each other. It is always the man—he dislikes how the wife does not pick up after him, or how she allows the kids to get away with everything, or how she would rather go out and eat instead of cook. She sometimes will say, "I do not like the way he sits in front of the TV, the way he leaves his stinky socks all over the place, or when he comes home drunk." Then we talk about that. "How could you help each other? For instance, you say he comes home drunk. Why does he want to drink?" "Well, because his friends drink." And I ask him, "Why do you drink?" He says, "She answered the question, because my friends drink." I say, "Could you go without drinking for a month even if your friends showed up?" "I don't know because I have not tried that."

I ask them on the third visit to tell each other a good, funny, sad or a sexy story. It is very difficult for men to be open in that way because they have never had that practice. They say, "We never talked like that, we never tell each other stories." On the other hand, some of the women talk about everything. She'll say, "He ignores me, he did not want to listen." I ask, "When was the last fight you had?" She says, "Yesterday, at ten o'clock, because he missed my appointment." He says, "Yeah, but it was your fault." I let them talk about that. I listen to them getting involved with each other. They stop and say, "What are we doing this for?"

We go back into communication. We talk about how we relate to each other as man and wife. I say, "This is getting pretty personal, but who is the most aggressive in your sexual stages and your making love?" The woman will say, "I am, because he doesn't want to touch me." "So you have to be the one to turn him on, do you?" He says, "Yeah, she does." I say, "Why is it so hard for you to turn her on?" "I don't know, I was always innocent. I did not do anything like that." It tells you a lot about how they grew up, how they felt about sex. "Is it dirty?" He says, "It was dirty." You find out a lot between a man and a woman when you get involved with their lives. It becomes their way of learning about each other. When you live with people you sometimes don't pay attention to relationships until somebody points them out. He says, "What does sex have to do with it?" I say, "Sex is beautiful. Don't you feel good after sex?" He'll say, "Well, that is pretty personal." "Yes, it is. But in order to make a relationship work, you both have to be honest with each other. Honesty has to come into this part of your life and you have to be honest when you are talking to her. She is honest with you." "Yeah, she is honest." This will go on for about eight weeks. We talk about everything they should be doing to know each other better, in order to make their marriage work. After we've talked about all of their things, they say, "Hey, we never paid any attention to that." I say, "That is true, nobody does."

"HE WAS A BEAUTI-FUL LOVER, HE WAS A BEAUTIFUL FRIEND."

My spouse and I always had fun together. Everything was a joke because he was a jolly person. Life to him was full of surprises. I was the quiet one—he grew up with a big family and I grew up in a different type of place. He always had fun in his life. There were times in my life when it was quiet and different. He understood me. He always told me his friends teased him about marrying a nun because I was so quiet. He was the one who woke me up, he woke my body up. He made me feel good. He talked and explained things to me I had never understood. He was a beautiful lover, he was a beautiful friend. He was a companion that was always there, encouraging, correcting and sharing my life. When you have problems, sit down and write out all the good things that you see in him whether you are mad at him or not. Look at the positive things he did that day or week and look at that against all of the bad things. If you look at just the bad things, that is all you will have in your mind. Look at the good things and see what he has done for you, the good things he did for you, and then communicate, talk to each other about it. It is good to get mad, it is normal to get mad. Once you get mad and you let it out, let it go. Do not bring it up again.

A relationship between a man and a woman is like being born, watching your baby being born. A marriage is like that. You are innocent and free with each other because you are just toddlers, just beginning. Then you go into different stages, like the stage of wanting to do things with your friends. "I want to go with my buddies, I want to go bowling." That makes you feel left out so you think, "Well, he is going to go that way, so I will go this way." That is another stage you go through. You always manage to work it out because you are still together.

Around about the eleventh through the fourteenth year, things start changing, couples start thinking and doing different things. Some men start sneaking out and sleeping with other women. Some women do the same. They are not happy with each other and they are not communicating. They are leaving out a lot of things they started out with, like that good feeling of taking care of each other and having the responsibility of a family. They start changing. When you are in your twentieth year, things start to settle down. Then one of you starts going through mid-life crisis and things are really topsy-turvy.

Maybe you lost your home, you don't have a job, you're having one heck of a time. That is where a lot of people divorce, leave each other, and try to go out and find something better and different. Then you leave the family and you leave the children with a real bad memory. But if you can work on it and communicate and talk it out, then you do not have to go through that. You save yourself the trouble of starting all over again and creating that second life for somebody else. Your children will wander and never have the support of a mother and father. They should always have the support of a mother and father. You become good friends if you can survive that long and that friendship is a lot better. A lot of things start happening, like when my mate got sick. He blamed everything on me forever. That was okay because I did not have that disease and I felt that was when he needed my support the most. I got to understanding his hurt, his fears, trying to be close to him, and making him feel comfortable. As time went on, he understood my feelings. He was always there as my companion, to support me and give me a pat on the back or correct me if I needed it.

Correcting people was always an important teaching in our Indian ways. A long time ago, if somebody corrected you, they always said, I correct you because I care for you, or I admire you, or I like what you are doing. When people corrected me I always thought, "Oh, they are always just giving me hell and I don't like that." Correction in the traditional way meant somebody cared for you and admired you and told you so after they corrected you. That is the way my husband was. That is the way people get eventually. I knew a young woman, she said, "Oh, I am anxious to get married. I want to be happy like you and Bob. You were always laughing every time I saw you. No matter what you were doing, you were always happy." And we were. We made each other be happy. We had hard times, rough times. We went through alcoholism, but we both survived that habit. We were teachers to our children, so now we have to watch them struggle. So again, the role model that people are to their families and their children is what becomes of the next generation.

Man and woman together are very beautiful. It all goes back to how they are taught and what they see in their home about love, understanding, and sharing. Or it could be just the opposite, of how they fight and how they set bad examples for their children. In these years, looking back at my family, my grandmother and great grandmothers and their husbands were together a long time. At that time, men could marry and have two women. Today this is not allowed. Some get married in the church and some get married traditionally. Either way, you look at the teachings and, again, we go back to spirituality. In the Indian way, they teach that you marry one time, always keep that woman, always keep that man, because that is the choice you made. That is who you should live with. It just goes way back. That is how my mate felt. He said, "You can't leave me, you can never leave me because we are together forever until I die or you die." I told him, "That is just the way the church talks." He said, "I am not the church, I am me." I said, "In other words, you don't want me to leave you." He said, "Don't ever leave me, you can't ever leave me." So he left me first, but our life was good.

You can make it good and you can make it bad. We are human. We can make a lot of things good in life because we choose to or we can make a lot of things bad in our life, if we choose to. That is our choice and that is just the way it was made. Good and bad or black and white, whatever you want to call it. There is always that balance of one or the other. Always that balance, however you and your mate want to make it. Many people do live together a long time. Many people who are not raised well in the home cannot make it a long time. It is up to you and me to teach our grandchildren about love. They knew their grandpa, they loved him and he taught them well. I feel that they will always have something to look forward to.

My oldest grandson is fourteen. He asks me, "Do you know who my dad is?" I told him, "Yes, I do." But he does not know who he is. I tell my grandson, "This is why I talk to you about your body, why I tell you to respect your body because it is beautiful. I also want to teach you to respect the girl's body because some day that body will give birth. Right now, because you ask me who your father is, I will tell you. Don't do that to a girl and then leave her. Someday that child will ask somebody in his family, "Do you know who my father is?" Is that what you want to do to your children?" "No." I said, "Well, remember that. Don't ever abuse a woman's body and then have her son not know you." Women and men today relate to each other in ways they are taught in the home. How they survive in marriage is what they make of it. They can make it good or make it bad, they have a choice.

BOOK THREE

PRACTICING OUR WAYS OF LIFE IS WHAT STRENGTHENS THE SPIRIT OF THE PEOPLE

Book Three focuses on how the application of traditional teachings in contemporary Native life can give new life to ourselves and our communities. These speakers show the feeling and vitality that comes when an individual walks with the spirit of their people. The moment in the change of perception from one way of life to another is told of by some, traditional teachings whose universal implications transcend cultural boundaries are discussed by others, and still others show how the return to traditional thought can revitalize our peoples.

On the brink of the twenty-first century, it is easy to question the relevance of traditional Native practices in the modern world. Yet a way of life is beyond a matter of rational, objective choice. It is a manifestation of one's innermost identity. A way of life does not begin and end with a generation. It is the thread joining our spirits to those of our ancestors and those of our people to come.

The speakers emphasize that the Native mind embraces the existence of spiritual and physical realities. The Native mind draws upon the guidance received from the spiritual world to determine thought and action in the physical world. Through prayer, they say, Native people acquire the direction and guidance needed to live in a way which supports the sacredness of life and not the desecration of it. Julian Lang speaks of the transformation he experienced when he brought the language and songs within and became "a totally different person." Vicky Vigil Downey emphasizes that prayer is a state of mind requiring practice to achieve sincerity. Fifteen-year old Poquin Vigil comments on her visit to a Tibetan community , "I want to give others the same uplifting feeling and unconditional love I received from the Dalai Lama." The speakers emphasize that it is our spiritual being that is responsible for continuing the ways of life of our peoples. Renee Senogles concludes this section with these words, "Our spiritual lives maintain the whole of creation."

These speakers demonstrate that we can practice our way of life in the twenty-first century when we come home to ourselves, families, clans, and nations. Our collective experience as Native peoples has been the shattering of our lifeways. We cannot join these splintered fragments into what once was; but moving together with the spirit of our people, we can breathe life and vitality into our languages, ceremonies, songs, dances, institutions and each other.

We Fell In Love Bringing

The Spirit Of The Songs To Life

CHAPTER ELEVEN

An interview with Julian Lang (Karuk)
and Lyn Risling.(Karuk, Yurok, Hupa)

Lyn Risling is of Karuk and Yurok descent and a member of the Hoopa Valley tribe. She is most noted as a traditional singer, maker of women's regalia, as well as a graphic artist, and most recently she has become involved in theater performance. She is currently leading a local effort to perform the Karuk puberty ceremony for girls, not held since 1870. Risling has two children, and administers a tutorial program at Humboldt State University.

Julian Lang is a ceremonial leader of the Katimiin, who as a language speaker has helped restore Native knowledge for tribal members. He is a writer, and fine artist, and a highly regarded traditional singer. Lang's book, *Ararapíkva* was published in 1994, and is believed to be the first book by a Native scholar in his own language. He founded the Institute of Native Knowledge in 1989 to discover ways to assert Native knowledge and beliefs (especially concerning sacred sites and philosophies) within Native and non-Native communities. The Institute supports Native scholarship of traditional knowledge, and, using various art forms, asserts this knowledge within the dominant society by collaborating with Native and non-Native artists and scholars. The Institute's philosophy is dedicated to the Fix the Earth Ceremony of the Karuk, Hupa, Yurok, and Wiyot peoples of northwestern California.

LYN: There is no beginning and no end to the work we are doing. It is ongoing. It is where we are coming from and where we are now.

JULIAN: Where we are now is a result of the choices we made in our lives. I remember having to make my choice. Did I want to administer programs or lobby in Washington, or did I want to do what I had planned to do earlier in my life: to work for my own people? I decided to quit the administrative job I had and use my abilities on behalf of my tribe. I had reached a burn-out point. I would either continue to focus on my career or return home in fulfillment of my idealism. That was the beginning for me, my first big choice for change.

The shocking reality I was forced to face in going back home after a ten year absence was that my tribe was deeply involved in ridiculous and self-destructive programs. I went home and after eight months I was fired. I wasn't willing to help create a tribal government based on a recipe prepared by the United States government. I wasn't willing to be a participant in creating that kind of tribal government (i.e. an Indian Reorganization Act). I thought we should assert our own identity and sovereignty. After a while of being a political stick-in-the-mud, they fired me. I left happily.

After that, my choices began to change. About the time that I first met Lyn, in the early 1980s, I decided that I was never going to work nine to five again. I committed myself to that. I had worked for eight straight years without any kind of a break or vacation. Instead of working, I committed myself to having nothing but fun for as long as I could. My "fun" was different. I was going to go to every Indian dance. My friends and I started going to every dance in our area. A new set of experiences set me on a new course in my life.

In 1980 I became what we call a *Fatavêenaan,* "prays-for-something," in the Karuk World Renewal Ceremony. I went into the sweat house where I was taught how to fix the Center of the World. When I came out my whole feel of the world was transformed. Finally, all the stuff that I was immersing myself in, which I now call Native knowledge, made sense. After the ceremony, I left and went home. All of a sudden I received a packet in the mail, it was music—eight or nine hours of our music, recorded in 1926. I took all of my rock and roll tapes and put them in this big box and stuffed it in the closet. I listened to those reels of music over and over again all summer. I painted, drew and thought about everything that had happened to me in the sweat house.

I spent that whole winter seeing few people. It was amazing. There were three hundred and sixty-five songs. When I started out, they all sounded the same, but by the end, I knew two hundred songs. I just listened continually to those songs, so much so that my son would say, "Oh, not that again." We heard the same thing over and over but it was fun. We would hear these songs, and then we would walk down a path and spontaneously start singing like birds. We'd be walking around and suddenly start singing for no reason. All these songs were bubbling out. That was my beginning.

That is where it started and there was no turning back. I also received language tapes recorded in 1949. Mysteriously, in the midst of learning all of these songs, here came the language tapes I had ordered. I put the tapes on and I sat there. I remember the moment, like when Kennedy was killed. Something like that, you remember the moment. I was sitting there and I turned on the tape. My heart sank a little bit because it sounded horrible, just mumble, mumble. You could barely hear the words. Oh no, I thought, it is going to be bad fidelity. Then all of a sudden these stories started coming out. The voices and the recordings were totally pristine.

All of these old people were telling what we call píkva stories. Some of the same songs on the old 1920s tapes were on the language tapes. It was all connected—from 1926 to 1949 to 1980. I was working with the elders at this time because I was home again and I knew much of our language. Suddenly, within a year's time of coming home, I had become a totally different person. I realized that this is where thought comes from—the language, the songs and bringing them inside. That is what needs to happen to everybody. The government programs do everything they can to keep that from happening.

"I HAD BECOME A TOTALLY DIFFERENT PERSON."

LYN: My work's direction comes from my grandfather. He was a strong influence in my life growing up because of his involvement with the culture. Like many of our parents and grandparents, he was sent to a boarding school and punished for using his language. He didn't teach his own children the language and or let them go to ceremonies. It was part of the breakdown in our whole ceremonial system. Either the ceremonies weren't done or, if they were, there was a lot of drinking involved. It wasn't until he got older and had grandchildren that he made a tremendous effort to try to bring back part of the ceremonial life, and, with it, the respect and the beauty of it.

In the beginning, he went outside, away from the ceremonies, and started teaching his grandchildren songs and dances which were demonstrated publicly to non-Indian people. We danced at the county fair for ten years to show people that we have a beautiful culture, that we weren't just savages. In doing that, we also brought pride to our people even though we were criticized for taking these things out of the ceremonial place or the reservation. My grandfather's mother was Karuk. His German father left when he was a young boy and his mother then married a Hupa man. He lived between Hoopa and his mother's family upriver. He married a Yurok woman. Growing up, I identified with all three.

I used to spend my summers on the Hupa reservation and that was my Indian life. I went back down to Modesto during the rest of the year to go to school. I was the only Indian I knew in my school other than my sisters and my brother. I was an Indian during the summer and I don't know what I was the rest of the time.

My earliest recollection of learning songs was in Hoopa, where I spent the summers with my aunt, uncles and grandmother. They all lived in this big house that they built. There was also a little house where my grandfather would stay and where he had all these Indian things, like dance regalia. I used to love to go over there because he was always working on dance stuff. He would be singing. He had all this ceremonial regalia that had been given to him in different ways through Karuk and the Hoopa side. That was my first exposure. All the cousins, aunts and uncles would get together and have our own little dance. The living room was where we started to learn to dance. We would have this little Brush Dance. We did it because it was fun, and to teach the younger ones. I learned my first song then, but I didn't understand what it was all about.

After I started dancing in the schools and at the Humboldt County Fair, I began to have some understanding of ceremony but not in the context of the culture because I was a member of the outside world too. It was not until I became older that I began to understand and feel

"HANG ON TO THE CEREMONIES AND NEVER STOP DANCING."

fortunate that I had the opportunity to learn some of our songs and dances, even though it was out of context. It was not the real thing. Sometimes other tribal cultures were incorporated into our performance. Our cousin went and traveled around learning different dances from other tribes. They were also taken out of context, but it still gave you a sense of what Indian people were culturally. As I became older, I began to understand why my grandfather did these things and why it was important. As he got older he tried harder and harder to get the message across that we needed to hang on to the culture, that we cannot let it die. He instructed us over and over again—I would think, "Oh yeah, he's told me that before." But those are the things I remember the most. And now I know why he repeated them over and over again. One idea I remember from him is that as Indian people, we have to keep dancing even if the world around us falls apart—that is what is going to hold us together as people. It is going to help in our struggles to survive. We have to hang on to the ceremonies and never stop dancing.

Respect is another thing he taught over and over. You respect each other and you respect the environment. You have to keep doing the ceremonies and that is what we need to do. I still did not understand fully what he meant but I do now. Over the past twenty years, a revival of the culture has begun among our people. More and more people are involved in the dances. There were hardly any girl singers when I was learning to sing, and few women singers. What you heard most was men. We have this dance called the Brush Dance that only unmarried girls dance in. After that time, their singing career is over. As an adult, I felt this emptiness in me because I love to sing. I would hear songs and want to sing and wish I could still be part of that. I did not dance in a ceremony until I was in my early twenties, which is unusual, because nowadays most girls don't dance after the age of eighteen because by then they are married. Among the Karuk people, women could dance until they had children.

More recently, I heard that my grandfather's mother had such a beautiful voice that in the Brush Dance they would allow her to sing. She would not be in the dancing but she would be allowed to sing from the outside. I did not have an opportunity to learn the songs because I did not know women singers. Women who were my elders, my father's and mother's generation, were not singers. My aunt knew a few songs and stories but I did not have an opportunity to learn the songs. I felt this loss. I knew a couple of women singers but you don't just say, "Hey, will you teach me your songs?" Songs are passed on in families or given to you by someone who knows you or who you've been around and watched, someone who knows you like to sing.

The songs brought Julian and me together. One day he asked me if I wanted to learn some old Karuk songs. I said, "Yes!" Since then, singing has been such a strong part of our relationship, it has really brought us together and has caused a real transformation within me.

JULIAN: Once this traditional path opened up, I reached a certain level of understanding. I learned to speak the language after being gone for ten years and then I relearned how to live the language. I learned all these songs and I had this spiritual experience in the sweat house. I began working with elders who suddenly realized that this guy understands and is beginning to learn. We would sit there and laugh and talk way into the night just telling old stories. We read the accounts of the "old days" that had been locked away for years and years, generations before. Most of the information that I was bringing back from the archives was gathered by linguists and anthropologists from the turn of the century into the 1920s. I was bringing back linguistic material primarily. Elders were hearing cultural knowledge that as children they had heard their parents talk about. This was cultural knowledge that was coming from people who were the age of their grandparents and their great-grandparents.

After a while we got to the point where we could either continue to accumulate and acquire knowledge or finally take it to the next step of applying what we had learned. I was reintroduced to a whole new level of involvement at the ceremonies with this new knowledge, which was actually old knowledge, and with these new songs, which were actually old songs. The past was coming back. Suddenly we woke up one day and time seemed to going the other way.

I had become aware of the GO Road case. The GO Road was a forest service road which threatened sacred sites critical to the continuation of our ceremonies. An activist friend, Chris Peters, asked us, "What do you guys want to do about this? We have to do something about this." Pretty soon it just ended up that only a few of us were standing there. I had no choice. I had to do something about the threat to ceremonies, but I had no idea what. I was into my artwork and I was actually making money painting. I ended up committing one year to doing whatever I could to work to resolve this issue. It took one year of community organizing and then the case was in the Supreme Court.

For one year I traveled all around this world–my country. It sounds like an old myth to me now. I went everywhere from Crescent City to Happy Camp to Pekwan, Hoopa, and Eureka. We went everywhere, to all these communities, telling people about the GO Road case and doing lots of things. Music helped, we would sing and people would come. It was a way of getting people to the point where they would realize what was at stake. The songs could make you feel so good. You can tell when someone's a good singer because everyone cries. That is the best singer. We would say, what is at stake is how we feel as a people. It's more than some kind of legal thing. For one year I did not do anything but that.

We raised a lot of money and incurred a lot of debt. The next thing we knew we were taking all these elders and people to Washington D.C. to accompany our case to the Supreme Court. Magic happened around it–everything that we needed just happened. Our faith and our belief made magic happen. Our stay in Washington D.C. was a very magical time. Everybody had a significant experience, even though we lost the case then. When I came back, it was kind of over. The external world places no virtue on sustaining these kinds of feelings. Once it is done, it is over. Once they close the book, it is old news. Move on to something new.

I ended up moving to the city and taking this job at the University of California at Berkeley, where I worked in the Phoebe Epperson Hearst Museum. This was opportunity extended to me as a result of working on the GO Road effort. I said "Yeah, I'll take it." The case was gone. People were doing nothing, so I went down there and found our cultural knowledge. There was so much of our stuff there that you could not believe it. The whole university was full of archives. All of these incredible stories, photographs and accounts that rarely saw the light of day. I started copying information and had notebooks filled with handwritten copies of handwritten notes recorded in 1902. I thought that I was on fire. I went into a whole different level of understanding. I produced ten times as much information as any other person I knew. It was fiendish–bringing this stuff back and taking pictures, as well as doing my job. Then I ran into one of the problems with academia–the whole idea of control. It felt like a strange weird competition, the negative side of western culture. I have never been very willing to compromise myself or my integrity. I ended up being asked to quit my job. I started writing and spent time with Malcolm Margolin, the editor of News from Native California. The GO Road kept bugging me. Then the Supreme Court decision came down that stripped us Indian people of the right to even declare a First Amendment case. No First Amendment religious question by Native peoples would be listened to after the GO Road decision. It made no sense. In the back of my mind, I was always thinking, what can we do? I begin thinking of a play, a theater experience of presenting the GO Road story. We could make people feel what we were losing. This is what is at stake, our feeling. Our experience as human beings is what can be lost here.

I conceived of this play in my mind. One day Margolin came and said "If somebody gave you a fully equipped theater with all the technical expertise and five thousand dollars, do you think you could make something up? These people just called and said that they had five thousand dollars and a theater. Could we do this thing?" I said I would get together the best people that I possibly could. People who have a voice and a message that can stand on its own, and bring them all in one place. And so he said, well, that sounds good.

"So, who are you going to call?" He was feeding me, taking me on. "Well, the first person I would like to call is Lyn Risling." He said, "I don't think I know her. Is she related to Dave Risling?" (President Emeritus of the DQ University, a Native college in Davis, California.) I said, "Yeah." He said, "Why her?" I said, "Because she is the best singer I know." I basically conceived this whole theater plan with her in mind and then this opportunity came. I called her up and gave her the same "what if" that I got from Margolin. "Would you do it?" I recall feeling my toes curl up. Then she said, "Yeah."

The next person I called was this guy, Paul Apodoca, from southern California. He is kind of a blustery, loud-voiced guy who laughs loud. He said yeah, too. Then I called Darryl Wilson. He is a rabble-rouser turned genteel writer. And he said he would do it. Then I talked to Brian Tripp because I thought he could do it. He said, "Yeah, yeah, when do we do it, when, when?" He wanted to get on stage. He was full of things people needed to hear.

The idea was that we would fix the world on stage for everybody. We would show them what the government was trying to mortally wound, this whole cultural, indigenous world that nobody knew existed. Simple story—this is our job in the world—to fix the earth and the reason why. We are here to fix the world, the earth. That is where we started out. We all arrived in San Francisco.

LYN: We did not have any rehearsal. We did not know exactly what would happen. Julian had this idea and vision. I knew I was part of that plan and it all came together.

JULIAN: I talked to each person individually. I knew Lyn and I would set the tone. Then all these strange things, like bumper sticker magic, began to happen. Buffy St. Marie was the one who said, "Magic is alive." It was good.

LYN: I started learning the songs as part of this. It was a heavy personal agenda and an opportunity to learn songs. I was part of that magic too. In a way it was always waiting to happen. It was something you wanted to happen.

JULIAN: I thought she would be indebted to me for the rest of her life.

LYN: It was a like a gift for me. I was this dormant person, asleep with my culture, and all these things were beginning.

JULIAN: We brought all these people together in one place. They kept asking what it was going to be. We said, "Just wait. You'll see something that has never been seen before." Basically holding the dogs at bay. Everybody had to be there and agree. We mutually defined their persona in relationship to everyone else.

We decided on a creation story. Lyn and I created the world with song. The second person to come on-stage was Paul Apodoca, the Historian. He brought the whole world from creation, through the ice age, through the age of the dinosaurs, to the age of the first human beings. He brought the whole audience up to the present and he had asked me, "Where do you want me to drop off the audience?" And I said, "What about the floor at Yosemite look-

"I WAS THIS DORMANT PERSON, ASLEEP WITH MY CULTURE."

ing at Half Dome?" He said, "Okay." So he created this whole story and at the end he said, "There they stood, this tribe of people looking up at Half Dome, like children looking up at their father." It was beautiful. Almost sappy but beautiful.

Then all of sudden Darryl Wilson came out, scratching his forehead with these papers. And he said, "You know, I got these papers and I thought I would bring them to you." He was the Activist coming out. Talking about the present and this whole relationship to the land. He read a letter he wrote to the head judge of the World Court while at university. Suddenly this whole different energy began to build. We created the world and nature had brought itself to this point.

Then Brian Tripp came out, and he was the Artist. He said, "I don't know what to say about those sacred mountains." He played his drum and then stopped. He said, "All I know is that some people use it and I use it, too, even though I don't go there. I use it by knowing that it is there." He drummed away. He was this totally individual person in relating his spirituality and his relationship with these mountains, these sacred places.

"THIS SONG SPONTANEOUSLY DEMANDED TO BE SUNG."

There was a guy in the theater, a set designer, who was creating the universe–constellations and the heavens. He was from San Diego and had been run out of Mexico because he was a nationalist Nahua Indian from Cuernavaca. He was up on this tall ladder, this cherry picker, with a staple gun, and he was creating the universe. We hired him. He was the Stranger. He told this Nahua story of the four worlds. How the first, second and third worlds were destroyed by people's greed. And how this is the fourth and last world. He said, we are sitting on the brink of destruction and we have to decide.

Then there was an intermission. The idea for the finale was that there would be a ceremony to fix the world. We gathered the best men and women, singers and dancers, the Pomo dancers from Santa Rosa. David Smith, Clarence Carillo, and a whole group. They were wild. The roundhouse was the world. It fit perfectly on the stage. They took everybody through

this series of dances that were incredible. Sweat flew off the dancers. It was incredibly, intensely good. They fixed the world and they ended the performance perfectly. I couldn't believe the power of it.

A couple of people called and talked about how good the performance was and asked what were we going to do next. I said, "I will teach Lyn a bunch of those songs recorded in the 1920s. She learned some songs for this particular event at the On the Water Theater in San Francisco. I am going to teach her more songs and then we will create a tape recording. Then we will make this available to tribal members, so people can begin learning these songs." That was the next project which has taken a couple of years. It is not completely finished yet. We have them recorded. It is just a matter of mixing them onto a master tape.

It was during that time that Lyn and I fell in love. We couldn't maintain the appropriate distance. I was content with being her friend and knowing that she is committed in the same way I am committed. We could be friends for the rest of our lives. When I started falling in love with her, I started getting unbearably hot. The more time we spent together, the more excuses I made to telephone her. In the end I talked to her two to three times a day. This was almost a year ago today.

LYN: That was when we were doing the recordings and practicing together. Some of those songs were so powerful. I think it was the magic and power of the songs, along with the full moon, that brought us together.

JULIAN: There is a short song that we sang, a song of the Pleiades *(ataynamtunvêechas)*, the stars, the seven sisters. It was not on the list of songs that we were recording. One evening, we were practicing and then suddenly we began singing this song completely unrehearsed. This song spontaneously demanded to be sung, so we began to sing it. It was like watching a lifeless plant, that somebody forgot to water, bring itself up. It was neglected, it was not dead. It was not anybody's fault. All it needed was nourishment. We were singing this song and then suddenly we were bringing it out. Singing it more and more, it brought this energy into our world. The singing filled up the room. It changed the chemistry in the air.

LYN: After a while the songs became more and more like that to me. The songs were an effort for me to learn because I am not familiar with the language. Julian made it more real.

I am more of a visual learner. I had to listen to the songs over and over again. Then pretty soon I could feel the songs. I would be driving somewhere and that star song would come. That song became a key part of me. I began to get this great feeling when I sang. It makes you feel good. I felt like I was bringing the songs back to life and connecting to the original people who recorded them. I felt like I was bringing the songs back to life in a spiritual sense. The songs themselves have their own spirit.

After recording the songs, we gave a public performance in Panámniik (Orleans), which is close to the mountains where these songs came from. The day before the performance we went to those mountains. We sang the songs to the mountains. It was like giving them back.

It was an exchange, a gift. We went down to the Klamath River and sang all the songs. My daughter came with us and she sat down by the river. We started singing all the songs just one more time before we sang them to everybody else. When we were singing, all these animals started coming around, a little lizard, ducks, an otter and an eagle. Everybody was there. Everybody was listening.

JULIAN: The night before the performance I spent the evening there sitting on the front porch of this little cabin. I practiced all the bird songs that we were going to be singing. Here came all those birds, they tromped out into the yard. When I started singing the quail song this quail was moving his head and his top-knot was bobbing as he walked. He walked in perfect rhythm with the quail song. The crane flew by and we sang a crane song. Everybody, all the birds, came around. They knew their songs were going to be sung.

LYN: We practiced the songs so many times our voices started tuning in to each other.

JULIAN: They called us the Indian Ike and Tina.

LYN: We tuned into each other's voices and knew exactly where the other person was going. That morning it came together. We took another cultural step by letting other people hear the songs. These songs belong to the people, too. They are not ours to keep for our enjoyment. We gave them back to the community.

"TO MAKE A DANCE ONE HAS TO HAVE COMMITMENT."

JULIAN: If we make these songs available to our people, they become available to others as well. For me this becomes a nationalist issue. These are Karuk songs and it is our responsibility to maintain their integrity. In the old days, people had to travel a long ways to hear these songs. We sang them on the radio one time, and later this woman came to a meeting and said, "I was singing that song along with you." This is the point where I have a hard time because I am a conservative person in a sense. I am not liberal minded when it comes to our cultural knowledge. I see songs as extensions of creation. I don't see them as a burst of energy that is shot into the future for us to receive. We are an extension of our past and we are responsible for maintaining that connection. Sharing songs with non-Karuk People is a difficult thing for me intellectually and philosophically.

LYN: Exploitation is all around us. People taking bits and pieces of ideas without really understanding them. We are connected to a particular place, where we come from. We are connected with the creation, the beginning of time. If you take a song out of context and sing it without understanding that connection, you lose something. Even though we are giving the songs back to our people, there is always the possibility of misusing them. Even our people may share a recorded song with somebody who does not have that understanding. They won't understand its meaning even though it might make them feel good and they might even understand the context, where the song came from, how and when it is supposed to be sung. On the one hand, we don't want to horde the songs and not share them. It is the whole idea of sharing the knowledge that has been given to you, like stories, songs and the language. Behind this dam there is all this knowledge. You want to let it out and share it. You don't want to share it chaotically, with people grabbing here and there without an understanding of what it all means.

JULIAN: After we finished the Creation Theater Project, we learned a lot about the issues surrounding Native knowledge and how to present it to people. There is a best way of doing things and then there are other ways. Not necessarily wrong ways, but other ways. I don't want to judge negatively but there is a best way to do things. This is the double-edged sword of the issue of sharing. The right way to do things is openly, publicly and making sure that those people who want to participate are able to participate. Consciousness extends out. Every step extends out.

For us, though, the next step extended inwards. Lyn has a daughter who is becoming a woman. We are committed to the plan of having an Ihuk Dance, a puberty ceremony, for her. There have been a couple of girls in the last five years whose parents wanted to have a Ihuk Dance, but it never happened.

LYN: I am in a master's program in social science with an emphasis in Native American studies. What appealed to me in this particular program was that I could do something that had to do with my culture. I was not motivated to do graduate work if I could not relate it to something I thought was important. I could not see myself just writing a thesis—it had to have an important meaning, something I could put my heart into. I talked to different people about this whole idea of an Ihuk Dance at different times. I thought it would be a wonderful thing to do because of all the problems our young women face. Everywhere with our people, there is a high rate of teenage pregnancy, drug and alcohol use, and poor self-image.

Traditional societies did not have "teenage problems." You were a child and you learned as you grew up. You were given certain responsibilities at certain times. You started learning at a young age what those responsibilities were and that eventually became your role as an adult. When you reached puberty, you became an adult. You went from childhood to adulthood. There was a puberty ceremony that helped that transition. This was done by tribes throughout the country, probably all over the world at one time.

I decided for my thesis to research this ceremony, which had not been done by the Karuk people for one hundred and twenty years. Then I started thinking of my own daughter and thinking it would be great if we could bring this ceremony back. I started my research and thought I could interview elders. Then I realized that there weren't elders living who had a complete knowledge because it had been so long since the ceremony had been done. There was some information available through what had been in done in the 1920s by J.P. Harrington, Alfred Kroeber and Helen H. Roberts. A lot of the information I gathered was through work Julian had done on language and stories, and ethnographic information he transcribed from original notes on microfilm. I went through a lot of that and I pulled out anything that had to do with puberty, menstruation, or the Ihuk Dance.

I had all this information and realized it was a puzzle that had pieces missing. I tried to make sense of it and how it all fit together. I realized that I was never going to find all the missing pieces. I felt overwhelmed. I had to keep searching for all this information. I finally reached a point where I felt stuck. I realized there was all this academic stuff I had to deal with. What I was doing did not fit my research method.

JULIAN: It was not an academic pursuit, it was a human cultural pursuit.

LYN: The other thing was the ceremony itself. I was at a loss as to how to make that happen. I did not have people to direct me and tell me what I needed to do. The people did not exist. I knew that it had to be a community effort. It was not just me doing this thing for my daughter. Making a ceremony happen involves a lot of people. I had this fear of getting my feet wet, taking the first steps, and running the risk of being criticized no matter what I did. All these things ran through my mind.

In the meantime, I had done some research on the Hupa puberty ceremony because the last one they did was in 1980. Their information was more complete. I did some research on that and interviewed a couple of people, including a woman who had gone through one. I did a comparison with Hupa ceremonies and ceremonies done in other tribes, to get an overall sense of what these puberty ceremonies were all about—the meaning, purpose, and symbolism behind them. I looked at the similarities and the differences within each tribe.

Last fall, Julian and I were asked to sing. I had been speaking with these people who wanted to reconstruct a puberty ceremony for one of their daughters. This was the Tsnungwe people who are related to the Hupa and live on the South Fork of the Trinity River. They are going through a process of tribal recognition and reconstruction of their culture. I had been talking to them quite a bit and exchanging information about the puberty ceremonies. Finally it was their daughter's time. They decided to have this ceremony. They called me up and asked if Julian and I would sing. We decided to help them. We brought my daughter, so she could be part of it, or just to be there. We sang some of the Ihuk Dance songs that have not been sung for over a hundred years. It was a great experience because we were singing the songs for their original purpose. Not just to be heard, but for that particular girl.

They learned from the Hupa ceremony but reached a point where they decided they needed to do something for their people and for that girl. They could not copy from the Hupas something they could not fully understand, even though they were related and some of their people lived together throughout the years. They could speak the language, as it was pretty similar. They finally decided that they needed to adapt this ceremony to their particular needs—for this particular girl, for this family, for this community, for this place. The ceremony took place at their village site.

I learned from that experience. After the ceremony, I interviewed the girl, the father, the mother, and the aunt that stood with the girl during the seclusion, fasting, and prayers. I also interviewed this young Tsnungwe man, who had done much of the research and helped the family perform this ceremony. One thing that I learned from talking to these people is that the family as a whole had to make a commitment to make this ceremony happen. They committed a full year of preparation—making regalia, preparing food, making arrangements for the location, etc. The whole family was involved in thinking about it, talking about it, and praying about it. At that point, I realized I had been talking and thinking about our Ihuk Dance but I had not really made the commitment necessary to make it happen.

I started thinking about what that meant and realized that I had to refocus my energies

from the academic thesis to the ceremony itself. I realized that I had been stuck in between. One day, after we went up the river and spent some time there, things started to change. Traditionally, there were two kinds of Ihuk Dance ceremonies. One was done every year. The ceremonial cycle began in the spring and ended in the fall, starting with the First Salmon Ceremony, the Ihuk and then the Brush dance. This Ihuk Dance represented the beginning of the annual cycle of rebirth, the blooming of all the girls that became women during that year. They would choose one girl to represent all the girls and she would dance in the ceremony.

The other Ihuk Dance would be given for a specific girl by her family. It would be done during her first period and it was given by wealthier families that could afford to feed everyone. In the old days, they would have as many as three different Ihuk ceremonies for one girl. If you had three dances, you were high status. The dances announced your daughter's status and eligibility for marriage. Negotiations for marriage would sometimes begin during the dance.

I realized we would not be able to reconstruct a ten-day ceremony exactly the way it was done a long time ago, beginning on the day my daughter started her period. It seemed so unrealistic. I thought that maybe we could combine both of the ceremonies by having it at the time the annual Ihuk Dance was traditionally done. We decided we would choose three girls, rather than one, who were at the same stage. One of the girls, who is my daughter's friend, has been dancing and singing with her, so they are connected in that way. The other is Julian's cousin who lives at the place where we want to have the dance, where it was done a long time ago.

JULIAN: We were raised on this flat where we knew the Ihuk Dance was once held. The last dance was done just before my great-grandmother was born. When we were kids she would say, "Oh, I wish you kids could see what I have seen." My greatest satisfaction will be knowing that there will be a dance on this flat that my great-grandmother never got to see. She

always talked about that place being the Ihuk dance grounds. "That land there was a place where they had Ihuk Dances for girls. That is what the land was for. The spirit in that place is to create luck for girls who will become women. That is the job of that land, that is its power." The land has not been used for that purpose for so long. The dance of that land is coming back.

There are some incredibly beautiful things that require a lot of work to make. They are tarnished and old now; they need a lot of work to bring them back and make them sparkly and brilliant the way they used to be. One is language. My great-grandmother always used to laugh and say, "Where did you ever learn how to speak Indian?" It always surprised her that I knew of so many things. I learned from people, as well as from books. At a certain level of understanding, you are free to think and to create yourself, your own identity.

Making a ceremony is an incredible amount of work. The dance grounds themselves have to be delineated. We walked all over the flat. I asked my cousin, "Where do you think it is?" He said, "Maybe it was over there where the sweat house is." We walked around and I said, "It could have been there." I took him to where I thought it was. To me, it is a perfectly natural place, this dance ground. We have to make the dance ground, too.

We have to gather and collect incredible amounts of various things like iris (to make string), and something we call Indian potatoes (brodaea), and maple which was stripped for bark dresses. You have to make feather visors from blue jay tail feathers which fit over the girls' eyes. To symbolize that they are new women, you have to make gray squirrel capes. We have to make deer hoof rattles. There is even a part of the dance where they have to wear what we call hooks—*ikríkir*—sea lion tusk headdresses. Then there is all of the cooking and the preparation of the food. That all has to be done.

There has to be a general understanding of what the dance is. How does it happen? From where does it come? You have to know and create an understanding, a consciousness, that will sustain us and that will keep it happening afterwards. The songs have to be learned. Certain dance steps have to be literally created out of descriptions that are found in old stories and songs.

What is unique about this dance is that, before, we have always had elders who knew how to make dances. In this one, there are no elders that know how to do it. Nobody has ever done it in over one hundred and twenty years, maybe one hundred and thirty years. My great-grandmother passed away in 1983 at the age of one hundred and fourteen. We have to make all of the dance by ourselves without being able to rely on the elders to make the prayers and give us the spiritual connection about how it all fits. We can't just do what we are told. We have to go and do it ourselves.

To make a dance one has to have commitment. It is like the word "commitment" has finally hit Indian Country. I have to fight hard to maintain my commitment.

The language helps to combine and unify everything. There is a story about the creation of the Ihuk Dance. The whole dance is ordained in this one story of how deer were lost and regained in the oldest days:

Before people, there were Spirit-people, animal-people. There was this couple, *Yupthúkirar* and *Ipatakéevriik*. *Yupthúkirar* was a panther man and his wife was a deer woman. *Ipatakéevriik* took a second wife, *Kachakâach*, from another tribe. His first wife moved out when the new wife came, and she and her daughter lived together in another house. Every day, she cooked him acorn soup and the daughter, who like her mother was a deer, brought it to her father. But every day, the second wife spilled it and told her husband it wasn't any good.

One day, the father grabbed the acorn soup away from his daughter before the second wife could get to it. He tasted the acorn soup and realized that it was the best soup in the world, and his second wife had been eating it herself all along. He beat her and she ran away, and turned into a blue jay. His daughter went back to her mother and told her what had happened, and the mother took her and they went back to their home in heaven, where they had a red house.

When they left this earth, they took everything that was theirs back to heaven with

133

them. They took everything that was made out of deer. In those times, everything that men used here to live, hunt, and gather was all based on deer. When the mother and daughter left, it was like the end of the world. The world could not exist without the deer. Finally, the men had to go and get the deer.

The panther father had a little brother, who was a wildcat. The Panther had given up hope, and they say that he became thin as a blanket. He just lay on the ground because he had nothing to eat. There was no acorn soup because his wife was gone. Wildcat was young and full of hope. He went hunting every day, even though the deer were gone.

One night, he had a dream that he needed spots on his body, so he painted himself and out hunting. After a while, he found his way to heaven, where he found the deer people. They were all dancing in heaven, because the deer daughter had become a woman. They were having the very first Ihuk dance. Because he had spots, wildcat was able to hide among the deer children, who sat on the roof of a house, watching the dance. They didn't notice that he was a wildcat, because he was spotted like they were. He watched the dance, and when he left, he grabbed one of the fawns. He gave it to the starving panther, who ate it and regained his strength. The wildcat's name was Akviish. He started telling Panther about his trip into heaven, where the deer people lived. He told his brother, "There's a red house in the middle of the sky there. The deer are having a dance for your daughter. She's become a woman. They're having a dance to make luck for her. A pole stands there and they put the girl on top of the pole during the dance. We can wait on top of the red house, grab her, and bring her back."

The deer people started to dance. The deer mother started singing a luck song for her daughter. Then she sang another song: "I smell his blood, I smell the panther's blood. I smell his blood, he's here. He's come to get his child." That's when they grabbed the daughter and brought her back to earth. The deer people followed them back. They stood on the hill above Panther's village. That's where they turned into deer, as we know them today. They said, "From now on, you must have a dance like ours for your daughters; then, we will be your food. But you have to make luck for your daughters. You have to make this Ihuk dance."

Contained in the traditional story form, we have found clue after clue about how the dance goes, how it happens, the sequence of events, and the whole purpose of the dance. These various clues are not evident in the English version of the story. In English, it's a nice story about deer, and finding the deer having a puberty dance. The Karuk language version of the story is a living thing.

LYN: All of these things are unfolding. We have an idea but we don't know the exact details. Every day we talk about it. In the beginning, I thought it was me who had to create this whole thing and then tell people what to do—even though I knew that that is not how it was supposed to be, that it had to be a community thing. I did not quite know how to reach out to the community. As things are unfolding right now, that is the shift for me. By including the families of the other girls, it became a group effort. Everybody had something to contribute: different resources, talent and more commitment. Their families started branching out and then it became this community effort. As we talked to people, pretty soon other ideas came into it and then everybody contributed who wanted to be involved, instead of our saying, "Okay, just he and I are going to figure it all out. We are not going to tell anybody until the end and then we'll just tell them what to do. If you want to come, fine, if not, don't." It has to be a community effort. There is a right way. It is not already mapped out for us, but as you go along, there is a right way of little steps that you take. Where there are pieces missing, somehow we will know as they come to us.

JULIAN: That is where faith comes in. The language is absolutely essential as well because just talking to a non-speaker for a few minutes, you realize that they are limited in their understanding. You can only go so far because they don't have the Indian language to guide them in the end. When you get so close you can almost touch it but you can't, then what do you do? When you almost know and are willing to commit fully to it but you can't, then what do you do? You need that one little bit of information, that one nod, that one indication. Lots of times you find it in the language, within the verb ending. You know that it is in a circle because of how the word is used in the story. It gives you the proper tense, the time, the sense of direction. Invariably, we have incredible clues built into the language.

LYN: Julian's understanding of the language is a bridge for me and the other people. Through the language we get a better understanding of the Ihuk. We can see how the dance works within our cultural context. I see this Ihuk dance as a baby. It is in the womb right now and at the end of this year it will be born. Then the dance will be a baby and next year it will be in the toddler stage. Eventually it will reach adulthood. We will look back and say, "Remember when we were giving birth to this dance? Look at it now, it is a woman now."

CHAPTER TWELVE

An interview with Poquin Theresa Downey (Tets'ugeh and Wylaki),
her mother, Vicky Downey, and her grandmother, Priscilla Vigil

Poquin Downey, Tewa and Wailaki, is a student at the Santa Fe Indian School. She lives with her mother's family at the Tewa-speaking Tets'ugeh Pueblo in New Mexico. The Vigils are a strong traditional family and are actively involved in ceremonial life, language instruction, traditional agriculture, and rebuilding traditional pueblo homes. Poquin's mother, Vicky Downey, is a language instructor at the Tets'ugeh Day School, and her grandparents, Priscilla and Mark Vigil, are respected elders in their community.

POQUIN: When I went to India, I met people on the other side of the world, but they were almost the same as the people here. They looked the same, acted the same and had pretty much the same values. The first week I was there we traveled around. We saw so many poor people, thousands and thousands of poor Indian people. They did not have any expression on their face. You would look at them and they would stare. You would have this feeling like you weren't wanted. They would come up to you and beg for money. I did not like that part of going to India. In that first week I got real homesick and I wanted to come home. I did not want to be there anymore.

Then we went to the Tibetan Children's Village. When we first got there, the director took us to the house where we would be staying. It was a Saturday, and the children were all getting ready for a celebration, so they were cleaning. Everybody was working outside and they were all happy and had smiles on their faces. We felt like we were wanted and had something to be there for. Everybody wanted to know who we were. We got introduced and pretty soon we had friends. Everybody was glad to be there because it was peaceful. It was way out in the mountains. The Tibetans were nice people and we had this good feeling from them. We were having fun and we weren't homesick anymore.

We would go to Tibetan shops and they would start talking to us in Tibetan. We did not know what they were saying, so we would try to explain to them that we were from the United States. Some of them were saying, "No, no, the same, the same," and touching their faces. The older Tibetans, they looked Pueblo. They looked like people from here.

"THEY ALWAYS
DISPLAY THE LOVE
THEY HAVE FOR
EACH OTHER."

The Tibetans are brought up to love everybody and respect each other. They help other people, they think of other people before they think of themselves. That is what we are supposed to do here, respect others and try to help everybody. It is different now because young people, people my age, don't really care. They don't care whether they know their traditions or not. There are a lot of people at my school like that. Some of them are really into their traditions, some of them don't really care, and some of them don't even know about them.

The students over there take care of each other. They are always hugging each other. They always display the love that they have for each other. Over there, you would see two guys walking and they would have their arms around each other. If you did that at our school, somebody would make fun of you or say things about you. Over there it is just the way that they view things. When we first got over there, it was hard because people would just come up and put their arms around us. They would walk with you and we did not know what to think. Then afterwards we got used to it and we would go up to anybody and put our arms around them, and walk with them and visit with them.

"I TAKE PART IN MY
TRADITIONAL WAYS.
THAT IS WHO I AM."

I participate in our dances. They are important to me because they are a part of how I was brought up. It is important to my mom and my grandma. They value it. Their values are passed on and that is what I value in myself, what is important to me. I am a part of my grandma, a part of my mom and my dad, and a part of all the people that teach me. That is all mixed, all a part of me. They all contributed to making me who I am. I am a fifteen-year-old Tewa and Wailaki. I take part in my traditional ways. That is who I am.

VICKY: We teach Poquin to be herself. In order to be herself, she has to feel good about who she is. To feel good about who she is, she has to know her dances, her songs, her language, her ceremonies. In our instructions, we are told to recognize one another as relatives, whether it is in a community or outside or with non-Indian people. You look at people as your brother or sister, your aunt or uncle, your grandma or grandpa. We are taught to respect all life, from the air to the water, to the trees, to the moon, the stars, the people, the insects, everything in life. In our language we use the word "life" a lot. The main ingredient is to respect and love life. That is all that matters in this world or when you pass on to the next world.

We are taught to love and care for one another. Caring for one another is a universal concept. It isn't just an Indian concept—it's supposed to be like that everywhere. When you are with the Tibetan kids, they already have that concept. It is stronger there than it is here. The education and social life we have in the United States and in Indian communities change those feelings. When I went to Ecuador, I saw the same thing. I saw little boys and girls car-

rying their little sisters and little brothers on their backs. You can just feel that caring for the family, that caring for the land.

When I was in Guatemala, people got up at five o'clock in the morning. That is how it used to be here. The first thing you do is pray for just waking up. In Guatemala, if somebody saw you on the road, they greeted you. They said, "good morning." No matter who it is, you greet them. Even if they are far away and you can't say good morning or good afternoon , then you raise your hand and wave to them. You give them some kind of acknowledgment; you greet them.

The prayers are done naturally. You pray in the morning and in the evening. In between, you can pray anytime or anyplace you want, even if you are in a car or at school. We also pray before meals. The other thing that we are taught is that we are supposed to plant corn and that means plant your food. Again, with the changes we have gone through, a lot of our people do not plant anymore. They go to the grocery store to buy their food. Yet that instruction is still here. We are still reminded every year that we have to plant, recognize our relatives, have respect and love, and care for one another.

"WE WANT POQUIN TO LEARN AND PRACTICE THESE THINGS ABOUT LOVING."

We want Poquin to learn and practice these things about loving. We just had the Corn Dance a couple of weeks ago. I was telling the kids, "Remember, when you get tired and really hot and thirsty, that is when you pray the most. Think about the people you love. When you are praying for that person, you do not feel the heat and the aches in your body as much because your thoughts are in concentration of prayer." Our children experience that when they are dancing.

We tell them they are not dancing to show off their costume, their jewelry or moccasins or whatever. They are dancing for life, for their own life, the life of the world, the universe. When they finish the dance they greet us by saying, "Life be to you." They have earned their life for themselves as individuals and for their community, the world.

Our kids who take part in traditions, ceremonies and songs know that, because they feel it in their hearts. They feel that energy. It is hard for our kids when they go to school. They are taught to be individuals and to make goals to become doctors, lawyers or teachers. This makes them forget the concept of others before self and so they are thinking about, "What do I want, what do I want to be?" We lose a lot of kids to that mainstream society. We lose them to drugs and alcohol and the cities. We have a lot of kids like that. But when they have sense of where they are coming from or who they are, usually we can get them back. We can get them back sometime in life. They might be thirty or fifty years old, but they still come back. They go through life as an experience and somewhere they realize, "This is who I am." So they eventually come back and become who they really are. We have a lot of people like that who do come back.

"IT IS HARD LIVING IN TWO WORLDS."

PRISCILLA: Each child, each individual, has to think for himself or herself. We can only show them the importance of our traditional ways of life, the importance of who they are. We only say the words to them. It is up to them to take it into their hearts, into their minds. And we don't just do it one time; we have to remind them. When they go to school in the non-Indian world, the teachers tell them to study hard and really be somebody, be a teacher, a professor, a doctor, a lawyer.

It is hard living in two worlds. Yes, they have to go to school; they have to learn. Their traditional way of learning is the first that they learn as they are starting to talk, walk, and hear things. They hear songs, birds, all the sounds outside. All that is learning. Sometimes it is hard. I am not just talking about my people, our ways. We go through a lot of hardships just like other tribes. Some of our young people find it so hard. They want to do their own thing. As grandparents, we have to remind them, time and time again, that we have to pray. Like the Tibetan children, we have to pray. They have that harmony through their prayers. They feel good about themselves. That is why they help their brothers and sisters or whomever they meet. That is a good feeling. That is the way with us—we have to be praying. Not just in the morning or in the evening. The way the world is going now, we have to pray whenever we think about it.

"WHEN PEOPLE STOP PRAYING, THEN EVERYTHING WILL BE IN TURMOIL."

Sometimes I go to bed and I can't go to sleep even if I am tired. When that happens, I don't just twist and turn. I start meditating and I talk to the spirit, and pretty soon I go to sleep. Sometimes early in the morning, I wake up. Once I wake up, I can't go back to sleep. Then again, I do more praying before I even get up. When I get up, I go outside; by that time, daylight is coming. Chief Leon (Shenandoah) says that is when the spirits are around; that's when they come to visit you. So I go outside and I talk to them. I do more praying and then I say, I already did my prayer while I was in my bed and now again I am telling you. The first thing I do is give my thanks. I give my thanks for this wonderful day. I tell them, this day here might be something that won't go right or will make me worry, but I leave that to you. You take care of that for me. Praying that way, I feel very good. I feel I am lifted and I can go on. I just let the great spirits take care of things for me through the day. I am praying all the

140

time for the youth, the children and those that are not even born.

When people stop praying, then everything will be in turmoil. I think that is what is happening now. We see on the television where people are shooting at one another. When I talk to Native people, I tell them our traditional way of life is what keeps us strong. Our language is so important because many of our prayers have to be said in our own language. I tell many people that, regardless of what race they are, they can still pray in whatever language they use. There is so much anger in this world, even in this community. Prayers can change the attitude of a person. They can bring peace and harmony. I see angry people here. I don't hate them. I don't judge them or tell them, "I don't like your attitude," or "I don't like the way that you treat other people." I just pray for them. Many times when I do my prayers I just give thanks to the Creator because I am blessed. My husband and I were blessed with our wonderful children. I can't thank the Creator enough.

Even if you are only going to have a small meeting with just a handful of people, always say a little prayer before you start. I guess by now people know that my prayers are strong, so they ask me to come and open up our meeting with a prayer. I am glad to do it. I am not asking anybody to put money into my hand. I leave that up to the spirit people and the Creator.

VICKY: People don't understand prayer. You say "prayer" and they think about kneeling down and saying words. A prayer, in the Indian sense, is a state of mind. It takes practice to achieve sincerity. You can pray in your mind—thoughts and words will come into your mind. It is not just thinking about it, it is achieving a state of mind. You have to believe and have faith in the Creator. You thank the Creator for whatever you are going to receive.

We teach the kids that whatever your thoughts are, they will come back to you. Be careful of what you are thinking. If you are thinking bad about somebody, it is going to turn around and come back. What you do is send good thoughts to whomever you see, so that good thoughts will come back to you. If you give your gifts freely, they will come back ten times what you gave. The gift does not always come in the same form that you gave. A lot of times it comes back in a different form. That is how it works. If you give anger, that is what you are going to get back. We are also not to judge people. That is hard, because you can't help but judge people. When I see a person staggering, in my mind I start labeling. I catch myself doing it and I try to work on it.

You are not loving them when you judge them. The idea is that you have to love everybody. The love that we are talking about is unconditional love. You cannot put conditions on love. You cannot say, I am not going to love that person because he is an alcoholic, or I am not going to love that person because he killed my son. It is hard, but that is what we are supposed to do. That is what everybody is supposed to do, not just Indians, but all races of people. That was the original instruction to both the Indian nations and the Christian world.

You forgive your enemy. Poquin didn't mention this, but the Chinese had come and invaded Tibet, killed the people, and destroyed the religion and taken over the whole country. The Tibetans had to flee that country and so they went into India, which is where many of them are living now as refugees. They want to go back to Tibet because that is their home. And yet, they have the compassion to forgive the Chinese for what they have done to the Tibetan people. Now, even young kids who are at the school have forgiven the Chinese because that compassion is part of their teachings. So, they have forgiven them. They are happy and sad at the same time because they want to go home. In order to save their religion, their ceremonies, they had to leave Tibet. They have survived and that is why they are still practicing their religion.

That is what happened to Indian communities when we were invaded. Many tribes had to go underground or go off secretly to practice the religion. Maybe they went to the mountains and they continued doing their ceremonies. That is why we still have ceremonies–because somebody took the time to hide and save their religion and language. They had to hide for a long time. It wasn't until the 1950s that they started coming out of hiding. Now that it is strong, everybody wants to follow the Indian's religion because they think that is the only true religion. But it is not. All it is again is practicing that unconditional love, caring and forgiveness. Our Indian communities still need to forgive and practice compassion. It's not easy, but we need to work on it

Ignorance is a big problem. A lot of people don't know who they are, where they are coming from, and where they are going. Indian people who know where we are going are really praying hard because of the situation in the world.

POQUIN: The biggest thing I learned when I went to India was about love and compassion. The Tibetans taught me to look at somebody and not judge them by how they looked or how they acted–just go up to them, talk, give them a hug or smile. When I came back, that's what I tried to do. It is hard because you go to school and everybody thinks that they are right and whatever they do is right. It was hard to talk to the students when I came back. I tried to teach them not to judge people and just accept them for who they are. That was hard because they didn't care or want to listen. When we tried to tell them how the Chinese came in and invaded Tibet, they did not really care or want to listen. It did not relate to their life, so they did not care. There were only a few people who wanted to listen, so we talked to them.

My best friend was the hardest because she did not understand what I experienced over there. We were really close and all of a sudden, I started going a different way. I changed a lot and I was trying not to hate people who I had hated before when I left. When I came back, I tried to let go of that anger. I tried, and she did not understand. She told me, "You said you did not like them and now you are trying to be nice." That was hard, because she was my best friend.

When I see people, I try not to judge them. It is still hard. I see a bum sitting on the street and right away I have a label to stick on him. Maybe he is not a bum; maybe that is the way he wants to live. I am already labeling people. I try not to; I try to give love and not judge. The most important thing to me is to share that love with people, but it has been hard.

I try to make people understand. I have to explain to them so that they can envision what I experienced and feel what I feel. When I was in Tuscarora, I was trying to explain to them. I think that is why a lot of them were crying because they could feel what I felt. It is hard, but you have to do it.

We have to be thankful for what we have. In India, they did not have any hot water. We had to go and take cold showers in the morning. We lived the way they lived. We did not have a Wal-Mart down the road to go to and buy whatever we needed. There was not any of that. There were just these poor people in the Tibetan village and they were so nice. They were always happy and smiling. You got this feeling from all of them, that they cared for you so much.

Once, in India, I had just gotten off the phone with my mom. She had told me that they were having a feast at home. We had been eating rice for four weeks. We wanted feast food, we wanted something good to eat. The next day, we were going to come home. I went back to my class and we had a break. Most of them go back to the dorms during breaks. That day I decided to stay and talk with a couple of guys in my class. They were asking about my home here. My friend, his name was Nygmar, was asking me, "So, you are ready to go home?" I said, "Yeah." He said, "Do you miss your mom? It has been a while since you saw your mother?" I said, "Yeah." He was real serious and he told me, "Most of us have not seen our parents in a long time." He said that he had not seen his parents in seven years, not since he had been at that school. He doesn't know when he is going to see his parents again. He was asking me, "Are you going to run to your mom and give her a hug?" And I said, "Yes, that is what I am going to do." He said "That is what I am going to do, too, when I get to see my mom." He is going to run to his mom and give her a hug.

It made me feel like I was being selfish because I had my mom to go home to. He couldn't just go home. He can't go home. He has to stay there and go to school. All those students, most of them don't have their parents. They have an infant place where they have all the little babies. When we saw them, they were all happy to see us and they were laughing. They don't have their parents either. They have foster parents who are taking care of them. When my friend told me that, I was thinking, "Even if I go to school Monday through Friday and I stay at school all during that time, I can still go home on the weekend and see my family. I am so lucky. I can go home and I can see my mom, my brothers, my grandparents, my aunts and my uncles—everybody is right there." In India, the Tibetans can't go back home.

Some of the students told us how long they had been at school. My friend, Yang Don, and her older sister, Kalsang, stayed in the same home as me. Yang Don was telling me that her mom died when she was little and that she had not seen her dad in five years. She did not know her mother. Every time I would talk about my grandma or my mom, they would get real happy. I was thinking, "That must be really hard." She was crying when she was telling me. I felt bad. Then she told me, "I am going to see my dad in April," so I felt better. I got happy and she was excited, too. When I came back home and April came around, I was thinking, she must be happy now.

When I came back, it was hard because the students here always say bad things about their parents—my mom is this, my dad is this, because they did not let me do something. They are always saying bad things about their parents. It made me mad inside because I thought, at least you have your parents. All those students over there, they don't have their parents. Some do because their parents are in India with them. But most of their parents are still in Tibet. They do not get to see them often. Nyngmar was telling me that he doesn't remember what his mom looks like anymore. They don't have pictures or cameras in Tibet. He never got a picture of his mom. I think he is about the same age as I am. The last time he saw his mom was seven years ago. Some of the students do not even remember what their parents look like, and it is just awful.

You come back here and the people don't care; they don't understand. You try to tell them, but they still don't know. You come back over here and you get caught up in the hate again. That is how I am. I will be sitting there at home. Then, me and my little brothers will start fighting. When we are really fighting, we will say, "I hate you, Mom." Then, every once in a while, I will be cleaning and digging through my stuff in my room and I will pick up a picture. I will pick it up and I will look at it and it will be Nyngmar and all my friends over there. They don't have their parents with them. None of them would ever say that. They would not say that to their parents or to their brothers. It reminds me all the time not to hate people or say bad things about them but to be thankful that they are here. It reminds me to be thankful for everything that I have. I have my mom and my grandma and everybody, and they are right here.

VICKY: Poquin wants people to send their prayers to Tibet for the young people so that they will able to go home sometime in the future and to pray for world peace. We want everybody in the world to pray.

POQUIN: The biggest thing I came back with is a feeling of being thankful for everything that is around me and all the people. You see the bum at Wal-Mart, or sitting on the street some-where. He is sitting there and he has a sleeping bag and all his stuff with him. Then you think about all the people in India and all they had was what they were wearing. You think, that bum, he is a rich bum. He has a lot. You don't really feel sorry for him because he does have a lot more than most people do. I am just thankful for everything that is around. I try to love everybody, not to judge them, just love them.

When I get mad, sometimes I go and take a walk. I pray the way I know how and I try to get away from things. I will take a walk in the hills and just try to think about everything, and then I go back. When I don't feel strong and I feel like crying, then I cry. When I cry, it helps me and I feel better. I write a lot. I do little things like that.

PRISCILLA: Prayer has to be a continuing thing. In Tewa, all the old people tell us that when-ever the spirit people can't forgive us for our mistakes, we have the lightning, hail, droughts, earthquakes, tornadoes. I call it the end of the world. We are not living right anymore. We are not praying. That is why all these disasters are happening. When we get ourselves straightened out, when we all start praying and living right, then things are going to be right, too. Not only Christians say that the end of the world is coming. I say, let it come. I am ready, I am ready to go. That is why, when I talk to people, I tell them we need prayers for one another. Forget the hate, forget bad-mouthing one another. That is what is creating all

these problems. We have to pray. The Creator is already showing us that if we do not behave ourselves, straighten up, and love our brothers and sisters, that it is going to happen. Many people have already been taken away.

I have been hurt by my relatives, but I have forgiven them. I can't go around with that grudge. I have to live my life. I am not going to worry about what they say or what they did. One time I told my brother, "I think I should go and tell my sister that I am sorry." He said, "It is not your place to go and ask her to forgive you. She was the one who did that to you. She is the one who owes you an apology." I said, "But she doesn't think about it. Maybe I should." Then, one night, I had a dream. I saw my mother in my dream and she said that we are to forgive one another for whatever happens. I went to work and I had that thought in my mind all day long. That afternoon, after the kids came home, we sat down. We always talk about how the day went, and if there is some problem, we talk about how to take care of it. So I just told them, "I am going over to my sister's house and I will be back." I went over and told my sister, "I came to see you." She told me to sit down. I said, "I had a dream last night of our mother, so I came over here as soon as I could." She said, "I have been thinking of that, too." So we forgave one another and we help each other. My two brothers, we have our misunderstandings too, but I can still talk freely with them and tell them things that are bothering me.

POQUIN: You learn the most when you travel. You learn to appreciate your family when you are away from them. I had to go to the other side of the world to realize what I have at home. If you are having problems at home, go stay with somebody else. When you are away from your family, that is when you realize what you have. When I was over in India, the people looked at you and they did not have an expression. I missed the people's smiles and their greetings in the morning. I missed people saying hello or waving. I missed somebody smiling at me. I missed my little brother. I thought about him when he was laughing. It irritates me when he laughs real loud—it just rings in your ears. But that is what I missed when I was over there. I missed his laugh, because I did not hear anybody laughing.

My message is to respect everybody and love them, try not to judge them. I know it is so hard to do. I try not to judge. My mom always told me that you have to love your enemy. I could not understand why. Now I do. Your enemies are going through a lot of pain, too. Whatever you send out, it is going to come back to you. If you are sending out hate, it is going to come back. When you send out love, love comes back.

It is neat with kids, because they don't care what color the other little kid is. It is just somebody to play with, and that is how you have to be. If you forget how to act, go to a nursery school to see the little kids play with each other. They don't care what color people are, how tall or fat they are, or what color hair they have. They are just people to play and have fun with. That is how you have to look at everybody. Don't try to find the bad in them. Look for the good.

When I was in India, I could be like the Tibetan children. Then I came back, and I had to be like everybody else at school. You have to take a risk and say, "Oh, I don't care what they think." You have to be who you want to be. You have to be able to say, "I don't care what you think about me. This is what I am doing." People are going to judge me but I have to let that go. I am going to make up my own mind. Inside, I still love them.

It is better when you go somewhere else because nobody knows how you were before. When I went to a Gathering at Tuscarora, I could say how I really felt inside, because I did not know those people. I didn't care what they thought. I think it is easier to love a stranger than it is to love someone you have known all your life. You know the mistakes they have made. You know all the bad things they have done to you or to other people. You have known your friends and enemies for a long time. You don't know a stranger. You don't know what they have done to people. You don't know what kind of person they are. For me, it is easier to love a stranger, because I don't know what they have done. I can't judge them because I don't know anything about them. If you think of everyone as a stranger, it is easier to share love.

I want to be able to give love, and respect everybody, and not judge them for what they have done. I want to be just like the Dalai Lama. Before we met him we thought, "What do we say to this person we have been reading about in books?" We did not know what to say to him. We went in there and were nervous. We thought, "Is he going to be real formal?" We walked in there and he was so happy. He had this smile and he welcomed us. He gave us all hugs. Then he asked us how the facilities were, the cold showers, the toilets, how we were getting along with the students. He was laughing and just real happy. You could feel the unconditional love. When you meet somebody like that, they make you so happy. They lift you up. That is how I want to be: to smile and laugh and share that love with people, to give them that same uplifting feeling that I got. That is what I want to do.

In Our Origin Legend, Woman Was
Named Winyan, "The Maker Of
Choices Who Is Complete"

CHAPTER THIRTEEN

An Interview With Charlotte Black Elk

(Lakota)

harlotte Black Elk is an Oglala Lakota. She lives on the Pine Ridge Reservation in South Dakota. She has spent ten years working intensively in Lakota oral tradition, interpretation and verification, using cultural teachings and ceremonial principles as the foundation for organizational design and development.

After a hundred-plus years on the reservation, we have reached a point where we have relative freedom from the interference of government agents in terms of how we structure our community services. I believe that we need to go back to our cultural traditions. If you look at our government, economy, social and judicial structures prior to the reservation era, they all are tied to the sacred teachings. These teachings give us a foundation. We need to go back to those teachings and incorporate them into all of our community structures, everything that is a part of our life.

We have the oldest tribal buffalo herd in Indian Country or anywhere in the United States. The present buffalo pasture in Allen was put together by the Civilian Conservation Corps. I don't think we ever branded our buffalo, but short of that, they were raised like domestic ranch cattle. I spent some time working with the Tribal Parks and Recreation Authority. We looked at how we treat the buffalo as a sacred animal—how we function with today's property rules, but respect the dignity and integrity of the buffalo. How can we show that we have a continuing relationship with this animal that is so principal to our sacred teachings and traditional culture?

I was involved in looking at the ceremony of the buffalo dance, the *ptewacipi*. This is a dance performed by a man who has a vision through which he is taught the dance. The drumming starts very slow. "A buffalo nation is approaching dancing. It comes dancing. Behold the buffalo nation, it comes dancing." The young man somersaults forward to start the dance. It is a shaky dance at the beginning and then it gets stronger and stronger. Then the drumbeat slows down and the dance becomes a measured walk, until finally, at the end of the song, the dancer lies down. The dance shows the life cycle of the buffalo from birth to the first walking, trotting through the buffalo's life, and death of old age. In performing the ceremony, the dancer becomes the buffalo. As the buffalo dies, he has new life. There is this strong relationship. I live because the buffalo gave up his life. Because I live now, the buffalo continues to live. The only way the buffalo will continue to live is if I respect his right to life. I participate in making sure that he lives. We translate that teaching into a management concept.

We need to look at those things within our governmental structure that incorporate a traditional decision-making process, the traditional caring for the greater world. Lakota society was not anthropocentric, it was not focused totally on humans. It respected the dignity of everything that lives. We were told as Lakota people that, "At the time you die, your life on earth should have been as though you always stood on shells, so that there is no destruction in your path and the earth is not harmed."

Those teachings respect the dignity of others. American society has the notion that if people have possessions or academic status, then somehow they are better than other people. Lakota society says everyone has value. You have to respect the skills of every person. Some people may be more skilled in some things than others, but that does not give them any greater rights. We need to look at making sure that in our tribal programs, we don't limit services to just those people who have access in the white world. We need to incorporate these teachings into our services so that they are respectful of our culture and are culturally based. Sometimes you are limited by economic or facilities factors. This should not prevent any tribe from looking at why we do things the way we do. We can no longer allow ourselves to separate our culture from the rest of our life. We did not live that way before white contact.

The judicial structure came from our sacred teachings. Our social rules came from our sacred teachings. Our philosophical practices and beliefs came from our sacred teachings. Our theology was incorporated through all of our life. I think we need to go back to that. I think it is more than just attempting to learn a few words or having a few of the ceremonies. We need to look at the everyday life of the entire tribe as a celebration, not a powwow. I think we can move back in that direction. It is there. It does not matter that there are computers, vehicles, or paved roads in this day and age. Our teachings go beyond the technology and economy that we have in today's society.

Another teaching we have comes from our origin legend. After the earth was created, Unk was created. Unk later created the realm of evil. Our story says that Unk mated with her brother and had a son; she mated with her son, and had a grandson, with whom she mated as well. In our origin legend, we are told that incest is wrong. In our social structure, we have the teaching that there are two types of scent—one you can smell with your nose and the other which your body smells. We have these prohibitions against incest in our social structure because we have knowledge of these two scents. We were prohibited from doing certain things. A woman doesn't sit on her brother's, father's, or son's bedding. A man does not sit on his daughter's belongings or bedding. When a woman prepared her son's leggings or moccasins, she always covered her lap with a part of the hide, which was taken from just below the back part of the smoke area at the top of the teepee, so that her scent that only the body can smell would not transfer onto his belongings. Today, we know about pheromones, and so we have these types of teachings. I think we need to look at those things in our social structure which allow us to maintain these teachings.

The penalty for those people who committed incest was death. That was just not allowed, so you removed the source of the problem. You cut off the sore. In today's society, if our police were to go and hang someone for incest, you would have the wrath of the federal government come down on you. So, while you can't do that, those teachings can continue. The societal rules, the kind that prohibit a woman from sitting on the bare ground, are separate from that judicial structure.

One of our sacred ceremonies is the keeping and releasing of the spirit. We are told that, during the time that we are keeping the spirit, we don't scratch ourselves. That is discipline. When you scratch yourself, who benefits? Society does not benefit. You please yourself; you focus your attention on yourself when you scratch. So, by consciously forcing yourself not to scratch yourself, you teach yourself to take the focus away from your own person and care for the good of the community. If you are not always worried about yourself, maybe you can look beyond.

The person who is the keeper of the spirit is not allowed to cut their own meat during this ceremonial time. The teaching is, "Unless you are good to people, they will not cut your meat for you." It teaches you to be good to people, to always think about them. When you are good to people and think about others, they will understand that you can't cut your meat and they will cut it for you.

There are a lot of social teachings that teach us to care for each other. We need to look at how those attitudes translate into everyday life. What are the things you can do as a direct progression from the ceremony? Our ceremony of *hanbleciya* has always been called a vision quest. People set up a circle and stay inside it. We have a tendency to focus on sacred ceremonies. We have a lot of teaching ceremonies that are supportive of, and related to, the sacred ceremonies. One of the problems is that many sacred ceremonies are expensive to do. My daughter did the tossing of the ball ceremony. It is a sacred ceremony. The cultural tradition is that she tosses the ball five times, and each person that catches the ball is given a buffalo robe or a horse. Those are not easy items to come by in today's society. It is a ceremony that you have to plan for, and because of the resources required, not every young girl can perform it. We have other ceremonies that teach responsibilities.

We have seven ceremonies among the Lakota that follow the stars of a constellation that we call the Bull of the Horn, the one they call Ursa Major, the big dipper. Each ceremony touches one of those seven principal stars. The first ceremony is the Red Earrings. In pre-

"SHE WAS TAUGHT THAT SACRED KNOWLEDGE IS VERY BEAUTIFUL."

contact times, the cape of the domesticated wolf and buffalo hair were taken and woven into beautiful earrings. Red earth paint was brought from the Black Hills. The young girl's earrings were painted red. She was taught that sacred knowledge is very beautiful. It is blessed and adorned just like the earrings. The sacred teachings all weave together and create a beautiful pattern. Just as in the piercing of the ears, there was pain. She learned that this knowledge would be painful to keep and care for. Sometimes it will hang on you and can pull at you, but it is very beautiful. When you understand, it will not be heavy; it will be beautiful. You have the responsibility to keep this knowledge.

The first teaching for young boys comes from going out to fish. He is taught everything he needs to know about fishing. Then he is sent out to fish. When he brings home that first fish, it is painted with red earth from the Black Hills. It is cooked and a bigger meal is prepared with it. The young boy has to walk and give everyone present a piece of that fish. He gets the last piece. He is told that from this day forward, you must always make sure that everyone else has food before you eat; you must always share your food and take care of other people. The community is told that no one has to go hungry because among you lives a man who can fish and who can get food. How do you translate that in this day and age? It is an important teaching for our children, to show them that they are responsible for the greater community.

I have an uncle, Raymond Hollow Horn. You can walk with him any season of the year. He can point native grass out to you in all four seasons, tell you its Lakota name and what it is used for. Some of us only recognize trees when they are in leaf, or grasses when they are green, but not in winter when they are in stasis. For those of us who are in our original homelands, we ought to require that we and our children know the names of every indigenous tree and grass, principal places and geological landmarks in Lakota. We should know the names of all the birds. We need to advocate and require that our schools teach that. The schools are the vehicle of the loss of culture and language. We were put in boarding schools, removed from our families, and the schools became the vehicles of genocide. While it might not have actually been chopping off the heads of Indian children, they were removed from their culture and taken from their spiritual foundations. This is spiritual and social genocide. We are in a position to control those schools now, particularly on this reservation, where we have tribal schools. We need to require that they atone for their sins and become the vehicles for the restoration of that knowledge. Our people had this as common knowledge, which we were forced to give up. We need to regain the knowledge that was once in every household, and a lot of other things will flow from that.

Our special places have names that go back in our history; for example, the Bear Lodge's Sacred Pipe, initially called the Bear Lodge–Ptehesan. Our stories say that the animals had this great race around the Black Hills. All of a sudden, the land started to swell and lifted up. After the race, when they went to this place and peeled back the land, there was a home for the bear. Our story says that much later, this was where the sacred pipe was brought to our people. On maps, it is now called Devil's Tower. Devil's Tower does not connote any sacred teachings to the Lakota people. When you say the "Bear Lodge," you learn that relationship, your place in greater creation, and are also taught geology. This is a volcanic plug which rose very quickly. As the soil around it eroded, this volcanic plug was left. All of those teachings are strengthening to our people.

All of these stories give you greater teachings with the universe because the stories meet the tests of biology, geology, civics and chemistry. They give us sacred teachings, our philosophical foundations, judicial and social structures, and the foundation for our economy. We have to look at these as more than just stories. What are they telling us? Whatever viewpoint you examine the story from gives you foundation. I think that is what we need to do. We need to make sure that we are not just people of Native American ancestry living on the face of the earth. Lakota is more than just an ethnicity. It has to do with something greater than having Indian blood. It has to do with an attitude and a lifeway.

Some of our tribal governments are poor examples of white man's institutions. Others are more successful imitations. Where do we have traditional structure incorporated into government? As you look throughout the United States, Canada, and Mexico, you don't find that. We have to get away from that. I think the time to do it is now.

In our origin legend, the story is told that when the earth wanted covering for herself, she understood she had to create her covering out of herself, as a part of herself. She decided her covering would be her children. She took of herself and created her first child, the growing and moving; and then she created her second child, the winged; then she created her third child, the four-legged; and then she created the fourth child and decided this two-legged would be her special child. So she named that child Mato, "I am esteemed." This is the bear. So her four children lived well. Then she decided she would have a child who made choices. She decided this child would be two-legged, but would not be another bear. She took of herself, created bone and covered it with flesh, gave this being hands and named this woman, this maker of choices, Winyan—"You are complete." Then she decided to make a companion for the maker of choices who was complete, so she took of herself, created bone, covered it with flesh, and named this being Wica, "A step from completion." This is man.

In our sacred teachings, we are told that woman was created to make choices and man was to be her companion. The ceremonies for women reinforce the need to make good strong choices for all of the people. The ceremonies for men teach the need to care for the people physically, to make sure they have food and shelter and are protected from enemies and the elements. This teaching of making choices is strong within our sacred teachings and social structure. It has been said that Lakota people have taken individualism to heights that no other society on the face of the earth has ever done. Yet when we examine our culture, we allowed the individual to flourish with the restriction that the life of all of the people was most important. No one person or people, trees, grasses, buffalos, birds—everything that lives—was more important than any other.

The teaching was also that humans don't have a greater right to survival than anything else that lives. We have a strong symbiotic relationship with all of creation. Some of creation we use for food, and so we make sure that the food survives. We would go back and make sure that our campsites had trees. We did not live in the same area, but left an area for seven years after using it. When we came back, there were new trees. We always had a supply of firewood and a supply of wild berries. Caring for everything that was there allowed us to survive and be very strong individuals within the greater belief that all life has to survive.

"I SEE EVEN GREATER HOPE FOR THIS GENERATION OF GRANDCHILDREN."

When I was young girl, I grew up knowing about and participating in many of these ceremonies. I was fortunate to live in a community where there were still a lot of very old people and I had access to them; I could question them. Back in those days, there were many things you did not talk about publicly. If you went to the sweat lodge, you did not talk about it to people who didn't also go to the sweat lodge. Certainly, when you left your home community, you never spoke about those things. My children are open practitioners of Lakota reli-

gion and culture. My sons and nephews are all singers. When I was young, people did not sing sacred songs publicly, or even admit they sang them at all. You might admit to singing powwow songs but not sacred songs.

My father, Henry Black Elk, talks about how sacred songs were the only ones he knew. One of the young boys at the mission said, "Henry, teach me some Indian songs." So he taught him sweat lodge and ceremonial songs. That poor boy was beaten. He did not know what he was singing because his parents had made the decision not to teach him their language in order to spare him from beatings. They taught him only English and he still got abused. So, our people have gone from being abused for practicing their traditions, to being very quiet, to openly talking about their singing like my children do in elementary school. I see even greater hope for this generation of grandchildren. They are going to be Lakota in a way we have not been for almost two hundred years.

The last grand Sun Dance was held in 1882. We didn't hold one again until 1929, a time when buffalo was not available. At this time, Hollow Horn danced the Sun Dance. The bighorn sheep that were native to this part of the country were extinct, so we did not have the horn to carry the fire in. We have had to change those kinds of things, but we have been able to preserve the essence of the ceremonies and the teachings. The younger children are living in a great time. Having that openness and pride in who you are is so strengthening.

There is a difference in American Indian children who know who they are. When I was young, people would say, "Yeah, I'm an Indian." Now our children say, "I'm Lakota, I'm Navajo, I'm Cherokee." They are proud of that greater recognition. That choice is made by a lot of individuals. That is very powerful. When you share your ceremonies with other people, they see them and have a degree of participation. Hopefully they will have that ceremony for their own child, or for their own grandchild, and the blossoming will continue.

"WE DON'T HAVE THE RIGHT TO GIVE UP THINGS THAT BELONG TO CHILDREN YET UNBORN."

Many things that come from our teachings can be done in contemporary life. It is our tradition that every woman has her own home. I have worked with women who stayed in very abusive relationships because they had nowhere else to go. In this day and age, we must teach people that every woman has to have her own home. Fathers need to learn how to build houses to make sure their daughters have their own homes. This will ensure that their daughters will not be in situations where they are prevented from making their own choices.

The movement towards sober government is good. Decision-makers have to be able to make free choices that are their own. Instead of saying that we want the economic benefit of gaming, and so we are going to give up jurisdiction to get gaming devices, we as a people have to make sure that we are not put in those situations. If your option is giving up jurisdiction, then the logical choice ought to be not to do it. We don't have the right to give up things that belong to children yet unborn.

The Black Hills are a prime example of a place where we have been able to keep our principles. When I was growing up I went to Pine Ridge. I came back and I asked my grandmother, what does it mean when people say, "Toksa [it will be good] when I get my Black Hills"? I had never heard that expression; I come from Crazy Horse's people. My grandmother said, "Don't ever talk about that." That was the time when some men got drunk and allowed themselves to be sodomized for payment in canned goods. I grew up in a community where I did not know what a treaty was, because Crazy Horse never participated in any of that. When I finally read about it, I found that people who were probably well-meaning gave up all this territory for rations. They gave up a whole lifestyle for allotments. We always say in this community that "They sold the Black Hills for wool pantaloons."

Fortunately, since the 1970s, as people got more in tune with Lakota culture and history, they have taken the position that the Black Hills are not for sale. In 1980, the Supreme Court ruled, "Yes, we stole your land. We did it legally, fair and square, and now we are going to pay you." The attitude of the Lakota people was that the land is not for sale; we're not taking that money. Weekly Reader came out and did a story with children in this community. Moses Little Moon, a seventh grader, said, "The Black Hills are my land. They are my home and they are not for sale." It is wonderful to have our children be that aware and open.

They started with the "nits make lice" policy of genocide, killing the women so they wouldn't have children and killing the children so they wouldn't grow up and keep fighting. Everything that followed after that was genocide by bureaucracy, from the treaty-making era to the Dawes Allotment Act.

The attitude of the federal government is, "Well, you're not really Indian anymore. We'll give you money to run your own schools, but the schools have to be accredited. The accreditation process says that instruction has to be in English. We have an obligation to provide housing, and so we will give you houses—you have your choice of cluster or high-rise." Instead of being a cluster of the traditional extended family that was capable of maintaining organization, we were put in artificial communities. Those housing clusters have tremendous law enforcement and social problems. When you look at children who have been removed from their homes, they are not generally from homes where people are living on their own land. They are coming from those clusters. The way you get nice paved roads on the reservation is by giving up law enforcement jurisdiction. The whole financial relationship with the United States government and even private groups is genocide by bureaucracy. If the private school on the reservation provides better academic services, it only takes Catholic children. The way you document that you're Catholic is you get baptized, and then they want you to go to church. That is another part of that whole cultural, social and tribal genocide. Kill them with paper work and let them do themselves in. Remove all their choices and have them give up even more after they've given up the right to make choices.

"A WELL-DRESSED LAKOTA WOMAN ALWAYS HAS A BELT FROM WHICH KNIVES HANG."

The fourth of our seven sacred ceremonies marked the transition in the life of a young woman from childhood to adulthood. It was a ceremony of knives. The young women were asked to make knives, tools, for this young woman. We have an expression that a well-dressed Lakota woman always has a belt from which knives hang. Having a tool meant you knew how to use it, you possessed a skill.

At the ceremony, the young girl was brought to the center. The women would come and put knives on her belt. When she was given a sewing awl, she was told how that awl is made, cared for, and used, and the legend of the awl. The spider woman weaves her web and holds the universe in place. She's always taking care of it. When she is not careful, a star will fall or explode. She has to take care of her environment and always be diligent. Then she would be given, let's say, a fleshing knife. She was taught how to take care of it, how the tool is made, how it is sharpened, if it is replaced seasonally or used once and discarded, or put to some other use. In this process, she received all of the tools for fleshing and scraping, and a turnip digging post. She was told how to prepare and use them. In this ceremony, as each woman took her turn, they would then put red earth paint on the tool and give it to the young woman.

The final item she was given is what we call a rare knife. These were passed down through families and were generally made of obsidian or meteorite. *Maza* is our word for meteorite. They were the hardest thing we had before we got steel knives from Europeans. She was told that she should live her life without ever using that rare knife for either of its two purposes. One was cutting off the head of the man who abused her, because by abusing her he prevented her from making her own choices. She had to make choices she was responsible for. The other use of that knife was cutting the head off the man who abused her children. Our name for children is wakanyeja, the seeds of the sacred. When you abuse a child, our teaching is that you are committing desecration because they are a gifts from God. What was good was that it forced a young woman to really examine any man she wanted to have a relationship with. Is this someone whose head I am going to have to cut off? Will he abuse me or my children? It made you look at the outcome of the choice. It taught you that everything in life was a conscious choice.

In this day and age, you don't want to advocate cutting anyone's head off. I think that we should advocate teaching young women all of the skills necessary for survival. They need to have the tools. We need to teach young girls to examine the possible outcomes of anything they do, not just on Indian reservations, but throughout the whole world. Children, who have not been taught anything, are having children. When you compound that by two or three generations, you end up with people who have no recent family history of having any life skills. The teaching we need to incorporate is that everything you do is a conscious choice that has an impact.

We have tribal or governmental policies that were sent down from the Bureau of Indian Affairs that say that you need to establish a blood quantum to see who is an Indian. They tie it to governmental services. You have tribes buying into that, saying, "I'm at least a quarter-degree Indian, therefore I have legal status as an Indian." We have no problem with adopting other people, bringing in new blood or new people, or marrying outside our people. We had citizenship. That is very different from membership. I can be a member of the Knights of Columbus or the Ku Klux Klan but that does not give me citizenship anywhere. We need to get away from the notion of membership and laws that are foreign to our traditions. That policy forced us to violate our traditional laws against committing incest.

Among the Lakota, an Oglala should not marry an Oglala. And certainly someone from the Oyurpe should not marry an Oyurpe. In order to meet the government test of "Indian-ness" and qualify for these resources which we gave up tremendous amounts of real estate to receive, all of a sudden we are having to violate our own laws on incest. Tribal members are marrying tribal members to make sure that their children will be tribal members. That was not our tradition.

To be a good leader, you have to be a careful person. The qualities of leaders were people that were careful. We talk about men who were raised by good women, so that they were respectful. They were careful in their attitudes and they were listeners. One of our traditions, a ceremony for teaching women, is to have four days and four nights without food or water. You sit still and shut up. The teaching was that, before you could learn anything, you had to learn to listen. The only way you were going to listen was to be quiet. When you learn to listen, you learn more because you hear more than humans. You could hear from the earth. It is clearing your mind to hear what is out there and being open to the song of the universe. These were people who would listen, who would take the time to understand something, before making a decision.

"WE NEED TO REALLY LOOK AT BEING THAT PERSON WHO IS LAKOTA."

The other thing that we did, that you see happening less now, and that you almost never see in the white society, is greeting your extended family by how you are related to them. If everybody is a relative, you have to treat each other better. When you met people, you addressed them as aunt, uncle, brother, niece, nephew, grandmother, or grandfather. It was very strengthening. We don't do that in today's society. We need to do it more.

Many times in tribal government—I am speaking generally—we end up picking the dumbest person for a job so they can't do too much damage. This guy is a crook, but the other guy is a dumb crook, so at least he can't do too much harm. We need to get away from that attitude. When we step away from our cultural traditions, we have a breakdown in communities and society that we see everywhere, not just in Indian Country. People are not respectful of each other, there is homelessness, children are being raised without knowing both parents. It was never our tradition that people had to live together after they had children, but that child had equal support from both parents and from the broader community. Many times, we don't look at ourselves as teachers of other people's children, yet that was our tradition. When you saw a child doing something that wasn't proper or correct, you explained to them why we don't do those things. We have abdicated our community responsibility for the education of our children to schools. We have not gone to those schools and made sure that what they are teaching is what we want taught. It is not just that our children are being taught that Columbus discovered America and that there was a bunch of savages in the New World. Our academic institutions are socializing us to be white people. We have to get away from that.

"WHEN YOU UNDERSTAND THE LANGUAGE, YOU APPRECIATE THE DEPTH OF OUR PEOPLE'S KNOWLEDGE."

The Lakota have a sense of belonging to a place, belonging to a people, knowing you have support there, that you have roots. Every family has its own interpretation or manifestation of pre-contact or pre-reservation ceremonial activities. When I go out into the non-Indian community, I am always struck by the fact that those people say they are from the house that they live in or the place where they were born, even when, for the most part, they don't have any ties to that community anymore. Ninety-nine percent of the people I meet are not able to say, "Well, my family came to Iowa from Germany and they have lived in Iowa for two or three hundred years and before that they came from this particular village in Germany." They are divorced from their family's biological history. In Indian communities, despite all the genocidal policies that we have had to put up with, Indians can say "This is where I am from, this is who I am." We have strong foundations for our identity. In some cases, we need to reinforce that and move it back to a pre-reservation tribal identity, so that it is not just, "I am from the Pine Ridge Reservation" or such-and-such an Indian community. We need to really look at being that person who is Lakota, and knowing what it means to be from that people.

There are many ways to bring about this change in our communities. Some of it is just the way you live your own life–being sober, responsible, good to people. On another level, I think we need to make sure we get involved in the curricula of our schools, so that our children are no longer being taught that Columbus discovered a land of savages. We need to advocate for changes in our tribal government's structures. We need to develop leaders from within that traditional pre-reservation mold. I feel sad and happy when I go to the Crow reservation and I see the people who are 85% bilingual. When you go to Crow General Council meetings, everyone is speaking Crow. I am glad to see that. I think that is really wonderful. On the other hand, I feel saddened by the fact that it is not true with all the other tribes. Some tribes have completely lost their languages. We need to make sure that our languages are preserved because so much of our cultural teachings and social structure is best taught in that language.

We have to be advocates in maintaining our language, in teaching it to people who had to give it up, not by their own choice, but as a means of survival. Someone made the choice. Some people decided to say, "I don't want my children beaten, so I am not going to teach them our language. I want to spare them the physical pain and humiliation of being beaten, so I will not pass the language on." That was done for so many of our people. Their parents and grandparents wanted to spare them. The language was not passed on. Nobody is beating us for speaking our language now, so we have to work to restore our language.

We have to get away from that attitude of having someone from the outside tell us what to do. We have in Lakota country what we call the *ateyapi* complex, the superintendent complex. Unless some white guy in a suit tells you that something is real, it is not real. It is like some people think it is only real if they read it in the paper. In many areas of Indian Country, particularly reservations in the western United States, the notion is that the government agent sits next to God. If he says it is good, it is good. And if he says it isn't good, it isn't good. We still have this notion that someone from the outside has to validate us. We need to get away from that attitude because we know it isn't right.

One of the things that I really want to ensure for those of us who live on reservations is that those plants with a cultural, special and sacred relationship to us, are openly available and all people know what they are. I think the goal of Lakota biologists is to know the names of all the trees and grasses, in Lakota, English and Latin. We need to know where we live and who we are.

The Ceremony of Making Peace

Is A Way of Life

CHAPTER FOURTEEN

An Interview With Philmer Bluehouse

(Diné)

hilmer Bluehouse is a member of the Red House Clan and was born to the To Walk Around You Clan. He is the coordinator of the Navajo Nation judicial branch of the Navajo Peacemaker Court, and is responsible for seven judicial districts throughout the Nation. The majority of the Navajo Nation, the largest native nation in the United States, is located within the boundary of the state of Arizona, but it also extends into portions of Utah and New Mexico.

After a seventeen-year career in law enforcement, Philmer is currently is working towards a degree in public administration at Northern Arizona University, Flagstaff. Since 1991, he, Freddie Miller, and Anita Roan have created peacemaker courts in 56 districts and trained 140 peacemakers throughout the Navajo Nation. Elder Freddie Miller observed and contributed to this interview.

My background in law enforcement is in the application of man-made law. The peacemaker process utilizes natural law. I discovered that in a journey I had to take after coming out of the "war way" process of law enforcement. My journey took me to a place behind Windowrock. I drew an imaginary line in this little place, twenty feet by twenty feet, and sat down. I did this three to four hours at a time for two weeks. I asked, "Tell me how to do what I need to do." I started looking. We all have eyes but sometimes we can't see. We have ears but sometimes we can't hear. We have feelings but sometimes we can't feel. I asked nature to provide me with that information.

I discovered that in the mineral world there are things that are put together in unique ways. I started seeing different colorations. Two little black things that I picked up and put together bounced apart. Apparently there was magnetism, the holy language. I could see them as they began to attract or reject one another.

The next thing I started looking at was the vegetation, the trees, grass and the different variations. I saw approximately thirty-four different species of plants in this little area I drew to seek my knowledge. I started seeing patterns. Certain plants and blades of grass grew in certain ways. At the same time the male and female beings that existed in those things started to present themselves together as a family. I saw them moving every time the wind blew them. I realized it was the air and that the air can be dangerous or cruel.

Then I started recognizing that I am built in a certain way. That is a natural phenomenon, a natural law of who I am. I have feelings, abilities, and limitations at the same time. I can't exist like a tree and a tree can't exist like me, although there are similarities. It digests certain things and I digest certain things. I am mobile and it is mobile, but not in the same sense. I think that was when I rediscovered that natural law exists and creates. There is a beginning and an ending. All these things started to come back to me. Those are the principles I started applying to the peacemaking court process.

I accepted this job with the Navajo Nation and was harnessed with the responsibility of developing the peacemaking court process. The peacemaker court process and the ceremony itself come from Navajo philosophy.

Picture yourself in a healing ceremony in some hogan in the middle of the Navajo nation, where the only light is coming through the smoke hole. Extended clan relatives, family members, are sitting around drawing on the floor of the hogan with different colors of sand.

The dry painting, also known as sand painting, depicts the first man and first woman as the Navajo perceive them. This pictograph is our understanding of the creation of all things within the universe. This is a holy way of writing, we call it *diyin k'ehigo `nq` asdeoh* or *'iikááh*—to draw with sand. What you see is a representation, not the exact image. The power would be lost if we drew the exact image.

The person who is directing the drawing and participating in the drawing is talking. This healer, chanter, and philosopher all rolled into one is teaching the people. He is describing the universe, which is depicted by the representation on our left-hand side as we look at the pictograph; and on the right-hand side by representations of corn, squash, beans and tobacco. This describes the order of things in the universe—how things are created, how things are placed and how they ought to be. It describes the nurturing characteristics of our Mother the Earth, and the protecting characteristics of our Father, the Universe. Likewise we as human beings on the earth's surface have those same characteristics or attributes. The female in our society, we consider as a nurturing and gentle individual who provides all the nutrients for the people on the earth's surface. On the other hand, the man is allocated the responsibility of protecting and bearing the weapons of war. These characteristics are drawn out and established in the painting itself.

This drawing is the original creation of the first man and the first woman. We believe that there is a male and a female existence in everything, that within protons, neutrons, electrons or even within emptiness, those dual beings exist. Those dual beings assist and help, rather than resist and fight, one another. That is the concept of *hózho* in our language, which means the perfect state of being, harmony, peace, and beauty. Navajo philosophy is about forever trying to achieve this perfect state of existence—this perfect state of being—as individuals and as a group of people, while understanding at the same time that other beings have the same purpose for their existence. In other words, we all have a common objective and that is to have peace, to exist together as a perfect unit, as a perfect group. That is the objective of hózho. And how do we achieve that?

To achieve that perfect state of being is a continuous evolutionary process in our minds. When we are on our journey to achieve this perfect state of existence, there are two philosophies that coexist with one another. One of the philosophies we call, *hashkééjí* which means war way planning. *Hashkééjí* suggests that there is something dangerous that can be contained within that policy, procedural rules, or regulatory matters that involve the way of war. In the peacemaking process, we use a lot of the information that is contained in our origin and journey narratives. These narratives are recitations of the origin and journey songs and prayers. They are the sources where we gather information about structure, development, how we relate and perceive that information.

Peace way and war way information systems come out of those songs, prayers and journey narratives. The positive and negative aspects of all creation began at some point. There was a beginning somewhere and we are all a product of that, we are all aware that somewhere there was a beginning.

We gather information from the war way system policy, procedures, and rules being assembled in that realm. On the other hand, we have the peace way information and the policies, procedures, and rules taken out of that realm. Our journey is to take information from both realms and to use them for our survival and our existence which is directed toward peace and harmony. As Navajo, we want to get to that apex of our lives where we are in perfect harmony with the rest of the universe and the earth. That is the objective of all beings now. In our origin and journey narratives, there are descriptions of other tribes that are on this journey.

When we take the information from both the war realm and the peace realm, our objective is to restore harmony. That is a continuous process. Every morning we get up, how we make it through the day is up to us. Sometimes we can use anger, gentle persuasion or whatever else to accomplish our intended goal. That is a natural given phenomenon that all of us possess and that is the source of who we are.

In the Navajo language, we call our left hand *nishtt'ají*; in other words, "it is difficult to decide." Our right hand is *nish'nááji*, which means "it is alive." Things can be done with this side. Our hands represent the duality within human beings where there are things that can be difficult, in the way of the war; and things that can be alive and beautiful, in the way of peace. Those two beings are within each individual. We have the ability to get angry and the ability to love, care, and share. We also have the ability to protect, be angry, and hope. All those things we have within us. To restore harmony, we have to understand those things and how to use them to restore that balance within self.

The journey of restoring harmony is called *hózho nááhasdli'i* which means "harmony restored." *Hózho* means harmony, peace, tranquillity, perfect state of being. *Nááhasdli'i* means "it has returned" or "we have been able to reorganize and create that perfect existence." We do those things in a continuous evolutionary process on a daily basis. Our lives come into war and peace on a continuous basis.

We are forever in that evolutionary process. The daily achievement of the restoration of peace and harmony began at the very creation. The creation basically thought, ntséskees. In other words, the thought was projected outwards. Whatever this being thought was the first thing that happened. At that point in time, the creation began. *Ntséheekees doo bizaad k'ehgo adahoo`teed*. In other words, the thinking process, the planning and organizational aspects of all things were created at that point. The word was spoken and according to that word, things came to life, started moving, coming together and projected outward into the universe.

Navajo people have our command center, our brain. We have those capabilities, so therefore we were created in the image of that being. We also have the ability to communicate, whether it is body language, verbal language, or eye contact. In the Navajo way, we talk about the *diyin k'egoh sáád* or "the holy way language." The first language in our creation and journey narratives is the signaling or attraction process. Protons and neutrons in a holy way get together or split and go separate ways. That level is the source of our communication process.

"THERE ARE FIVE CHARACTERISTICS OF GOD."

Our language is very precise in its interpretation of God. In the greater society, God is God, and that is it. There is no description. For us, there is the description of the characteristics of God. This establishes in the Navajo way that we are monotheistic. We believe there is one God who allocates responsibility to representatives of himself or herself. I have to say himself or herself because in our description of God we don't give a gender. It is not a him and it is not totally a her. It is a combination of the two. That is one of the five characteristics of what is commonly known as God.

Secondly, the description refers to the center of the universe, to that which was nurtured in the center of the universe. Then the third characteristic, *tàa`i naagahii*, says that God is singular, mobile, and omnipresent. *Yá althene' nihoni káádi, Yá althne'naayannii, làa'i naagahii nil'chi diyinnii*. In other words, that the holy being is air, or spirit if you will. That is the fourth characteristic. *Shi'tsóí yéhé* is the last characteristic. *Shi'tsóí* means, I am its offspring. It is my grandfather or grandmother and I am its grandchild. In other words, we are created in that image. Then, as in our wedding ceremonies, *shi'tsóí yéhé, yéhé* refers to the fact that we are through holy matrimony connected. Through the holiness of this being, we are created like it and it is like us. We are describing the essence of who God is in our mind and how we perceive him or her.

"OUR BELIEF SYSTEM REGULATES OUR SPIRITUAL, PSYCHO-LOGICAL AND PHYSICAL BEING."

We are monotheistic. Anthropologists and missionaries have come to this region, saying that we, their lesser brothers, believe in all these different gods—gods of the rocks, plants and air. They say we are a multi-god system, so we are a lesser brother. That is not true. There is a single God. That being, or singularity, as I am going to call it, delegates and authorizes responsibility to carry various functions out to holy beings or the *diyin dine'e*. We are a product of this spirit world in physical form. It is on that level in the holy realm where the planning, organization, direction, control—the thou-shalls and thou-shall-nots—were all perpetrated for human beings to absorb, digest, think about and decide on for themselves.

Our belief system is the foundation of right and wrong, decision making, planning, organizational development. All these things need to happen at that spiritual level and are subsequently furnished to us. We are representations in human form of spirit beings on the earth's surface. We are able to articulate and share that information among ourselves. The information from that realm is carried on through our physical being where we are able to apply, use, assist and regulate each other with it. Our belief system regulates our psychological being, spiritual being and physical being. These things are all-inclusive, we do not separate them.

We started the peacemaking system in 1982. The Navajo Nation incorporated the peacemaking manual into its Supreme Court rules. Until 1991, the peacemaking process was not used extensively—only fifty-six times in a formal setting within the Navajo Nation Court system. We were able to secure a grant and three of us—Eddie, Taron, and I—started the peacemaking court process for the Navajo Nation. We identified twenty-five chapter houses and each selected peacemakers to be certified and trained. Chapters are community meeting centers in rural areas which are the source of services for decision-making and recommendations back to the central government in Windowrock. We found we had an abundance of money left over from the grant because we minimized spending the money we had. We decided to involve more chapters. At the end of the grant year we had fifty-six chapters that were certified and one hundred and forty peacemakers who were trained and in place to implement the peacemaking court system. Those are our humble beginnings.

The first year we had less than one hundred and fifty cases. The following year the caseload nearly doubled. In Shiprock Agency alone this year, I calculated we would have more than four hundred cases of peacemaking. We have seven judicial districts. We are talking four hundred per judicial district times seven, nearly twenty-eight hundred cases projected for this year. The Navajo people have asked, "Where have you folks been? We have been wanting responsibility. We don't want the central tribal government or the federal government telling us what to do. We are capable and know who we are out here in the country. We have decision-making skills. We have empowerment skills. Now you have implemented this and we will use the system."

The process starts with a prayer. We try to keep the rules very simple with establishing respect. We say there is no yelling, shouting, or posturing as far as body language, giving each other the eye. We have to respect one another. We are in here on common ground and we need to have these things understood. "If we don't abide by these rules, then we will refer this back to the adversarial system and you can tell them your problems there. If you cannot allow yourself to be humble, understand, learn about yourself, and your fellow human being, this is not the place for you." The rules are established and the prayers are offered.

After the prayer is offered, we go to the investigation and questioning phrase. The objective is to discover the root of the problem. A lot of times we start with denial. Let's take a domestic violence situation. The husband will intellectualize and rationalize. "No, I never

"WE DON'T POINT THE FINGER IN PEACEMAKING."

beat my wife, I don't do those kinds of things. I am a very humble person." All that comes to the table. The woman is over there shriveling up, sitting in the corner and trying to say her piece. Why is she responding the way she is? Why is this guy denying he does those things? You start uncovering and unraveling the mystery. Everybody is pulling at the cords of this mystery to get down to the problem.

"YOU PETITION THE CREATOR AND YOU GET A RESPONSE"

When we as Navajos ask something from nature, we have to give something in return. That is respect. The precious jewel offering to ask an herb, "I know I am going to have to take your life in order for you to sustain me, but I have something to give in return. Therefore, I offer this prayer." It is a petitioning process. You petition and you get a response. This whole process in itself can be applied to the peace making process. *Nalyéé* means bringing things together where people can share and give, take and receive. At the point when these two things contact, that is called nalyée. I learned that the other day. I have been trying to find out for a long time what that meant. The way it was described to me was, "When there was a problem, people would bring their best horses with full saddle and bridle, and with full packages of food. Both sides would have that to offer to begin their conference of peace making. That in essence is the bottom line of *nalyée*—bring things together.

In the egalitarian system everything is considered equal. People say, "We cannot allow domestic violence to go into peace making because there is imbalance of power. The woman is powerless and the man is flexing his muscles." I say, "That is all the more reason why you should bring domestic violence into peace making because it balances things between people. You are empowering the woman by saying, we know you are fearful of this individual. Let's talk about ways to build yourself back up to the proper level of who you should be. We are here to help, offer advice, give you information and support in the peace making session. Man, come back down to earth. Who do you think you are? Why are you injuring our own people? Why are you acting as if you don't have relatives and the ability to support them? We are all related. Why are you doing this? Why are you hurting us?"

We don't point the finger in peacemaking. We put the problem on the table. We acknowledge that there are problems, but this is not the place to point fingers and have shouting matches. We talk about the problem. It is like peeling an onion. You take it layer by layer and finally get down to the sweet little green center of that onion. After you discover that, then we close it back up and repair the individual with good information, knowledge, and empowerment. The objective in peacemaking is to do just that. Biblically speaking, it is re-dressing oneself in the armor of God for the purpose of peace.

When we are teaching peacemakers the Navajo justice system, we talk about the vertical system of justice. The vertical system of justice was imported with the European people when they first came to this country. Their experience and their way of surviving was adversarial because they believed in a class structure. They believed in things that egalitarian societies did not believe in. The vertical system of justice can be bought. The more money you have, the better chance you have of winning in a court of law. That is true ninety-nine percent of the time. I am stating a generality, but look around you.

The adversarial system uses force with force. Our jails are full. People are hurting one another. Brothers and sisters, families are fighting with one another. People don't know who their relatives are anymore. "That is my cousin but he lives on the other side of the world. I don't care what happens to him."

The adversarial system uses aggression, force, and coercion. It uses things that are conducted in the "way of war," as we perceive it. My brother, Justice Bluehouse with the Navajo Nation Supreme Court, was on the bench for a long time and retired two years ago. "The adversarial system," he said, "is not fair. I have had people come into my courtroom, come before me on the bench, and at the end we find that it is not fair. I see my own relatives walking out the door. One group is dancing around with their tails up in the air. The other group is moping and walking out with their tails dragging on the carpet." The adversarial system is a win/lose situation.

We are not looking at the broad picture anymore. We are only looking at specific aspects of human life and the event. What about emotions? What about the physical comfort that all human beings desire? When you go into an adversarial court, you don't address those things.

Here, we look at the overall objective, not just specific issues, although we can go to a specific issue and then expand outwards. Investigation is done. Now the peacemaker gets directly involved. On the outside, in alternative or dispute resolution, the intermediary has a role of remaining impartial. In peacemaking, this is not so. You do not go into a session as a peacemaker acting as if you don't have relatives. In other words, you have a contribution to make because you are concerned about these individuals with this problem. You will give suggestions or offerings of information. At some point in time you may scold, using the war way posturing, to get whatever is needed brought onto the table. Then again it may not be the peacemaker who decides that. That natural scolding, the probation and parole function, usually was the responsibility of an uncle or an aunt.

The Navajo Nation has a clan system. When we go into session, all your relatives are right there. The Navajo clan system is a living legal system. Everywhere in the world, the clan system process is unbalanced. There are wars going on between clans. The purpose of clans is to allow sharing, caring and articulation of information. The original design along the way has been corrupted. The clans establish for us the thou shalls and the thou shall nots. In other words, we cannot marry into our own clan. If we do, we are interfering with natural law. When we interfere with natural law, we are going to have Redhouse Clan members with legs sticking out of their heads. That is law, that is the way it is.

The next phase is a problem solving process. We have unraveled this whole mystery and we know what the problem is. Let's talk about the problem that sits here on the table before us. Let's talk about it, break it down, and figure out how we are going to rebuild this thing. How are we going to fix it? This is not shaming, not pointing fingers at one another, not saying "you are right and I am wrong." It is not black and white. It is reparation and healing. It has nothing to do with force or aggression.

We say, we understand you did something wrong—now what are you going to do to repair what you did to the rest of the family? What are you going to do to show us that you are not going to do it again? We will accept you back into our lives. You are here. We just can't allow you to go anywhere else.

There are societies that have shunning, or banishment, where they allow the person to leave the tribe. That was a form of correcting people. The Navajo form of banishment is what we call killing with eyes. If a person perpetrated wrong in a community, everybody would watch everything he did. While he slept, there was somebody there to watch him. At some point, the person would say, "Why is everybody watching me?" They'd say, "Let's talk about it. Do you understand what happened? You finally realize that we are trying to allow you to recognize that there is a problem. We see the problem. Let's talk about it, let's get rid of that problem. Let's kill that monster and allow you to continue to live within our society." The whole objective is to allow people to stay within the community by using banishment through eye contact. It is a subtle form of force.

When problem solving occurs, statements are made by all persons who wish to speak. Judges, lawyers, and police are not allowed to participate in their official capacities. We do not allow lawyers into peacemaking, period. We don't need to have someone say, "I object to that line of questioning. That is a Fifth Amendment issue." That is not the point. The point is to allow people to use their natural abilities to heal and repair. Everyone has the natural ability to sit down and talk, rather than denying the problem. The state of denial has gotten so big that it is a great big monster. It is a stumbling stone in human life. The adversarial system has caused that.

After the problem solving statements have occurred, we move towards commitment and resolution. We are moving towards the conclusion of peacemaking. We encourage people to interact, to talk when the person is shy, we allow them the time to come out of their shell. A peacemaker put it this way the other day, he said, "Get rid of all the vomit. Get it out, it is a poison." When you get it out you feel better afterwards. You have to get these emotions out to start feeling safe. You have to deal with hate and love. We all naturally have those abilities. Why are we suppressing them? Why should we suppress them? These are tools that help us revive ourselves, help us to grow."

Peacemaking seeks commitment from all the participants. They sign an agreement and they may even go to the extent of asking the judge for a judgment. The court can step in at their request, it is not forced upon them. Sometimes they will leave with a simple handshake and not sign an agreement. Way back before paper ever was, agreements were formed with just a handshake. That is very powerful. People make long-term commitments. You do find people who violate that commitment and the next thing you know we are back in court. That was their choice, it had nothing to do with the process. It was an individual choice they made and therefore they are responsible for it.

As Navajos, we are reviving some of the learning that has withered away through our journey with the United States government. We are going back to the peacemaking process. We must also look within. I took a journey within and built outward from there. I reconfirmed some of that information by talking to people who already possess that knowledge, the medicine men and women, the chanters, the star gazers, the people who have supernatural abilities to understand the nature of things, the holy and physical realms. Those things have been confirmed.

I feel like we are walking down the right path with this knowledge and information. We are bringing people into the peacemaking process, sharing this knowledge, and giving them the empowerment to say we all have problems but we have the skills to solve them. That is what peacemaking is all about.

There are various stages of erosion of being Indian. Some people say they have lost their traditions. They ask, "How do we rediscover our ways?" I talk about going back into nature, seeing with your eyes, listening to what is said in the forest, rediscovering those things and applying them to yourself. Rediscovering those things is very important. Your DNA, your roots, source, and Indianness are contained there. The knowledge, the book of Indianness, is already contained in your genes. All we need to do is go back, re-evaluate and look at those things. We all have that ability. We can either ignore it or go back and rediscover it.

The other source that we can turn to is the elderly people, who still possess information about the way creation is, the way things really are. A lot of people have said this is voodoo, we don't want that any more, we want to go with the Western technology. But Western technology is not working. The jails are full. People are killing each other. Are we going to walk in those same footsteps? As Native Americans we ought to say, "This is what we have to offer." We have been saying this for the last four hundred years. Finally people are saying, "We have got to go back and rediscover kinship, respect for nature, respect for human beings. We can't be continuing to go blindly down this path and fighting against each other." That is not the original creation. Peacemaking is a way of life.

Your Spiritual Life Is Responsible For

Maintaining The Whole Of Creation

CHAPTER FIFTEEN

An interview with Renee Senogles

(Anishinaabe)

The work of Renee Senogles, an Anishinaabe from the Red Lake Ojibwe Nation, is based on her belief that Native people have all we need within our culture and traditions to reclaim our strength. She strongly believes that all the issues facing Native people can be traced to colonialism and its attacks on Native culture. Renee has been involved in Indian women's issues and concerns and worked in Minneapolis as a family therapist. A published writer, Jingle Dress dancer, and beadworker, Renee grew up in Northern Minnesota. She lives in Bemidji, near Red Lake, with her children Simone, Migizi, and Anna.

Renee formed an indigenous women's writing collective to reduce the isolation of Native women writers and to showcase the wealth of their creative expression. She is writing a book with the working title *Healing the Generations*. Renee directed an environmental project at Red Lake designed to promote experiential learning for youth while providing a service for the community. The project worked in partnership with reservation programs, agencies, and elders and received funding under the Corporation for National and Community Service. Funding for the program was renewed in 1994. Renee was recently selected as a fellow in the Kellogg Foundation National Fellowship Program.

Accountability is a delicate balance. Nobody has the authority to go out and speak for their whole community but we have a lot of that in political activism. People take that upon themselves without being accountable to the communities they say they represent. Yet, at the same time, we need to take independent action. It is a balance to go ahead and act with personal integrity and do what you know to be right, while at the same time letting people in your community know what you are about in building communities.

I do not know if "building communities" is a phrase that I would use. I believe that our communities are already really strong. The fact that we have survived and are even here to

talk about the incredible genocidal onslaught of the Western world shows how powerful and strong our ways and people are. So I don't think in terms of building or rebuilding communities. I think in terms of feeling real honored if I can, in any way, help to strengthen what is already there, or if I have an opportunity to live the values that are already there as our strengths. I believe that we already have everything that we need. We have the information that we need. Even if we don't have access to it, we can pray about it. We have our way of life, our religious way of life, which is powerful and alive. We have a lot of people who can go between different worlds and get information.

When people talk about their ways of life being lost, I do not believe that they are lost. We do have access to them, but it means that you have to develop your character, your inner life. You have to train yourself and be strong in your mind. If you take action without that inner work, things do happen, but there is always a missing element. In order to have spiritually based activism, you have to do your own inner work. Take a really deep look at your motivations, your own drive, your reasons for doing what you are doing. If there are things that you want out of it, if you are driven by your ego, personal ambition, or even the desire for honor or respect, that will hurt your activism. That will make your work less effective.

What I have come to understand, through watching people and seeing the effect of activism without inner life, is that you can't have real social transformation without inner transformation, because then it is just reform and not real revolution. If you want real revolutionary change in your work in the outside world, you have to do revolutionary work inside yourself. I believe that with all my heart. It is not that things don't happen in the outside world without it. Attention is brought to different issues. Sometimes, groups of people will organize around certain issues that they feel are threatening to our people. It is good and I do not question that it is important. But for myself, I can't put myself ahead of what I really feel on the inside.

Western society is based on a lot of destructive things. I think it is based on woman hatred. Hatred of women is directly tied to overpowering the land. They don't say "rape the land" for no reason. In the sense that sexuality is creativity, it is the overpowering of the natural world. I believe that woman hatred is the basis of this thinking. If we want to rebalance, it means looking real deep at ourselves, looking really deep at our own cultures and our original instruction, looking seriously at what it means to respect Mother Earth. People say that real lightly, "Oh, Mother Earth, Mother Earth, respect Mother Earth." Meanwhile, they are abusive or disrespectful to women.

I do not believe that you can honor Mother Earth and be disrespectful to women. Women represent that creative principle in all of the created world. We now live in a world of male dominance. Our communities were not like that at the time of the invasion. They are now, with the imposition of the tribal council system. The land is owned by men, in the same way that women and children are owned by men. That is the imposition of a foreign way, that we have to find our way out of. In just a few generations, that alien system has become ingrained in us. There was such massive indoctrination into that way of thinking that Mother Earth is now real estate. It is the objectification of the sacred, so that it is other, and so there is no responsibility. That is how women are treated, even in our own communities.

In political activism, we cannot afford to have a separation of church and state. We can't afford to have politics and spirituality as two different issues, so that people can be political activists and not be held accountable for their inner selves, their attitudes, their ways of thinking and looking. It is misleading to our people, it creates confusion and brings sorrow to our families. If we want to have healthy communities, we have to do what it takes to be healthy individually and be responsible. In this generation, we carry the burden of the abuse of our generations before us. We are the ones who have the awareness, consciousness and direction to become well; to take action, so that our kids don't have to grow up in grief, sorrow, and pain. Our children are healthy and they know their way of life, their Indian ways, to be really good. They do not have wait until they are adults to come into their consciousness and their awareness of themselves.

"YOU CAN'T HAVE SOCIAL TRANSFOR-MATION WITHOUT INNER TRANSFOR-MATION."

"OUR CHILDREN WILL COME INTO THEIR CONSCIOUS-NESS AND AWARE-NESS OF THEM-SELVES BEFORE THEY BECOME ADULTS."

This kind of inner transformation is radical, but I believe that if you really want to change the system, you have to change your indoctrination, instead of just reacting to each issue that comes forward as it threatens the well-being of the people. The whole system, the whole Western industrialized way of looking at the world objectifies the natural world, women and children and the earth, as property. We can't come to our responsibility until we really perceive ourselves as part of, and responsible for, the whole. In order to do that we have to get right with ourselves.

Everybody's life is this interesting process of growing awareness and consciousness. All I can say for my own self, is that it has been a beautiful, terrible, agonizing and joyous life. I am grateful for that. It has been really hard at times. It has to do with facing the reality of what happened to our people, and facing life head on without running or making excuses; just embracing all of it, embracing the sadness of it; not running away from it, not being afraid, or even if you are afraid, going ahead anyway. Facing what happened to our people takes a lot of courage, but it can be real liberating.

I think we have the right to expect our spiritual people and our political leaders to be, not better, but to work harder to strive for personal integrity and excellence. Sometimes people say that I am harsh in asking for absolute honesty and integrity. People have told me I should be more compassionate. But I say that if you put yourself in that position, then you have to be accountable. When they aren't, it hurts everybody. We have everything we need. We have the ceremonies, we have elder people, and we have people who are coming into these under-standings.

We have to really ask for help with that. I don't think anybody can do that by them-selves. You have to go to those who know how to think about these things. This can start with prayers. I want to do what is right; not what makes me feel good, but what is right. I want to do what is good. There are a lot of people who are that way.

"FOR ME, THE MOST
IMPORTANT THING
IS TO ALWAYS TRY
TO BE HONEST
ABOUT WHAT I AM
EXPERIENCING."

I think in political work, and even spiritual work, one of the most damaging and seduc-tive things is the honor and respect people in the field are given. People give them respect and honor them. If a person is not internally strong and not clear on the inside when they start going forward, they can turn to doing that work to serve their egos. Even though the words and the results can be good, it often makes the work less effective when people start going into it for personal satisfaction.

One of the ways of avoiding that is to have a group of people that you are always accountable to, whether it is your tribal council or a group of community people; people that you answer to for your behavior and attitude. Even in doing that, the community is strength-ened. I believe that "leaders don't lead, they serve." I believe that is the way it should be. I really dislike the kind of elitism that happens, in even grassroots political activism. Real com-munity-based grassroots stuff that involves everybody is revolutionary.

Making decisions from the top down is the way that things are done now and even in grassroots politics, people will define issues. They will say, "Oh, that is an issue and our peo-ple should know about it." We'll get together with other political activists from other tribes, unite, and overcome the problem. Meanwhile, the people in their community do not know

what is going on because they are on the outside. It is self-serving. I am concerned about the national stuff that goes on because the same group of people meet with each other, over and over. They talk to each other about what is going on. They think that they are united, but they are not because they don't have the strength of their communities behind them. Some do, and those people are effective in organizing their communities; although, it is not that they really "organize their communities." Even saying it that way sounds disrespectful to me. They are accountable to their communities. If they have tools that their community can use, then they make them available in any way that they can. I hate paternalism when it creeps into my language. I mean, even saying, "community organizer"–how arrogant.

"IN THIS PROJECT, EVERYBODY WAS WORKING SIDE BY SIDE."

Strength of character can manifest itself in so many beautiful ways. I think mostly for me, in my own life, it has to do with self-honesty–looking at my motivations all the time, a stringent self-scrutiny. What am I thinking, what am I feeling? Thought is energy and you are responsible for your spiritual life. Your spiritual life is actually responsible for maintaining the whole of creation. You have that much power. Each person has that much power, has that much authority in the world. That is a lot of responsibility.

For me, the most important thing is to always try to be honest about what I am experiencing. As a recovering alcoholic, I learned that language of looking at yourself through trying to deal with addiction. In those programs, I learned how to be honest with myself and that was real helpful to me. I take it even further than that. You see things the way they are. Once you get to a certain point, any kind of self-deception creates a lot of inner discomfort that interferes with peace of mind. Peace of mind is my driving force.

If there is something that is interfering with my peace of mind, I know it is either my reaction to the situation or a faultiness in my spiritual perception. For me, one of the clearest indicators that I am off is that I get resentful towards others. When that happens, I feel bad, uncomfortable, I can't sleep; other people are responsible for me. When I start feeling resentful towards others, that is a real indication that I had better look at myself and see how I am thinking and perceiving the situation. It does not mean that you accept what other people do and the fault is always yours. Definitely, sometimes people have bad intentions toward you. Community people are capable of incredible pettiness and it is terrible. It does not mean that you accept anything. You still make your stand. It is important to be clear in your own thinking, what you know to be true, and to be able to speak it.

I am really drawn to the idea that certain people whom I know can't be bought. You can't buy them with love, you can't buy them with honor, you can't buy their allegiance with money. They state, "This will not be bought." I really respect that. They stay true to themselves, to what they have come to understand as their own values. It is not that they never compromise. If they decide to bend on an issue, it is done with clarity of mind. They know what they are doing, what it is about, that there may be repercussions. They are willing to accept the responsibility for their own actions. That is what I respect and what I think strength of character is. I am real happy to say that I know some people like that. They are inspirational to me.

I was involved with a project that reflects these beliefs about community work. It was a really great project. It started out in a partnership mode in Red Lake. All these different community agencies were partners in this project. There were fifty kids—there actually ended up being forty-seven kids and nine supervisors. We had two projects going, one cutting brush and making a mile-long interpretive trail through the woods at Ponemah, which is the traditional community at Red Lake. The Medicine Lodge is real strong up there. They never had a church; they do many ceremonies. There are a lot of native speakers.

The other project was at the town of Red Lake, where a creek runs right through town. It is called Pike Creek. When I was little, we used to swim in that creek. We would swing on the trees and jump out in the middle of the swimming hole. There was a bridge. The creek was real clean and freshwater springs flowed into it. We used to haul water from there in the winter, when the town pump did not work. It was really cold, but that water was delicious.

Over the last twenty to thirty years, Pike Creek became a total dump. The area in this little valley was full of garbage and dirty. Kids would go back there and skip school. It goes right through town, there is a culvert under the road.

"WE MADE A REAL POINT OF HAVING OUR TRADITIONAL PEOPLE AS THE AUTHORITIES."

They have representatives from the four districts on the tribal council in Red Lake: Ponemah, Red Bee, Red Lake and Little Rock. Each of those districts had young people who were involved in this project. This was really good because it meant that youth from Ponemah would work side by side with the youth from Red Lake or Little Rock. There was a cultural interaction as a result of that. Sometimes Ponemah kids would stick to themselves, or the Red Lake kids would stick to themselves. In this project, everybody was working side by side.

When we did the work, we split up into two teams—half would work on the Pike Creek project and half would work on the Ponemah project. Some of the parents would say, like from Ponemah, that Red Lake is 30 miles away and they would have to go all the way to Red Lake and then go back. They would say "It would be easier if the kids from Ponemah could just work on the Ponemah project." But I said, "No." It needed to be about this broader thing. We would count them out and some would go down here and others would go there. We would switch them back and forth, so that all the teams would have ownership in both these projects. At the end, we brought everybody together to finish up each one.

We would start out each morning and each day in a circle, to stay unified. I was always giving them all kinds of pep talks, telling them that this project was going to change the community and bring all kinds of awareness. I brought in extra trainers, so that they could develop their working teams. We did not want it to be just a cleanup project. We wanted it to be based on a philosophy of environmental awareness, so we incorporated history.

We would start each week with a tobacco ceremony. Different young people would do that ceremony every Monday, so that each one would have the chance to conduct our ceremonies. We prayed together with tobacco and then we would go into a classroom. We had different elders from the community come in and talk about what they were doing. They would talk to them about their relationship with the water. They would talk about the history of Pike Creek, where the traditional chiefs resisted allotment. Red Lake is a closed reservation now; our land base is tribally held, and we were not broken up into allotments. No individual owns that land; it is all held tribally. The traditional chiefs, who met at Pike Creek, resisted allotment and refused to sign. Allotment is the most destructive thing that ever happened. The youth began to feel like they were part of their own history. They got educated about what went on at that time, what they were participating in, and what the relationship of Pike Creek is to the rest of the community. They learned their real history.

The elders would come in and talk to them about their relationship with the water and spiritual things. They would talk about moose, deer, the trees, forests, the fish, Red Lake and the spirits that live there. We made a real point of having our traditional people as the authorities on all of this. They can tell when anything is out of balance with the water, with the land. They are just so tuned in. They helped these young people to see their true relationship to the land and to come to understand sovereignty in a deeper way than they had before. They got to know that they are the sovereign people of this continent and that everything they learned in school about themselves is not true. They developed a lot of cultural and national pride. We did a history of Red Lake from creation to now, from our original instruction,

"THE WHOLE COMMUNITY WAS INSPIRED."

through allotments, treaties, boarding schools. They really learned the history of Red Lake.

We worked closely with the tribal Department of Natural Resources, the water quality specialist, biologists, the fish people. We used all of these people for backup because they would always say the same thing that the traditional people would say. We never had the white scientist be our authority. The authority was our own knowledge, our own cultural knowledge. I think this turned the heads of these young people in their ideas about themselves. It was really a powerful experience for everyone involved.

We made this trail an outdoor classroom in Ponemah. Those young people worked hard. They cut this mile-long trail with chain saws and brush cutters and cleaned the whole creek in eight weeks. They completely finished two heavy-duty environmental projects in eight

weeks. Where other people would have used all kinds of machinery, they just went through it by hand. They were real committed to it. The interpretive trail in Ponemah was a concept started by the grade school. They did not have the money or the manpower, so it became part of our project. Manpower!—we are so conditioned. Anyway, work power, elbow grease. They cut the trail through the woods. It was beautiful. We had these metal signs and there was a picture and two words etched on each sign designating different fish, animals, birds and trees that live in that area. They made posts, put these metal signs on them, and spaced them along this interpretive trail. For example, there would be a picture of an eagle etched in the metal and then a great big Ojibwe word. It would say "Migizi." Way at the bottom underneath in parenthesis, it would say (eagle). And again we wanted to say, this is who we are, we are Ojibwe. Your way is good, you don't have to be anybody else. All of these things impacted these young people on many different levels.

A lot of the young people started out with this project to make money but then they became committed. The whole community was inspired. We had two community days, when the whole community came out. At different times, people would come by and help because we did not have enough equipment, or enough chainsaws. We did not have enough trucks. We had to haul all kinds of brush and garbage and these young people did it by hand. Different families would drive up in their pickups and spend the day hauling brush. When they were finishing the interpretive trail, the forestry department came out. The whole Red Lake Forestry came out and cleared more brush that was beyond the scope of our project, so that people who walked along the interpretive trail could see the lake. They cleared out the underbrush and hauled it away.

Our housing department gave us all kinds of technical assistance. Indian Action brought their bobcats down and spread gravel. Everybody helped. On our community days, the whole community turned out. There was one community day, when we had four hundred extra people down at Pike Creek helping out. The tribal chairman was down there with his chainsaw and his hard hat cleaning out debris. The DNR built two bridges across Pike Creek. There were kids playing in that creek for the first time in twenty years. I have pictures of it. Older people were so happy to see this kind of respect.

It had a ripple effect; some of the other youth projects went to other parts of the reservation and started clean up projects on their own. We want to ultimately develop a park board, for the maintenance of these areas. They got picnic tables and built two bridges across that creek. It is beautiful, just beautiful down there now.

I got a call a couple of weeks ago from one of the teachers at the Ponemah Elementary School thanking us for what we did because they use the outdoor classroom. The teachers from the elementary school take their kids out there almost every day. It was really a successful project in every way. Everybody was changed by it. I know I was.

BOOKFOUR

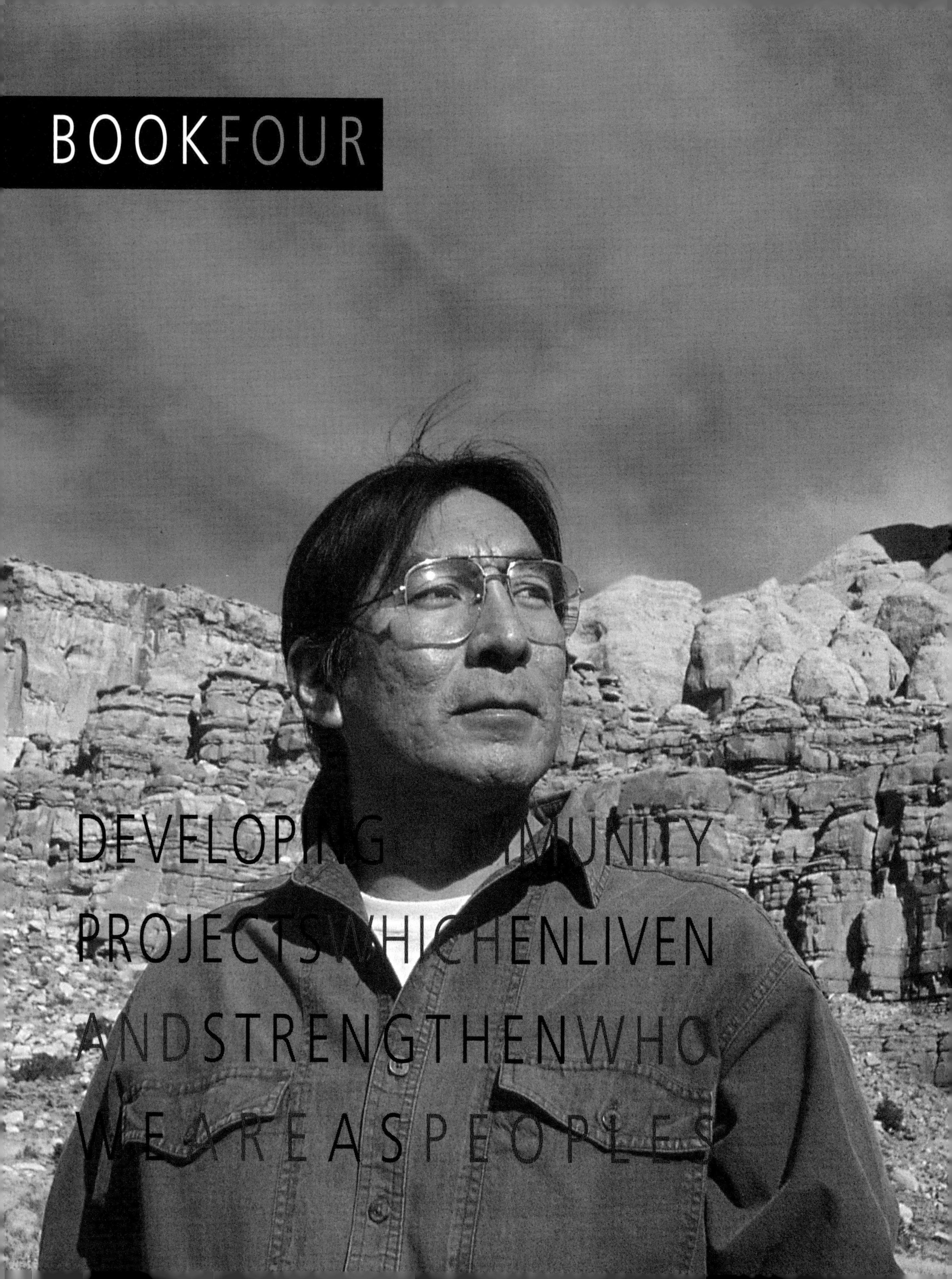

DEVELOPING COMMUNITY
PROJECTS WHICH ENLIVEN
AND STRENGTHEN WHO
WE ARE AS PEOPLES

Book Four contains interviews with individuals who make it clear that the prophecy of the seventh fire is being manifested in this generation. Throughout Native America, communities are concentrating on enlivening Native ways of life based on traditional principles and thought. These individuals, tribes and organizations demonstrate a regenerative movement based on original knowledge and lifeways. Taken together, these projects represent a composite of what Native nations could do to become strong again.

Our lifeways are based upon belief systems which are rooted in positive human behavior and interaction with all life. Revitalizing these beliefs forms the essence of a powerful movement to bring about the healing and empowerment of Native individuals, communities and nations. Native development is a process which comes from individuals within communities working in real and vital ways with the issues of our survival.

This book contains specific examples of community-based efforts to reintroduce Native lifeways, language, and teachings into contemporary Native life. Darryl Kipp speaking from his experience in revitalizing the Blackfoot language states that "If you lose your mother tongue, you become like a museum, a dusty room full of decomposing artifacts." Mililani Trask, Kia'aina of Ka Lahui Hawaii, speaks of the traditional teaching which gives them strength to overcome the many obstacles they encounter in giving rebirth to their nation. She says, "A difficult birth does not make the baby any less beautiful."

These people and their projects share a common framework derived from their unique experience but which has universal application among all Native nations: the renewal of our belief systems, cultures, and languages provides solutions to the contemporary problems we face to revitalize our communities; integrated approaches to Native development incorporate the spiritual, emotional, physical and mental well-being of each respective community; the healing of Native individuals, families, and communities comes from the pragmatic reality we create from our traditional beliefs and principles; Native institutions addressing economic, governmental, cultural, educational, and social needs address the whole person and community; the external issues of protecting lands, environment and sovereignty are balanced with the internal issue of empowering Native peoples' belief within ourselves to determine our futures and find solutions to our problems; the resolution of the factionalism and political divisiveness is found in the reinstatement of traditional values of peace, consensus building, and dispute resolution; finally, viable Native economic systems simultaneously support the way of life and meet basic human needs for food, shelter, and income.

The Blackfeet Language Is A

Journey Back Toward Ourselves

CHAPTER SIXTEEN

An interview with Darrell R. Kipp

(Blackfeet)

D arrell R. Kipp was raised on the Blackfeet Indian Reservation in Blackfoot, Montana. He graduated from Eastern Montana State College, earned a master's degree from Harvard University in Social Policy and Planning/Education, and in 1982 received a master of fine arts degree in writing from Goddard College. Darrell is the director of the Piegan Institute. Other founders include Dorothy Still Smoking, a graduate of Concordia College, University of South Dakota, and doctoral candidate in Educational Administration at Montana State University; and Edward Little Plume, a rancher. Both are fluent speakers of the tribal language. The Piegan Institute, a private non-profit organization founded seven years ago, is dedicated to researching, preserving, and promoting Native American languages, in particular the Blackfoot language.

I am a member of the Blackfeet Tribe in Montana, a member of the Blackfoot Confederacy which includes the Bloods, Northern Piegans, and Blackfoot in Alberta, Canada. We represent a language group currently estimated by the year 2000 to number approximately forty thousand individuals. In the 1990 United States Census, thirty-two thousand people nationwide indicated that they considered themselves Blackfeet Indians. The number of individuals who have an alliance or affiliation with the Confederacy probably exceeds fifty thousand.

In 1836, when the first major inroads were made by outsiders, the estimated population was about twenty thousand Blackfeet alone, which could be projected to saying about fifty to sixty thousand Blackfoot Confederacy members. From 1830 to 1900, the people of the Blackfoot Confederacy suffered enormously through smallpox epidemics, which eliminated about three-fifths of the population. In 1896, the Blackfeet Tribe of Montana reached its lowest ebb with only fourteen hundred members left. We were on the verge of extinction. We now look forward to the year 2010, when we should have twenty thousand enrolled members with one-quarter blood or more. If we eliminate the quarter-blood requirement, then the numbers could easily swell to over thirty thousand.

They tried to annihilate the Blackfeet people. We are still here and we are growing. Although we did not go away, our land, language, religion and philosophy went away. We all know how and why. They were physically taken. The basis of America's so-called "Indian problem" is that they did not eliminate the Indian. That presents the problem. Had the Blackfeet been eliminated, there would be no "Blackfeet problem" today. They would have the choice lands we live on. They would not have to oppress our language, because there would not be one. They would not have to worry about where they would confine us, because there would be none of us.

In the book Earth Household, Gary Snyder writes a reference to the Viet Cong, during the Vietnam War. I like the line and quote it a lot. If we take it in context today he says, "The American Indian is a vengeful ghost lurking in the back of a troubled American mind." We are viewed with great suspicion because of long-standing stereotypes attached to us as Indian people. Over the years those stereotypes, rather than being erased, have been reinforced through movies, distorted reporting, the pre-conceived notions of individuals who want to study us, and the long-standing institutional racism that is rampant in the public school systems and universities. An Indian artifact is viewed as valuable if it is a museum piece or a piece of art. There is a great market for it. This is why the majority of lovers of Indian art and artifacts are in bed with grave robbers. Where things that represent dead Indians are valuable, nothing that represents live Indians appears to be of any worth. This stereotype is the way that Indians are viewed today.

Our languages particularly are viewed as worthless entities. But they are living. Where we would spend millions of dollars to save twenty-six California condors, nothing like that has ever been spent to save Native American languages.

The irony is that, after all has been said and done, Indians did not go away. We were merely stripped of all our possessions. I do not blame American society for the condition of our community. We have a community of nine thousand people. We have one store, two cafes; most of the downtown area is blighted, burned-out and made up of old abandoned buildings. There has not been anything new built here on this reserve in many years, except for HUD houses, new schools, and a mortuary. I think that it defines us. Schools for our children, houses to live in, and a place to be buried. What about the rest? American society is faced with the dilemma of what to do. I feel that if they were to leave Indian tribes alone for a while, and we could have a moment of repose away from the continual siege, we might find ways to develop self-sufficiency and self-realization.

What are we going to do in the year 2010, if we lose all of our land and are confined to HUD housing, within the confines of the reservation agency-towns, the last piece of land we are able to hold onto; if we no longer have our language because it has been taken from us; if we have not made the transition to American society that was established for us? Even those who were capable of moving into the American mainstream found themselves uncomfortable and rejected enough to understand that the melting pot is a lie. What will be left? In the year

2000, will we have survived and multiplied from the fourteen hundred survivors of the starvation winter of 1884 only to find ourselves confined to a refugee camp called Browning, Montana—stripped of what dignity we had left, stripped of our culture, because we have lost our language?

Our culture emanates from language. Those who say they want to preserve their culture, if they do not say they wish to preserve their culture and language, are naïve. You cannot keep a culture alive in a dynamic way unless you have a language. If you lose your mother tongue, you become like a museum. You become a dusty room full of artifacts. Gradually, those artifacts lose their meaning. They decompose until they become archetypes viewed as rare objects from a previous age. The human mind and the human being cannot be turned into artifacts. They will not do well in a refugee camp.

What is the alternative after all the economic development schemes that have been brought to reservations have failed so blatantly? If you take a short ride around the reservation, I could drive you by at least eight rusting monuments to the short-sightedness of agencies such as the EDA, HUD and CDBG. Who brought us a pencil factory, paid minimum wage, and said they would save us? They subsidized it for twenty years and still it has never been successful. Who brought us an aging factory from Massachusetts that did not save us? Who brought us a race track that sits rusting in the only decent riverbed near this town? They not only desecrated a beautiful valley, but they left us a hulking, rusting piece of wasted vision. I can take you to the state-of-the-art livestock center they built with millions of dollars that sits empty, torn apart, home to pigeons. You can go around and see the abandoned, wasted, hulk-

"IS THIS HOW WE ARE GOING TO SAVE A NATION OF PEOPLE?"

ing, rusting, fallen-down sawmills, factories, race tracks, and say to yourself, "Is this how we are going to save a nation of people?"

In 1983, it was through a strange combination of events that my eyes were opened to the fallacy of this kind of approach. It happened in a very innocent way. I was a professor at the Blackfeet Community College where I had been a long-time member of a group of Blackfeet people that wanted a place to exist and survive. One day, we went to one of the public schools and interviewed a group of sixth-grade Blackfeet children. We were going to evaluate how much they knew about their tribe. One of the questions we asked was a toss-off question, not really meant to be serious, just a lead-in—"Are you an Indian?" These kids ducked their heads, covered their faces with their hands, and would not answer. No matter what we told or asked them, it was obvious they were so ashamed of being Indians that they were unhealthy. From that point on, it occurred to me that this long legacy, which we had watched and participated in, had to be looked at from a different perspective. I decided I would attempt to find a different perspective. That was the beginning of our work as it is today.

In 1983, the first language effort ever made on the Blackfeet Reservation on any large scale was carried out by a colleague of mine named Dorothy Still Smoking. Dorothy was a successful grant-writer for the tribe. For the first time, the tribe submitted a bilingual teacher-training grant for the community college. Many tribes at that point were submitting grants. The bilingual initiative on Indian reservations was just beginning. The unexpected occurred: she wrote a successful grant for a three-year program to train Blackfeet people as teachers in bilingual education. Once the grant was approved and everything was ready to

begin, they advertised the jobs in the community. There was a director, a curriculum coordinator, and professors. Much to everybody's shock and bewilderment, nobody ever applied for the jobs. Here you are on a reservation where good professional jobs are hard to come by, and here is this beautiful series of jobs that intertwine standard education with training in something you would think everybody would be interested in–the Blackfeet language. They advertised these jobs, and they advertised them, and nobody ever applied.

Finally, in a last-minute act, Dorothy resigned her position as Chairman of the Native American Studies Department and took over as Director of the Bilingual Program on a sabbatical arrangement, since no one else would take the job. I had been an English professor at the College for several years and worked as a technical writer for many tribes in Canada and the United States. Dorothy came to my home and asked if I would take the curriculum developer's job temporarily, so we could get the program going. I finally agreed, reluctantly.

We were both baffled by the lack of interest in the language. We were aware of a high interest in learning to dance, learning the music, and all other aspects of being Blackfeet, but it did not include the language. That baffled us, as members of the tribe and as academic people. We are academic in some of our approaches, but on the other hand, we come from very traditional backgrounds and families. In fact, we were somewhat worried because of our reluctance to get involved. We used to sit and question, why did we feel so reluctant to go all out on this?

One day we simply sat down at a table and said, "Well, how are we going to do this?" There were some typical guidelines in the grant, but no one knew exactly how you would teach Blackfoot 101, Blackfoot 102 or advanced Blackfoot.

At that point, we came to deeply respect and admire the work of the few people who had been advocates of studying the Blackfoot language. For many years on this reservation, long before anyone ever thought about studying tribal languages, Nellie Reevis went about the community in her calm way, teaching the language in many places. The other lady was Elizabeth Butterfly, who had taught as a teacher's aid in the Browning Public Schools for many years. She taught Blackfoot and had been a part of one of the first books written about the language.

We were stumped as to why everybody had such a negative view of the language. It was a real catch-22 situation. The community surveys from which this grant had been derived, asked people on the reservation what they wanted their children to be taught. They would always say their culture and history. The assumption was that language was part of that. But probably not, because very few people were interested in the language.

One of the first things we did was produce a three-part Blackfoot lecture series to kick off the program. The last one, on Blackfeet language and ethnology, was entitled, "What is Left of Our Voice?" The second one, on Blackfeet history, culture and tradition, was called, "Who Has Written Our Past?" The first one, on Blackfeet art and design, was titled "Where Are Our Images?" Ironically, for that, we brought back the ethnologists, now in their seventies, who had studied our tribe as young men and women. Dr. John Ewers, who was a longtime curator at the museum, returned and did a slide show of Indian artifacts and artwork of the Blackfoot. The place was packed. It was so huge, we had to hold it at the hotel in East Glacier. It was unbelievable.

In the second lecture "Who Has Written Our Past?" we had Dr. Hugh Dempsey, who

"WE BECAME CONCERNED THAT THERE WAS SO MUCH NEGATIVE FEELING ABOUT OUR LANGUAGE."

has written many books, primarily on the Blood but extending also to the Blackfoot Confederacy—the same thing, the place was packed. Everybody had read Ewers' and Dempsey's books about the Blackfeet, so two or three hundred people showed up. Very few people showed up to the last seminar we produced on the Blackfoot language. No one could speak about the language; in fact, many got up and refused to speak. Some very strange statements came out of that seminar. People said that the old Blackfoot was gone. The new Blackfoot was something else. The most bizarre statements I heard were, "You can't make soup out of your language," "What good is it in New York City or Great Falls, Montana?" and "Can you use your language at K-Mart?" It was a negative and disappointing meeting, but it stuck in our minds.

I had been a teacher of English for all these years. I had advocated the "love of language" and I had an MFA in writing. I had taught Indian children on my own reservation to love the beauty of language. I was always talking about the English language. I was not talking about the Blackfoot language. Now I am faced with wondering why is it that we do not love our own mother tongue like we love our stepmother. A Native American English teacher is a rare person because there are not very many of us who are able to master English to the extent that we become teachers of English. Out of fourteen thousand Blackfeet, only three hundred of us have BA degrees or better. I was in this very ironic position of being a lover of language, but not of my own.

Dorothy, and by that time Ed Littleplume, and I, were all beginning to become conscious of a built-in hypocrisy we all shared. Mr. Littleplume is considered the most fluent speaker of the Blackfoot language in the entire Confederacy. Yet, when we approached him, he was reluctant to help us. In fact, he refused until the third or fourth time that we asked him. We sat together for the first three or four months and questioned, "Why is this so difficult; why are we so overwhelmed by this? It should be something that is natural, something that we would love to do, and aspire to do." Yet no one did and no one wanted to.

Then the strangest thing happened—we began to get comfortable with it. We got more comfortable with each passing day studying our language. In the beginning, Dorothy and I literally had to sit at a table and walk our way back through the language because we were not fluent speakers like Ed. We were asking, "Should we study grammar, do we write words out, how do we do it?" Suddenly, we started feeling better. It was amazing. I started enjoying it. I noticed that something was beginning to happen to me—I began to become enlightened about the language. It dawned on me that I had been taught to hate the language. Naturally, deep down, I did love it, but I had been taught it was worthless and of no value. I had been taught that it was not as good as English. I had been taught that English could fulfill all of my needs. I had been taught that I could not learn another language. All of these strange fallacies became apparent within the first year.

We became concerned then that there was so much negative feeling about our language. We were shocked in several instances when members of our tribe found out we were studying the language, came to our office, and to put it mildly, admonished us. On one occasion, a woman told us the language was like a glass bowl that had been tossed to the ground and was broken. She said, "You are trying to pick up the pieces and put them back together. You will never be able to do it. You should leave it alone and let it rest." On another occasion, a man and a woman came in and told us, "You are sinners, pagans, and godless. You should know better than to study the language. You are anti-Christian." On another occasion, we were told that, as educated Blackfeet, we were not in a position to do what we were doing.

Everybody ignored who our parents and grandparents were, but saw us as educated people who were stealing the language. After a while, we realized that an oppressed group that has no solid definition of itself will give itself many definitions. Each person had a separate definition of what Blackfeet should be and what they should do. We were presenting a dilemma to both sides. On one hand, we presented a dilemma to people who saw us as educated and observed that we were not able to speak the language well. We presented a dilemma to them as people that would take the language. On the other hand, those who aspired to be educated and wanted to move away from tribal culture and language saw us as traitors. They saw us as individuals who had been given the opportunity to have the best education and now we were wasting it. Instead of extending our efforts in a non-Indian way and supporting the tribe in economic development, technical writing and education, we were wasting this formal education by spending our time studying something as lowly as our mother tongue.

"WHEN YOU THROW AWAY A LANGUAGE YOU ARE THROWING AWAY A UNIVERSE."

This all baffled us, but later on became revealing. The process itself became an enormously powerful teacher to me, Dorothy, and Ed. One of the first mistakes we made, in typical Western fashion, was in dealing with the fact that the grant provided for the training of ten teachers. We were having this enormously difficult time getting people to participate in the program. Suddenly, when we advertised for trainees, twenty-three people applied. This shocked us. We were going to pick ten out of the twenty-three and then we said, "Wait a minute, this is insane. On one hand, we can't get anyone to join us and now we get twenty-three people to join us, and we are going to tell thirteen of them that they can't? This is crazy." We sat down and worked it out so that all twenty-three could participate.

The first thing we did was a Blackfoot language study conducted by the twenty-three interns. Dorothy and I designed the survey objectively and scientifically to measure the extent of the language on the Blackfeet Reservation. We found that the language was going to die in what we estimated would be thirty years. The majority of the fluent speakers on the reservation were over the age of fifty. Approximately twenty-five percent of the population speaks Blackfeet on a regular basis. We knew then that the language was already in a very precarious and fragile position. Most of the fluent speakers of Blackfeet are older members of the community. Younger members speak, or are strongly influenced by the language, but are less proficient in its usage. A large percentage of English-speakers are not as proficient in English as fluent Blackfeet-speakers are in Blackfeet.

As the transition between Blackfeet and English continued, a general decline in language proficiency occurred on the reservation. It happened all over the United States. The Christian and government schools should have simply added English to the Blackfeet repertoire. Their method was to eliminate the Blackfeet language and replace it with English, a method which is now considered barbaric and unenlightened. They tried to strip away the values system, language, culture, and a wide range of activities, and put something else in their places. The transition did not come. What we found was that for generations they tried to switch

"WE CONVINCED PEOPLE, AND WE CONVINCED OUR-SELVES, THAT WE COULD LEARN THE LANGUAGE."

our people over, but they never became proficient English-speakers.

The Blackfeet language was not, as stereotype would have it, a series of grunts and groans. It was, in fact, highly sophisticated. The entirety of the Blackfeet people is in their language. When you throw away a language, you are throwing away extremely detailed and long-standing information. You are throwing away a universe, an enormous library, and one of the greatest laboratories a group of people could ever ask for. And what was it replaced with? They replaced it with English. In the reservation school system, our children take the Iowa Test for Basic Skills. The Blackfeet people have been at the bottom percentile for the last forty years. They have never come out of it. Our children are at the bottom of the United States in terms of English language acquisition. Their ability to master English never happened.

It was ironic that this beautiful language was replaced with a very primitive form of English. We have never been able to rise above the level that we now master in English. Sixty-five percent of Blackfeet today do not possess a tenth-grade education. The majority of our tribe has, if I may, been essentially de-languaged. We found that the most proficient English-speakers on our reserve are not as proficient in language as the most proficient Blackfeet-speakers. It is important to realize that taking away our language and replacing it with English was in fact an anti-intellectual movement, and it accomplished its goals.

The long-standing dogma that the Blackfeet language was bad transferred to mean that all language was bad. We never really put our hearts and our minds into learning English. The punitive measures used against the Blackfeet for speaking our language for so many years took a serious toll on us and left us in a sorry state. You now have our school systems spending enormous amounts of money on gadgetry to teach the Blackfeet English. The record indicates they can't do it. One of the major problems faced in the school systems of today is the inability to teach Blackfeet children to read and write. If we are a society of functionally illiterate people, how can we then be expected to achieve any form of self-determination and realization? Being functionally illiterate handicaps us in a literate world.

The next thing we found out was that Blackfeet-speaking parents were not passing the language along to their children. When they did, there was a tendency for the children to be less proficient with the language than their parents. We knew then that the Blackfoot language was in a steady state of decline. All Blackfeet advocated the use of the language, but in reality, we were puzzled as to how this could be accomplished. A great deal of confusion existed about the merits of teaching Blackfeet, as well as the techniques to be used.

The myth in America, that it is impossible to learn another language, is strong and supported by the ineffectiveness of the teaching methods. We realized we had to overcome that. Unless we could convince or show people that it is possible to learn the Blackfeet language, then there was no point in going any further. It became irrelevant. If you are advocating the restoration of language and cannot come up with a way to teach the language, then it is a strange catch-22. You are advocating something that cannot be done to other people who are already convinced that it can't be done.

One of the things we found was that the Blackfeet are not familiar with the tenets of their own language. Fallacies abound with regard to methods of maintaining the language. Everybody believed that the language should be learned in the home. We said the home was not transferring it. We convinced people, and we convinced ourselves, that we could learn the language. That was a major breakthrough for us.

One of the things we became interested in was why and how all of us lived in homes where our grandparents did not speak English and our parents used Blackfoot as a first language, yet we could never speak it. We spent a lot of time asking questions and researching. We came up with a lot of reasons, but ultimately felt that the first answer given to us was in fact the answer.

"I BELIEVE WE WERE PICKED BY THE LANGUAGE."

One of the hallmarks of our work is that we constantly interview a wide range of people, relatives, friends, all over this reservation. They said, "We did not want to teach you the language because we did not want you punished the way we were. We did not want you to suffer the kinds of indignities we did when we spoke Blackfoot." They did not pass the language down to us because they loved us. You could say our language began to die out of an act of love. They were so denigrated, punished, and disgraced because they spoke their language, they could not bring themselves to allow their own children to be humiliated as they had been. It is love that kept the language from us.

We say, then, it is out of our love for our parents and our tribe that we reconcile this. It was not right that they did not pass the language on to us, but it was not their fault. They did not do it out of hate or spite or to deprive us. They did it because they loved us and did not want us humiliated. This is reconcilable. I can say because of the great love my parents had for me they denied me something, but I can correct that, in the name of love, for them and my tribe. We view the act of relearning and working toward a better understanding of our language as an act of love, reconciliation and, more powerfully, as an act of healing.

"IT IS A JOURNEY BACK TOWARD YOURSELF."

People ask us, even today, "Why do you do all this?" It doesn't make sense to the secular technical mind. I say, because it is the way to healthy people. We must first become healthy Indian people. We know that no matter what they bring us, if we are unhealthy, we can't use it. It is only when we are whole again that we will be able to accomplish powerful things. They won't need to bring us some run-down factory. Healthy people can do anything they want and create utopias. Unless we become healthy, we are going to suffer the same type of setbacks that have been with us all this time.

The Piegan Institute has been viewed as a lone-horse organization. Tribal colleges were put on reservations to become independent and to represent the needs of the reservation. One of the weaknesses of the tribal colleges is that many got lured into believing that they could become universities. Instead of developing models of tribal intellectual pursuit, they emulated nearby universities. You saw tribal colleges offering Viking Mythology and failing to offer their own tribe's genesis and origin; offering Victorian History and failing to offer their own tribal history; offering ballet and failing to offer their own tribal dance; offering Western

music and failing to offer their own music; offering Spanish and French, but failing to offer their own tribal languages. In other words, committing the same mistakes that the overall education system had for years, all in their quest to be accepted as the equivalent of the Western model of education. This college was no different. After the third year of the language program, when the money ran out, instead of obtaining other moneys to keep it going, they chose to close the program. This is a tribal college that essentially kicked out its own tribal language.

We left then and said, "We are not giving it up." I believe we were picked by the language. We said, "This is strange, but we were chosen to work with this language." Even though the college got rid of it and we were back to step one, now there was a group of people including the group of twenty-three interns, which had grown to about fifty, plus three or four other people. We were all inside the language and remain so today. We could not just pack up and leave.

In 1985, we formed the Piegan Institute, a private non-profit organization. We devoted our energies to writing out a long-range plan of things we hoped to accomplish in the next five to ten years. We obtained a tribal charter and IRS paperwork. A friend of ours loaned us his house. We began very quietly. We did not want to draw fire anymore. We also decided that we would try to change the attitude that our language was bad. Our five year plan consisted of one page. Then we went about our business of doing it. One of the things we said we would do was change the community's thoughts about the language from negative to positive.

When we needed something, it would suddenly appear. We never worried. Our work never interfered with our lives. It enhanced our lives. We began to see how much impact it had on us as human beings and as Blackfeet people. None of that formal education meant much until we began to balance our lives with education that reflected ourselves. The emptiness that we felt began to be filled. You gain respect and power by helping, sharing, and following the tenets of the tribe, not of your Western education. Western education teaches you to be competitive, and capitalistic, to take care of yourself at the expense of all those around you. The language of the Blackfeet teaches you differently. It teaches you that acts of sharing and generosity overcome all things, that being cooperative with the world around you is the way to go, not being competitive.

Suddenly, we began to realize that this was the life we were now leading. The spirituality within the language is so powerful that we were brought back. By understanding my language, I have come to a greater understanding of myself. Others that are deeply involved with restoration of the language will tell you the same thing. They will tell you, "It is a journey back toward yourself." Everything else that has been brought to Indians has been a journey away from ourselves. Our being sent to college was a journey away from ourselves. Our refusal to teach and learn our own language was a journey away from ourselves. We have always been placed on the road away from ourselves.

We did achieve our goal of changing the attitude of the community. It took us about five years of intensive going about the community, talking to a lot of people, and putting on seminars at the drop of a hat. The consensus among us is that we need to start total immersion schools where fifty or so community members start a private school, support it, and hire the most fluent speaker in the community to teach the children. Tribes need to produce fluent speakers at a very young age. Any tribe actively trying to save its language should, without any delay, build a one-room immersion school. When that school fills up, go to another section of their community and build another one room school.

The number of speakers is limited in all tribes. We know about two hundred tribes that still have their language. If we sit back and ask, "Do you or do you not wish to save your language?" and you say, "I do not wish to," and then don't do anything, the language will disappear within the next fifty years. No one will escape. By the year 2050 maybe the Chippewa, Cree, the Navajo, Northern Diné, their relations on the Arctic Circle, and no more than ten other tribes by the most liberal figures, will still have their language. All the rest of the languages will be gone. So the real crucial question is, "What good is saving it?" The truth is revealed in the process of trying.

We have found that once people embark on the study of their Native language, they never stop. You will never stop, regardless of how much you get frustrated, hear another calling, want to go do something else. You may try to give up, but you never will. Just in your weakest moment, something nice will happen to you and reaffirm that there is a reason to speak your mother tongue. We asked when we started, "If you were walking down the road and saw your fragile grandmother sitting beside the road, would you walk on past her?" I think that analogy still holds. We view our languages today as our fragile grandparents. If we walk past them, we have become brutal people ourselves. This is not where we should end. I think that any tribe that saves its language will never allow it to be taken away a second time.

A Difficult Birth Does Not Make The
Baby Any Less Beautiful: The Rebirth
of the Sovereign Hawai'ian Nation

CHAPTER SEVENTEEN

A statement by Mililani Trask

(Hawai'ian)

Mililani B. Trask is the first Kia'aina (prime minister) of Ka Lahui Hawai'i, the Sovereign Nation of Hawai'i. The Nation, overthrown by the United States in 1893, was recently re-formed. Native Hawai'ian people live in communities scattered throughout the islands of Oahu, Maui, Kauai, Hawai'i, and Molokai. Mililani received her law degree from the University of Santa Clara in 1978. She is an attorney and executive director of the Gibson Foundation, which provides affordable housing for Native Hawai'ians on their homelands. An outspoken environmentalist and Hawai'ian rights activist, she has developed expertise in the legal background of Native Hawai'ian land trusts, Hawai'ian homelands and ceded lands, and natural resources related to them. The following is adapted from a statement delivered by Mililani at the 1993 International Indian Rights Council hosted by the Cherokee Nation in Tahlequah, Oklahoma.

Aloha! Owau o Mililani Trask keia—I am Mililani Trask. I am the first elected *Kia'aina* of the *Ka Lahui Hawai'i*, Native Hawai'ian Sovereign Nation, which has only recently been formed. In the beginning of any undertaking, it is part of our culture and tradition to first call upon the Creator to bless us all so that our hearts and minds might come together as one *ohana*, one family. If you would join me at this time for the oldest of traditional prayers of our people…

NA' AUMAKUA

Na 'aumakua mai ka la hiki a ka la kau
The ancestral deities from the rising to the setting

Mai ka ho'okui a ka halawai!

From the zenith to the horizon!

Na 'aumakua ia ka hina kua, ia ka hina alo!
The ancestral deities who stand at our
back and our front!

La ka 'akau i ka lani!
You gods who stand at the right side!

O kiha i ka lani
A breathing in the heavens

Owe i ka lani
An utterance in the heavens

Nunulu i ka lani
A clear, ringing voice in the heavens!

Kaholo i ka lani!
A voice reverberating in the heavens!

Eia ka pulapula a 'oukou o Ka Lahui Hawai'i
Here are your children of the Hawai'ian
Nation

E malama oukou ia makou
Safeguard us

E ulu i ka lani
That we may grow in the heavens

E ulu i ka honua
That we may grow on the earth

E ulu i ka pae 'aina o Hawai'i
That we may flourish in the islands
of Hawai'i

E homai ka 'ike
Grant us knowledge

E homai ka ikaika
Grant us strength

E homai ka ikaika
Grant us intelligence

E homai ka maopopo pono
Grant us true understanding

E homai ka 'ike papalua
Grant us a way of communication

E homai ka mana
Grant us divine power.

This year marks the hundredth anniversary of the overthrow of the Kingdom of Hawai'i by the armed military forces of the United States of America. Many people do not know that in 1893, the United States landed military forces on Oahu Island to overthrow our Queen. At that time the Kingdom of Hawai'i had twenty-two international treaties and was part of the world family of nations. For over one hundred years the voices of our people have called for justice and asked for recognition from the American government. We are the only Native peoples in the United States of America who are not recognized. America does not recognize our existence.

We see that our brothers and sisters in Indian Country have heard our call. By inviting us to share and sit at your table, you honor us. It is a great pleasure and honor for our people to be here to support you at this momentous time. I want to thank and congratulate Wilma Mankiller and the Cherokee Nation for having the foresight, insight and integrity to preserve our culture and tradition, to defend our land, and to come forward. We stand steadfast together in the cause of what is just and what is right for Mother Earth. Thank you for recognizing and honoring us and providing us with a place at your table.

There are one hundred and thirty-five thousand Kanaka Maolis, Native Hawai'ian people, residing in the State of Hawai'i. Federal census figures indicate that there are about seventy-five thousand more who live on the continent and elsewhere in the world. When Captain James Cook, our alleged discoverer, sailed into Hawai'i in 1778, he came to an archipelago that was heavily populated. At the time James Cook landed at Kealakekua Bay, there were one million Kanaka Maolis residing in the archipelegic region on our traditional land base. By the time of the overthrow in 1893, within one and a half generations, only thirty-nine thousand of our peoples remained. Our history, the tragedy of our loss of life, culture, tradition, language and jurisdiction over our land, is one that I will not belabor because you as Native peoples shared this history with us.

In 1992, there were those who celebrated the coming of the discoverers—the big theft by Columbus, Cook and Cortez—but we all know the truth. The Native peoples populated the piihonua, the lands of the earth. They were already well populated with Native peoples who suffered the loss. Many people believe that we have vanished, but we have not. This gathering demonstrates that we have great strength in our hearts and resiliency for the cause of justice and self-determination.

The values and traditional underpinnings of our culture are, I believe, similar to those of other Native peoples in this continent and globally. The tourist industry would have you believe that "aloha" is the only cultural value we have. When you read the translation in an American-Hawai'ian dictionary, it says aloha means hello, good-bye and love. This is not the meaning of aloha nor is it the greatest value of our people. *Lokahi* is the greatest of the traditions, values and practices of our people. When you see the circle or the diamond in the Pacific Island cultures, it is the symbol for *Lokahi*. There are three points in the triangle: the Creator, *Akua*; the peoples of the earth; the land, *aina*. These three things have a reciprocal relationship.

The Creator provides the earth and the gods to nurture and sustain the people. The people acknowledge the Creator's call to act as sacred guardians of the lands, waters, and all the things that be, the ones who live in the ocean, the ones that are winged and go in the sky, and those that walk as we do on the land. We are the guardians and the keepers of all of the children of the earth. In this way we understand our appropriate place in the cosmos and our appropriate place on aina, the land.

The second greatest value of our people is *Aloha Aina Malama Aina*. *Aloha Aina* means the love and nurturing that you have for your land. *Malama Aina* means the care that you demonstrate when you embrace the earth. These are basic and fundamental principles.

When you read the history books, they will tell you that this is "old" knowledge. This is traditional knowledge, it is not old or archaic. This is the fundamental basis upon which Native nations will resurrect themselves. The papa, the teachings, are the foundation that will lift up our people and give sustenance to our Nation. The traditional teachings of our people are kept under the guidance of our *kupuna*, our elders, who by virtue of their experience and knowledge know much more than the younger adults. These teachings are in our *kupuna* so they must also become part of our government—whether they are part of the official govern-

"THE TOURIST INDUSTRY WOULD HAVE YOU BELIEVE THAT 'ALOHA' IS THE ONLY CULTURAL VALUE WE HAVE."

ment of Ka Lahui Hawai'i, or whether they are guiding us in ceremony, teaching us prayers or ways of healing. This is the basis upon which we will lift up our nation and change governmental policies. We must never lose sight of our culture and tradition.

Our government was overthrown in 1893. For many years we sent messages to Washington asking them to assist our Nation. When our Queen was taken from the throne, she was jailed for many years. The Americans went with their weapons and guns to her home and lined up a cannon. In response, Hawai'ians had come armed to defend her. She told them to lay down their arms, that there would not be blood shed on the land of the people. Instead, she said, all of our people were to pray for the enlightened justice of American wisdom. She died with her prayers but never did our people relinquish the hope in their hearts that someday there would be an awakening and justice for our people. We are still praying for that day. We are thankful that there are others who pray with us. We all know as Native people that there is no greater power than the prayer in the heart. That strength is truly the power that we rely upon.

In 1987, we decided that after ninety-three years of praying we should do more. Perhaps we should take a good look at ourselves and ask some tough questions. We spent over ninety years pointing the finger of blame at Washington. We had a lot of enmity and anger in our hearts. We had to reflect upon this. With the guidance of our *kupuna*, we looked in each other's eyes and asked ourselves, "Why have we not taken the Native initiative, why have we not come forward as Kanaka Maoli to put back together what was rent asunder when the American imperialist came to Hawai'i in 1893?" We realized that much of the blame was ours. We had the ability to come forward as Kanaka Maoli. America created the State of Hawai'i—would we and could we accept it, and be truly Hawai'ian? Of course not. We had waited ninety-three years with our tears and anger and had neglected to see the resilience and the capacity that we have within ourselves.

In 1987, we decided to call the Hawai'ian leadership of all the islands to come and put back together the fundamental documents and a constitution for Hawai'ians. We had no place to hold this meeting. We had a church that invited us to go there, so all the Native leaders went there. We had some tents, as you all do in Indian Country. We set up the tents and we worked. There were two hundred and fifty of us who came and wrote our own constitution. When we finished, we had a press release. Everyone laughed at us, called us fools and said, "You know you are nothing. You only have a paper. Where are the people? You think Hawai'ian people will support you? You don't control your land."

In 1920, the American government set aside land trusts for the Hawai'ian people. Two hundred thousand acres of Hawai'ian homeland were created by Congress that we might not be homeless. In seventy years, only six thousand of our people ever received their land. Thirty thousand families died waiting and twenty-two thousand are still waiting. At the time of statehood in 1959, 1.4 million acres of land were set aside to better the conditions of Native Hawai'ians. This is in writing in the statehood admission act but to this very day, not a single acre has ever been provided to the Hawai'ian Nation. As a matter of fact, in the last two years the state of Hawai'i with federal assistance has resolved the land claims of our people. We are the only class of Native Americans that are not allowed standing in the federal courts of the United States of America to bring claims for breach of trust. There are three groups of Americans who can't get into the federal court: children, retarded adults and Native Hawai'ians. We are legally deprived of access to the federal courts.

This is our current condition. When two hundred and fifty of us wrote the Ka Lahui Hawai'i constitution in 1987, people really laughed and thought we were crazy. In a few years, we went out and talked with our people. Hundreds of people came and sat on the ground to have meetings. We slept on the beaches, we went up the mountains. We had no place to go but our people came and our people listened. When we wrote the constitution it took us two years to take it to all the communities on all the islands. We took it to the leper colony of Kalenpapa, and even those who did not have fingers to hold a pen got someone to come and sign, so that they might join Ka Lahui Hawai'i, the Sovereign Nation of Hawai'i.

Today, Ka Lahui Hawai'i has about twenty thousand Native Hawai'ian citizens. Every week and month more enroll because they believe in the fundamental right to self-determination. Initially, those in power in the state and federal government laughed at us. Now, they are concerned that Native nationalism has not gone away. In the last two years, many questions have come from Senator Daniel Inouye to our people: "Why do you want a sovereign nation? Don't you want us to pass a Hawai'ian Reorganization Act? We did this on the continent, to make Indian nations." We are fortunate that we have treaty signatories among the American Indian nations and Canadian nations. The power of treaty-making is not just a chapter in tribal history books. It is something we are capable of doing here and now. Ka Lahui Hawai'i is a small nation but already we have treaties with all the Tlingit nations of Canada and America, the Pueblos of California, and in the last six months we signed a treaty with the Lakota Council in support of protecting the Black Hills.

"NATIVE HAWAI'I HAS NOT GONE AWAY."

You don't need federal recognition or the power of the *kala*, the federal dollar, to make yourself a strong nation. The strength of your nations is in the traditions of your people, the production of your minds, the labor of your hands, and the commitment in your hearts. These are the greatest resources that you have. We Kanaka Maoli are living proof that this is the truth. I always laugh when I come to meet with the American Indian people. We are all in a crisis. We all know that this is so. We have to gird our loins to prepare for the short and long-term battles we face on a daily basis. But we can never lose sight of some of the many things that we all share together.

Recently I was in Montana touring the Flathead reservation of the Salish and Kootenai people. They were showing us the different tribal buildings and their court. We came into a little room and they said, "This is where we hold our court." Then they kind of looked down and said, "You know it is not very big, it is not as good as a lot of the other tribes but it is the best that we can do." They cast their eyes down in shame when they showed this to me. In Hawai'i, we still do not have an acre of land. We don't have a building. We don't have a courtroom, we don't need a courtroom to resolve conflict among our people. If two neighbors are fighting or two island communities are in disagreement, you call the *kupunas* or the judges. I said, "Do not feel sad because your courtroom is small or you don't have too much money. We don't even have courtrooms. We hold court outside. We put up tents. If it is too rainy to go outside, we go down to the neighborhood McDonald's, buy coffee and sit down. We fight with each other until it is resolved. You don't need a courtroom to resolve conflict among yourselves. You have the inherent capacity to do this."

Then they looked at me and said "How is your judicial court established?" I told them that in our constitution, there are two ways to resolve conflict. Our citizens may choose. They can either go to the elected judge of their community or they can choose *hooponopono*, the traditional way of conflict resolution which is done by the elders. If they go into the court system and they do not like the first decision, they can go upstairs and make an appeal. If you go before the elders, there is no appeal. You do what the elders tell you. It is not something that occurs in a courtroom. If the elders tell you to fast for five days, swim in the ocean, take the *hookupu* offering to the volcano, you will do that. You do not eat, go to work or go home, you do as the *kupunas* direct. This is how we resolve conflict.

"PEOPLE HAVE THE RIGHT TO SELF-DETERMINATION."

Most of us are called upon to serve our peoples at home, and indeed that is where a great deal of our work needs to be done. I have been working for the rights of our people. We are indigenous to the earth. Under international law, people have the right to self-determination but "minorities," "ethnic populations," and "indigenous people" do not. For the last ten years the indigenous voices of the world have been in Geneva praying that we be recognized as "peoples-peoples." We are entitled to the fundamental rights and international standards given to all peoples.

Under the international covenant of civil and political rights, peoples have the right to self-determination by which we freely determine our political status. That is the nature of the debate at the United Nations. I am proud to say I went there for the first time in 1993. I was assisted in representing my people by those who had been there before me. Chief Oren Lyons, the faith keeper of the Haudenosaunee, and one of the chiefs of the Lakota Nation were there instructing us in what we have to do. Geneva is far away but they are making international rules there that nations are using as excuses to deprive our peoples of the protection of fundamental human and civil rights. All Native leaders, all Native peoples, need to be aware that our work is not only here in our home base but also in the land of the foreigner. We cannot allow dominating nations to deprive our peoples and future generations of our human rights any longer.

One of the greatest and most difficult tasks of a Native nation today is taking a good look at ourselves and seeing what we need to do. For a long time in Hawai'i, we said that we as guardians of the sacred earth were called upon to protect the land. For a long time what we did was speak truth and enunciate our tradition. That was all. A few years ago, we came to the difficult understanding that the time in which we could limit ourselves to practicing our tradition had long since past. We are not living in traditional times any more. Our traditions, teachings, and ceremonies must be incorporated into our daily lives.

In Hawai'i, we can no longer stand up with dignity and call ourselves guardians of the sacred earth unless we acquire the necessary skills to be the guardians of the earth. In traditional times we could stand by the river and pray to the *Akua*, the Creator, to bless the river and take care of the river people. At present, this is not enough. You have to do your ceremony and get out there and understand what water quality is. You have to bring an understanding of natural resource management to your land. You are not going to get that assistance from the EPA or the state government. You must strengthen and build those capacities yourselves. We can't just pray in the forest and hope that the timber will be protected. We have to understand forest management and then go out there and test our soils and water for contamination.

In this day and age, if you as a Hawai'ian wish to be the guardian of the sacred earth, you must acquire and attire yourself with the weaponry for this battle. You are not going to stop people putting radiation and pollution in the water with a spear as we did in traditional times. Today, we need new weaponry. We have taken a good look at ourselves, come to this understanding, and committed ourselves as Native people, as Native nations, to strengthening our capacities to be natural resource managers. Then, we can say once again with integrity that we are guardians of this sacred earth.

We still have a long way to go. We still do not exercise jurisdiction over our land. When Senator Inouye said the United States would make us an Indian Reorganization Act government, we said, "No, thank you. We have a constitution." Then a Hawai'ian Claims Commission, like the Indian Claims Commission, was proposed by Inouye. We said, "No, thank you. If we have disagreement and conflict, we go to our elders or the judges of our nation." Last year he sent draft legislation to the State of Hawai'i. Hawai'i has become the first state to totally usurp Native self-determination by creating a state Hawai'ian nation. This state nation will have officials elected according to state rules but no land is provided in this state law.

They wish to crush the nation of Ka Lahui Hawai'i. That is what we face now. Without the dollar, without the ability for mass education, we prepare for this latest challenge. Your heart is always heavy when you struggle for your people. You can't help but be a little fearful, feel a little down-hearted. Whenever we get to this point, we need our elders to come forward and remind us of the motto of our nation which has carried us thus far. I want to leave you with our motto today because it is something that we share with all of our treaty signatories. The motto of Ka Lahui Hawai'i is "A difficult birth does not make the baby any less beautiful." We are committed to raising up this child so that it will be strong.

We are yet in the pains of birthing of our nation but we are taking heart. Even though the power brokers in Washington do not recognize our existence, we cannot help but celebrate that in a few years, we will come together. Already our brothers and sisters from throughout America recognize our existence. Times are hard, we are in crisis, but we have great strength and ability in our hearts, tradition, and the land we love.

"A DIFFICULT BIRTH DOES NOT MAKE THE BABY ANY LESS BEAUTIFUL."

t Is Easier Said Than Done To Base

Community Development On

The Values Of People: The Zuni

Pueblo Conservation Project

CHAPTER EIGHTEEN

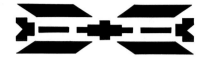

An interview with Jim Enote

(Zuni)

J im Enote is the Project Leader of the Zuni Conservation Project, a comprehensive and integrated program of action for sustainable resource development. Using modern technologies and traditional practices, the project works to restore damaged lands, protect wildlife, biodiversity and freshwater resources, and further local sustainable agriculture and forest management. This program, the most comprehensive tribal effort of its kind, was cited as a model project in the 1995 edition of State of the Earth.

Jim has worked with the Zuni Agency of the Bureau of Indian Affairs in many fields, including soil, forest, and range conservation. He has also worked with a number of wildlife studies for the Colorado Division of Wildlife. Jim associated with the International Union for the Conservation of Nature and the Native American Fish and Wildlife Society. He is a member of the President's Council on Sustainable Development Natural Resource Task Force and a Trustee of the A:shiwi A:wan Museum and Heritage Center.

Jim is a writer, and has contributed to the Zuni Land Claims History Newspaper. He also wrote *Saving the Land and Preserving the Culture: Environmentalism at the Pueblo of Zuni* and produced several videos concerning Zuni environment and development.

The Zuni Conservation Project started in 1992 after we brought a lawsuit against the United States in the 1970s for lands that were damaged as a result of federal improprieties related to Native trust responsibilities. We had two suits going on simultaneously, both of which were settled in 1990. The first was called the Zuni Indian Land Claim Settlement Act, and the second was the Zuni Land Conservation Act. The latter is what we are working under. The Zuni Land Conservation Act of 1990 is to correct all of the damages to our lands. Of course, expert witnesses for the United States government said that this damage was all naturally caused. The tribe's position was that these were problems exacerbated by federal mismanagement.

We settled out of court for twenty-five million dollars in each case. Attorneys' fees took a big chunk out of both. The one we are operating under, The Zuni Land Conservation Act, set aside a seventeen million dollar trust fund. The investment returns from the principal are being used to run this program to rehabilitate damaged lands and develop the means to ensure that our resources are available for future generations.

This program began in January of 1992 when the moneys from this settlement finally came through. The plan was first implemented in 1994, and the project staff has grown from myself and one student to over sixty-five people in just two years. We are working on water, grazing, range conservation, wildlife and fisheries, and sustainable agriculture. We have a Geographic Information System (GIS) office and a youth group, and we are conducting a cultural values study.

"IT IS A LOT EASIER SAID THAN DONE TO BASE COMMUNITY DEVELOPMENT ON THE VALUES OF PEOPLE."

We spent two years in planning. The program is based on the cultural values of the Zuni people. Many people will say that, but it is a lot easier said than done to base community development on the values of people. We read what was going on in the United States Forest Service and the Bureau of Land Management, which have standardized programs across the board throughout the United States. Their ways of doing things were not specific enough for us. We looked at programs in developing nations all around the world. Things looked very familiar to me as I read through plans for Ghana, Nepal, Bolivia and Mexico. I saw very similar scenarios.

I thought, why are we following these templates set up by the United States government for the city of Seattle or for Indians in Florida or North Dakota? Why can't we develop our own plans? So we did. The idea came from looking at what was happening in the communities of other developing nations.

We decided the program was going to be participatory. We were going to assess what people know. We were going to communicate in our own language as much as possible. We were going to have the farmers, land users, religious hunters, sports hunters, youth, and others tell us what they thought the priorities were. We were going to spend a lot of time and resources understanding the cultural values that affect land use. Values would be the foundation of our program. We needed to explain to people what we were doing so they would understand what we were about and begin to offer suggestions.

The vision for the work is rehabilitating the damaged lands and developing and implementing a mechanism for sustaining those resources. We are also reevaluating the way we do things now, so that the resources we have today are available for future generations—not just twenty-five years from now, but one or two hundred years into the future. We are thinking about the real possibility of a change in the economy and we want to be sure that resources are available for Zuni people. If the economy changes and our people have to continue to use firewood to heat their homes, we want to make sure that it will be there. Or if something catastrophic happens and, who knows, the dollar is worth very little, or the Indian jewelry market crashes, and people need to go back to farming, we want to be sure that they can.

We don't want to be stuck in a position where we rely on whatever economic system is

in place in the future. We want to have alternatives and follow the most stable and valuable resources we have—our lands, our water, seeds, soils, trees, animals, whatever. If we have those, we can make a go of it. We can survive. We have done it for thousands of years and if we have to do it again, I am sure we can.

We are restoring the damaged lands through watershed restoration programs and different kinds of erosion control. We are looking at different ways of using the land. We have to look at the concerns of religious and sports hunters. We have to be aware of the various needs for water—recreation, fishing, irrigation or drinking. Our work is basically rethinking how we are going to use our resources. In the past, we have followed some standards, but they have not all been the best for our land or for our people. We are rethinking, through the use of the widest spectrum of knowledge possible, an approach to sustaining those resources. On one hand, it is very traditional. On the other, it is very high-tech.

In traditional farming, most of the traditional knowledge is oral history passed on through families from farmer to farmer. Oral history is very tangible, easy to see, and clearly connected with religion and culture. "These are seeds my grandmother gave to me and I am giving them to you now." It means a lot to your heart, makes you feel good. It is important and has a lot of significance and strength. The modern technologies are very left-hemisphere oriented—absolute, provable, and logical. Once you learn the cookbooks or the patterns, you can manipulate them, change them, and build on them. You can work out equations to determine how fast water moves. You can figure out the kinds of plants animals eat, how many pounds per acre those animals eat per year, what they will require.

The traditional and modern are two different interpretations of reality. When you bring them together it gives you a wider perspective of what reality is. I am not one to say which is right or wrong. They are both part of the universal knowledge that is available. Today, it would be a tragedy if we relied on only one. Since we have the capability, we are using both. They can complement each other without one being dominant over the other.

We are advised by Zuni religious leaders. Their title of Cultural Resource Advisory Team is only used when they are being consulted with regard to projects. They are the recognized religious leaders in the community, who otherwise have no pieces of paper or titles. They have that title so they can be consulted as a body. They are respected people in the community with regular roles and difficult obligations to serve the Zuni people on religious aspects. Most of what they do is very secret and not discussed with the public. They can be consulted on things that are religiously important, like burials. They will all get together and give you their opinion.

If it is on non-Zuni land, there is not too much our religious leaders can do but say what they think. It is up to the federal processor to deliver after that. If it is on Zuni land, very often their decision is absolute. In many instances, they also provide guidance. "What do you think about us radio collaring deer? We will use telemetry and follow the deer and see where they have their young or where they spend the winter." And they can say, "No, you can't do that. It is not appropriate." Then we can say, "Okay, we will find alternatives then." They can tell us that we can't identify and learn a certain type of plants because they are reserved for a certain medicine society. We say, "Okay." They guide us in things that are appropriate. While we have the capability to store any kind of data, it would be a very sterile and shallow program if we were only relying on modern science and technology. It is possible, with this spectrum of knowledge, to do just about anything.

I would say the most important, and the most difficult, thing in a program like this is communication. If you fall back on public meetings and announce them on the radio and in newsletters, that is not enough. Not everybody goes to public meetings and even when they do, there will be a few outspoken people and the rest won't say too much because maybe they feel uncomfortable. We meet in traditional meeting places, out in the fields or over a meal or with women in cooking groups, things like that. Why try to construct an artificial meeting place, when there are already effective traditional means of communication in place? We are going back to what works.

Public meetings are basically worthless. Not everybody listens to the radio or reads newspapers. Although we will use newsletters and radio and we will have some public meetings, this is definitely not something we rely on. It is much more effective to go out and meet people face to face and spend three or four hours with them, talking. What did they grow out here fifty years ago? What do they remember their grandparents raising here? Tell us the story of this area. So our staff spends four or five hours talking with people out in the field, if that is what the land users want to do. We get a lot of information. We may spend a week and only reach ten people, but we may have one public meeting every two months and get twenty people. I think the better end of things is going out and meeting people. We try to cover as much of the spectrum as possible. When you have participation, you can start planning. Now we are through the planning stage and we are actually into the implementation.

We began to tell people that we would support them if they wanted to have a farming, livestock or youth organization. If you want to use our office meeting rooms, phones, copy machine, fax machine, whatever you need to use, we will support you. We will buy some filing cabinets if you want to come in and keep your records here. If you want to print up some bylaws or whatever, we will help you do that. We support them as they set themselves up in organization.

People used to see any government vehicle on a reservation and think it must belong to the BIA. It could be the Soil Conservation Service, the U.S. Geological Survey, the County Extension Agent, or any number of land-management type people, but still generally the people would think it was BIA. We are a Zuni tribal program. We have spent a lot of time letting Zuni tribal members know we are tribal and what we are about. This is what the extension service is about, this is what SCS is about, this is what the Forest Service and the BIA are about, and this is what they can all do. Now that you understand that, what do you think? Then people began to say, "Oh, I thought all you guys were BIA out here." Sometimes they would see somebody and ask, "Well, when are you going to put in a cattle guard?" and some extension agent would say, "It is not really my business, it isn't my responsibility." They would usually get angry and say, "Oh, you guys are no good." They do not understand who is doing what and what the responsibilities are. We tried to make that clear from the very beginning and of course that takes a long time.

We are mostly tribal members doing this for the people in our community. Our jobs here are not stepping stones to someplace else because we are going to be here anyway. As opposed to a lot of outsiders working here, we locals are careful about what we say and do and try to do what is right. If we do somebody wrong or give him bad information, we have to live with him for the rest of our lives. So we try to make sure that we do things right. The BIA has been promising us that for years and we do not want to be in their situation. At the same time, we are not going to carry people all the way either. That is why we will support people, but we will not do everything for them. We will give them all the support we possibly can and with that people begin to trust us. The trust of the people is one of the most important things you can have.

After communication, the second thing we put a lot of resources into is the training of our people. All but one person on our staff are Zuni. We have hired twenty permanent, and about forty-five seasonal, employees. Training involves having each staff member write down their individual goals, what they want to do with their career, what they want to be. Then we ask them to write down what they will need to get there, whether it is taking college courses, learning engineering, or learning how to work computers, design irrigation structures, or fix windmills. Each person on the staff makes a list of what they will need to do to attain that goal. When the opportunity comes up, I review them and help them obtain the training that falls within the scope of the plan they set up. We want the capability to do things ourselves. To make those goals a reality, we are matching the fiscal resources with these individual development plans. We have been able to match what funding foundations have provided us with, so that our training reaches the same level of importance as our communication efforts.

A lot of times people think that we are just training, training, training. I say, that is why we are so good at what we do. We are getting better and better at it. In-house, we have a scheduled cross-training program. So, for example, the fish and wildlife staff spends a day or two with the hydrology staff to learn how to do water quality sampling or sediment analysis, or to understand the geomorphology of arroyos and stream channels. Then the agricultural staff will spend several days with the GIS staff to understand how computers work, how maps are made, and what kinds of information the GIS people need to make the maps. Then the GIS staff will go out and spend time with Fish and Wildlife, so they know where all this data is coming from. Everybody knows what everybody else is doing. If one of the Zuni people asks one of the agricultural staff, "What are those guys doing out there?" instead of our agricultural staff saying, "I don't know, they are fish and wildlife guys," they can say, "Oh, they are doing waterfowl nesting surveys." Cross training is not only good for morale and team building, it helps build friendships, too.

This year, we plan some socio-economic work and a lot of policy evaluation with regard to definition and coordination of roles. There could be fifteen or sixteen different institutions involved in the natural resources or environment of the reservation from the Army Corps of Engineers to the Soil Conservation Service. If we are doing all these things around the reservation, but we are not doing it together, then we are spinning our wheels.

We are coordinating all the tribal, federal and state programs on the reservation through this project. We get all the people together and say, "This is what we do, this is what they do. I do not want to see your government vehicle and then find out that the Forest Service was out here last weekend or last week. I want to know what you are doing. If it has anything to do with our work, it might be redundant." Next year, we are going to require collaborative efforts. The Zuni Pueblo Conservation Office will be the authoritative clearing house for pulling it all together. This office will be responsible for making sure all the others know about the coordination. We want to do that in a way that does not hinder work. We do not want to be another bureaucracy, either. We want to be as quick and effective as possible, with the fewest hoops to jump through.

Through all of these programs there are a lot of growing pains. Many people are saying that we are a great success story, a global model. We are an ongoing project that has failures, but we learn from them, too. It means being very honest with ourselves and with each other. When we show and tell, we say here is where we screwed up, this is what worked in the end. After we tried these two other things, this one actually worked. One thing that really bothers me is going some place and just hearing success, success and success. I know it is not always like that. Being honest about your failures helps people just as much as being honest about your successes.

The Project has brought a lot of farming groups together. It has gone through ups and downs. Sometimes we are butting heads with the BIA and other times with the Council and sometimes it is very successful and everything works out well. I always tell the staff, just do this right. Do what is right. The first year, people think you are troublemakers, but at the end of the year, people are going to see that you have done some good things. Nobody can argue with that or condemn you for doing what is right. In fact, by then most people will be working with you because they want to be part of a good thing. I hope it works out that way. Many people are resistant to change, but change happens all the time. When it's good, people always follow.

I think those of us in this kind of work should think about the consequences of any actions. I am sure we do to some degree. If we are going to develop some part of our land, it is going to be beneficial for twenty or fifty years. What is going to happen in one hundred years? The consequences should be better thought out over the long term. We need to be aware that markets are artificial and will change. I think that change is a given. We need to be honest, try not to fool ourselves, and always be prepared.

The good work is a result of the efforts of the project and the community. It is also a combination and hybridization of the ideas that I picked up from developing communities in other parts of the world. We deal mostly with nations on different continents because they are the ones that can relate to us and we can relate to them. We are honest about development. The same issues that are confronting them confront us in many respects. As far as history goes, when we look at cities, we can see what could happen to us. When we look at developing nations, we can see where we were twenty-five, fifty and a hundred years ago. Then it is easier for us to see where we are now. It makes the idea that now is the time to decide which things are more important. It makes the picture a lot clearer.

The project is definitely a combination of things I have seen in different parts of the world. I have been to maybe sixteen or seventeen countries in Europe, South America, Central America, and Central Asia, and I have connections with some international development groups who are interested in the work here. I am comfortable with travel–I think it is in my blood. I have met with Native groups and rural communities in Brazil, Bolivia, India, Nepal and China. What is happening with the Tibetans, in terms of their cultural preservation and development efforts, is very similar to what is happening here with us. We may be working on the reservation and they may be working in the Tibet Autonomous Region, but we are talking about many of the same issues. In Nepal, the country is governed by His Majesty. Not too long ago, to get things done, you had to have an inside line to the palace. In Indian country, sometimes, to get things done you have to have an inside line to the tribal council. It is not that dissimilar. If tribes realize that they are developing their governments, judiciary branches, administration and all that, then we can begin to design what is going to work best for our communities. We don't have to be like everyone else. We can tailor-make it ourselves, using our own people in the most efficient way.

"WE DON'T HAVE TO BE LIKE EVERYONE ELSE."

CHAPTER NINETEEN

An interview with Larry Emerson

(Diné)

arry Emerson lives in the town of Shiprock, in the Navajo nation. He was the director of Ni Ha'alchini Ba Educational Programs and has helped to design a number of community projects, including the A'da'n Community Loan Fund Association, which is based on a model developed by a partnership between the First Nations Development Institute and the Lakota Loan Fund. He has worked with the Navajo Nation and Shiprock Alternative High School. He is Vice-President of the Navajo Community College Board of Regents, a board member of the Seventh Generation Fund, and a member of both the Shiprock Diné Philosophy for Wellness Group and the New Mexico Commission on Indian Affairs.

We began working on the A'da'n Community Loan Fund after reading some literature about micro-enterprise development by the First Nations Development Institute. I read about their philosophy, which includes concepts like community empowerment, culturally relevant economic approaches and people at the community level negotiating change for themselves, as they see necessary, instead of somebody else from the outside of the community defining their needs for them. I only vaguely understood some of the concepts about economics. I went and visited them in Virginia and we talked a little bit more in detail. Gradually, the concept started making sense, so I came back to Shiprock and organized three community meetings of forty or so people and we began to explore the idea.

There are two ways that ideas can take hold within communities. One way is that a community, by itself, independent of any outside sources, sees a need to do something and does it. The community organizer helps people move on the idea. This way is easier because people evolve into the understanding themselves. They take anything that needs changing, own it, and move with it toward resolution.

For us, change took hold in a second way. In this way, a really good new idea outside the

community has meaning to the people on the inside. They take the idea and move with it. This is what we have been used to—like the Bureau of Indian Affairs coming in, saying this is what you people need and then trying to make us implement it. That approach doesn't usually work. I had the idea that that was what community change shouldn't be. But here was a good idea, coming from the outside. We thought, how can we make it work for us?

People started to work on it right away. I had known all along that people sell the things they make, like quilts, bread, Indian foods, and farm produce. A lot of them do arts and crafts. Some work independently in other ways, irrigating farms for each other, baby-sitting, hauling wood and coal, or doing weavings. In Shiprock, most of the businesses, like the franchises, are non-Indian owned but they employ Indians. They are the formal private sector. We looked at the number of businesses in Shiprock. There were forty-five and about thirty-five were owned by non-Indian people who live outside Indian Country. That was, and is, a big irony. It is supposed to be the other way around if economic development is going to work.

Then I looked at what is called the informal sector, and these micro-enterprises were one hundred percent Indian-owned. It occurred to several of us that, logically, this was where the economic development empowerment should be. Then we looked at the Navajo Nation's approach, which seemed to be in the formal sector and only there—maybe stick a big factory in the middle of Shiprock and put hundreds of people to work doing menial labor to try and solve the economic problem that way. That seemed to be their approach—trying to move in large companies and rope off a certain area of Shiprock to become an economic development zone, or offer loan programs where the minimum loan would be ten thousand dollars. But what Navajo, given our forty-five percent unemployment rate, the poverty of our community and so on, is going to qualify for that? There is no way they could ever begin economic self-sufficiency at that level. No one has that kind of collateral.

We mainly learned about the micro-enterprise approach through the Lakota Fund in Pine Ridge, South Dakota. When we understood the approach, we said, "Hey, we can empower this one hundred percent Navajo-owned informal economic sector. If the Navajo Nation wants to take that other approach, then they can." To us, helping your people meant helping them at the micro-enterprise level. The problem with someone who is trying to, let's say, make quilts and sell them, is that often they don't speak English well and they do not know the formal skills of business planning. On the other hand, they are out there selling, saving, and keeping inventory. They are doing the same thing an entrepreneur does, but they are doing it out of common sense to supplement their family's income.

We asked: Which entity in the Navajo Nation is helping the micro-entrepreneurs? How large is this group? How much is it worth financially? We knew that Navajo dollars flow off in the millions to the border towns like Farmington. It is true that we spend our money outside our own community and end up financially supporting the non-Indian economy. We believe that the people who are circulating Navajo dollars among Navajos are the informal sector, the Navajo entrepreneurs. They are the ones that circulate the dollar among themselves in a more genuine way. Navajo people are providing goods and services to each other in an invisible way, through an underground economy. We reasoned in the Shiprock Agency, where there are thirty thousand Navajo people, that there is some statistical validity to what they are doing. We know there is validity to what they are doing in survival terms. They are already entrepreneurs.

With the help of the First Nations Development Institute, we did a study and looked at a lot of things. We looked at how, where, and for what the Navajo spend their dollars. We tried to get a reading of how big this invisible economy was. We surveyed one hundred and twenty families and found out that seventy percent of them had one or more individuals from the family who were informal microentrepreneurs. We reasoned that seventy percent of thirty thousand Navajo people is a pretty sizable number not to be recognized, and that they are being discriminated against. Some of these people can't put up a hundred dollars as collateral for a loan, but they are out there selling. Why not do like the Lakota Fund was doing and offer loans to these people? It made sense. At the same time, in exchange for collateral, have them volunteer to be trained, so that they could gain more insight into what they were doing. If we could offer that in lieu of collateral, would they do it? We tested that idea and a lot of people said they would.

People working at this level were responding in a natural way to the economics of Navajo Country. If you want to get a business started here on the Navajo, you can forget about starting next month. You have to assume that you are going to have to go through a whole bunch of crazy bureaucratic red tape. The joke is that, if it is done by Indians, it is red tape; if it is done by the BIA, it is white tape. Either way, you have to go through "tape" that can take years. Some people take ten years to get a business lease or a loan. It is a horror story in Navajo Country. We started understanding what these people on the micro-enter-prise level were saying, "The heck with that noise. Why bother?" Why put yourself through that stress? Our needs are not to conjure up ten or twenty or hundred-dollar businesses. It is ridiculous. We don't have that kind of money anywhere as collateral. Why fuss with that big red-tape mess?

In addition to that, it really does not work. If I am a single mom, I need to be home, taking care of my children. I can't be running off leaving them somewhere, especially if my family is broken up or dysfunctional or whatever. It makes sense for me to stay home, take care of my kids and make money. That is why I am doing what I am doing and weaving rugs at home. I enlist the support of Grandma, Grandpa, or my husband when I need to. I go out to the Shiprock Flea Market every day and sell my rugs. I call my own shots, buy my own materials, and am in charge of my own little operation. So what if it brings in twenty or a hundred dollars a day? It helps my lifestyle. It is more Navajo to be that way. No wonder no one is bothering with the formal sector. Why not work at home, speak your own language, and supplement the family income this way? The Navajo Nation, because of what we are doing at Shiprock, is seeing the value of micro-entrepreneurial empowerment.

The concept is that this rug-weaver lady, this single mom whose husband split on her with three kids, sits in a lending circle. Next to her might be a guy who hauls coal and wood to various homes in exchange for money or bartered goods. Our family used to exchange coal

"PEOPLE WORKING AT THIS LEVEL WERE RESPONDING IN A NATURAL WAY TO THE ECONOMICS OF NAVAJO INDIAN COUNTRY."

"THE PURPOSE OF THESE CIRCLES IS TO FORM A HUMAN BOND AND START HAVING THE CIRCLE WORK FOR THEM AS A COLLECTIVE."

213

for melons in the fall. The next person in this circle might be a guy who does arts and crafts to sell. The next guy might break and shoe horses. Then maybe the next lady might go around from door to door, office to office in Shiprock, selling sandwiches. The single mom with the three children may not speak English very well and may be ashamed of that. The guy who shoes horses might have an alcohol problem.

The purpose of these circles is to form a human bond and start the circle working for them as a collective. They struggle with the support of the group. In the circles they decide what their financial needs truly are. The rug-weaver may say, "I need six thousand dollars right away to get going." But then the horseshoe guy might say, "Well, do you really need six thousand? What is your real problem?" The sandwich lady might say, "I'd like to start a restaurant, and for that, I would need twenty thousand dollars, but is that realistic for me? No, what I need is a bigger stove, so I can make more sandwiches. I saw this huge stove; I just don't have the money. What I need is three hundred dollars." After talking in the circle, she decides that really, considering her situation, what she needs is a new stove. Then the rug-weaving lady will say, "Well, let me rethink this. I need to get my loom repaired, buy some wool and so on. That totals up to three hundred dollars." So they help each other that way. Finally, we tally up the needs and say it is fifteen hundred dollars for all five or six members.

What we do at the A'da'n Community Loan Fund Association is fund that circle at fifteen hundred dollars. They sign a regular loan contract that banks use, which legally binds them to paying it back at a going interest rate. They have to meet once or twice a month in order to check in with each other and see how they are doing. If the guy I mentioned who has an alcohol problem defaults on his loan because of drinking, it is up to the other members to counsel and remind him that he is a member of this circle. When he defaults on his payment, they have to pay it for him. That is a prior agreement.

Each member of the group brings five dollars to their monthly meetings and puts it in a kitty, in case someone defaults on a loan payment. They end up supporting, counseling, and working with each other in a group fashion to make this thing work. They know that ahead of time. At the same time, when they tell us they need certain types of training or information, it is up to us to go and provide it for them at their circle meetings. They learn how to problem solve and how to make a profit within their own endeavors. Gradually, they will grow—maybe three hundred dollars the first loan, five hundred the second, and eight hundred the third, until one day, the weaver opens her little store in her living room and needs two thousand dollars.

We have a lady with the First National Bank in Shiprock who has agreed to be on our technical advisory committee. We ask her to keep an eye on our people so that in the event that someone wants a five thousand dollar loan, she can vouch for the integrity and management skills of that person. We think in the long run that this is not the only way, but it is one way to help make the Navajo economic circles happy and healthy through empowerment and networking. We want to use the Navajo kinship system, the clan system, and the Navajo philosophy of learning and life to work in those circles and to help those people regain their self-concept.

What we are really saying is, let's measure ourselves against ourselves. Let's not always measure ourselves against the white man and the way he does things with a chamber of commerce. What are our standards of ethics, goodness, harmony and beauty? Let's measure ourselves against those Diné standards. You are beautiful because you are Diné women and you speak your language first and English second. You are doing a wonderful thing with your rug-making, despite all the odds. It may be the only thing that your mom taught you, but she did give you something to hang on to and develop. You may want to do that for your children. Maybe not passing on rug-making per se, but you may want to pass on those values of survival.

First things first—pat yourself on the back. Let's give each other affirmations and the loving, nourishing support that we need right now. We will try to be available to get the resources to help you increase your knowledge of whatever you think you need to know. That is what we are really doing as an economic project. We are trying to be part of healing and self-reliance. In the Navajo language, A'da'n means to be self-reliant, to know where you come from in terms of your culture and teachings; to know who you are as a Native person, as a holy earth-surface person; to know that you have your own mind, and that it is a gift. Something way within you has been damaged or interfered with, but it is in there. If you can open and tap into that, you are on your way as a self-reliant person who is part of a larger kinship. A'da'n means to be able to do for yourself, have pride in yourself, and know your real full worth as a Diné. Out of that sacred center, you can act and be your own leader. That is what A'da'n Nodilzin means.

As facilitators, we ask questions about how people's work fits within their tradition. Navajo woven rugs, silver work, and some of the crafts that we have done for a long time, are salable and a lot of people make them to sell. But we ask: what is the importance of these crafts and this artwork; what is its relevance to the Navajo people? What are the songs and stories behind it? Do you teach this to your children? Once, we ran a simulated circle in front of a larger group. They were acting. One guy says, "You make jewelry, right?" Another guy says, "Yeah, I make it." "Are you teaching your children what the designs mean and where they come from? Are you thanking the earth for that gift?" The jeweler says, "Well, I haven't thought about it." "Do you know the songs and stuff?" He says, "Yeah, I know the songs." "I wonder if you can teach them to your children, then." And he says, "Yeah, I guess I should." That way, you help stimulate thinking around the meaning of money in relation to the tradition.

We want the micro-entrepreneurs to run the circles the way Navajos have done all along. When you get in the circle, bring your clan with you while you are working with the people. Most of our elders say, "If there is one thing that can save the Navajo people, it is the kinship system, because within that, everything is held." The kinship system, called k'é, defines the relationship between man and woman, elders and youth, human beings and the natural world. If one embodies those rules, which can be learned at a basic level, that automatically invokes the cultural system. If they don't know how and want to learn, we want to be there with people to teach it, so that they can use it in their circle.

As thinkers in the community, we must make sure that things we would like to see are done—like being dutiful in the prayers, being in a reciprocal relationship with Mother Earth, always giving back from what you take and celebrating your success, not necessarily in the

"WE ASK THEM TO RUN THE CIRCLES BY DOING WHAT THE NAVAJOS HAVE DONE ALL ALONG."

American way, but in the Indian way; having made enough money for your family, one should give some of that away and not be unbalanced with money. You have to keep balance.

"THE A'DA'N FUND WILL TRY TO GIVE SEED MONEY TO FAMILIES THAT WORK AND THINK TOGETHER IN A HEALTHY WAY."

We want to work on a project to get families participating in circles for recovery. We put out a call around Shiprock Agency to get four families into recovery. The A'da'n group would help people deal with their problems and issues, like grief, shame, history, trans-generational trauma, ancestral responsibility, culture, and issues dealing with post-colonial psychology. The families would work on their issues first.

In the next phase, we would give them seed money to grow their own business as a family unit. We know that in America, the individual is the economic unit. In Navajo culture, the extended family is the economic unit. This is the *k'é* system. Here, we know that if we finance individuals to be millionaires, that really upsets the culture. We would give the family that works and thinks together in a healthy way seed money to grow whatever economic project they want to get involved in through the micro-enterprise model. We would help them with marketing and business management to make sure the project works for them, guided by their own *k'é*-based leadership.

My wife, Kathleen Wescott, was once told by an Ojibwe elder that Indian people in recovery need to include the Western concept of recovery, as well as our own. The reason is that we Native people, including myself, have assimilated a lot of Western values and thinking. We have also assimilated the materialistic dysfunction that comes with Western civilization. We have done a lot of assimilation, so that it is no longer possible to heal just the Indian way. The healing process would have to be bicultural, so to speak. I have accepted this as reality.

"IT IS IMPOSSIBLE THAT SOMETHING EXTERNAL TO YOU IS RESPONSIBLE FOR YOUR IDENTITY."

One important concept in becoming responsible is *T'áá Ho Aji Téego Jiináa Leb*, which means that only you stand for you. Only you can be you. Only you can understand where motivation comes from. Only you can make things happen. There is a deity within your life, the Creator, the mystery. You are the embodiment of all those things. It is impossible that something external to you is responsible for your motivation, self-concept or identity. You alone have to stand for who you are. You have to take the responsibility to look within. Once you do that, then you stand for you. You are a holy being, the earth, rainbow, streams and the rain. You are the male cloud, the female cloud, and the Earth Mother. You have to understand that. You are kin to the plants and animals. You are not the center of the world, you are part of the whole functioning system and you have a place in that whole world.

"WE ARE A MATRI-LINEAL CULTURE AND SHOULD DEVELOP MATRILINEAL INSTITUTIONS."

We will give ourselves a few years to develop a non-hierarchical board system—throw concepts like president and vice president out the window. We are using that conventional structure now because we do not know this other system well enough to jump right into it from day one. It is in our bylaws that we are going to phase out of this hierarchical system and into a Navajo-based system. We have discussed among ourselves that once we do that, make the circle Navajo-based, and bring the cedar and the sage back into our decision-making process, then automatically the outcomes of our decisions will be based on a traditional mode. We are not in a position right now to predict what will come from that. We can't force the circles to be Navajo. We can encourage them, set up models, and suggest ways for them to organize themselves non-hierarchically. We are a matrilineal culture and should develop corresponding matrilineal institutions rather than patriarchal Western systems that make no sense to us and oppress our spirit. It is better to start off in the early stages with a Navajo-based decision-making system, than to blindly haul in a patriarchal Wall Street system to govern ourselves.

Economics is also defined by the language itself. We don't have a word for economics in Navajo. There is something we do that is "economic" but we don't call it that. What is it? How can that serve as an "alternative" model for thinking? What is the nature of this activity and what are the goals implicit in the meanings of our system? That is what we want to find out. Let's stand up to Wall Street, so to speak, and say we have a whole different system here because we don't have that word. Our economics are a different realm, a challenge, and way of life. It is the paradigm shift that some of the non-Indian people are always talking about. It is a way of life, a relationship to the earth and the sky.

This is not to say that English is wrong or not useful. Diné is equivalent, you might say, to the English language, in terms of importance for describing human phenomena. English tends to be anthropocentric, whereas Indian language is everything but that. Diné language diffuses humans as the center of the world and makes them part of systems nesting within systems.

I am not a fluent Navajo speaker, but I know enough of our language to know that it represents a radically different way of life. It is its own stand-alone system at the same time. I can step outside and say Navajo is a philosophy, a system, a paradigm, a method, an epistemological system, a way of measuring yourself, and so on–those words that you use to define science. It can be described in these terms, but then only from the outside. The inside does not rely on those descriptors or concepts to be itself. It happens to be something in addition to those things that modern people can't understand.

The meaning of money, the coins and paper money, is just two hundred years old for Navajo people and a lot of other tribes. We do not traditionally have a word for money. We use the word "héeso" which is borrowed from the Spanish "peso." In order to understand economics, we have to know what has happened over the past two hundred years and how we absorbed that concept, and also how things were prior to that word.

I understand in Western tradition, the coin has a material value on one side and a spiritual value on the other side. According to King Solomon and his philosophy in the Western tradition, you are supposed to spend money so that everybody can be spiritual. Money is meant to buy things so that the outcome is spiritual growth. It never worked that way. It turned into something quite different from that.

"WE DON'T HAVE A WORD FOR ECONOMICS IN NAVAJO."

217

Native tradition did not have money at all in the Western way. We had a whole different concept. In the Navajo world view, hard goods meant shells, turquoise, and certain stones that came from the mountains that you put in your medicine bundle. That was wealth, but it was tied to the mountains and the songs that go with the mountains. That is what they considered wealth. They never sold it or bought it; it was just a lot of exchanging and bartering governed by a kinship system. That is the way they did things, without this extra entity called money. It was not necessary for shelter, clothing, food or happiness.

We were blamed for it, discriminated against, called savages and uncivilized, because we did not have money. In the long run, we will be credited with achieving a civilization that didn't need money to survive for thousands of years. It had education without schools, land without ownership, no system of taxation, no peasants and no kings and queens, no banks, no totalitarian regime, no such thing as unemployment because there was no employment. There was justice without jail, no such things as attorneys. We did not have policemen. Those are all things that the American people are struggling with: crime, jails, courts, lawyers, taxes, and financing a government that is supposed to be for the people. We lived without that. We never even bothered with it. What kind of a people is that? To me, really good people, really smart people. I see it as more of a utopian society than the societies European writers have described. Their assumption is that money has to be there, goods and services, supply and demand, have to be there. The Native people did without that.

There is something about that system that is really valid. It is just as valid for a United

States government that is trillions of dollars in debt and can't build enough jails and schools. We have an answer that totally challenges them. Why don't you have education without schools? Why don't you try to have justice without courts and jails? Why don't you eliminate your police force—do you really need one? Do you really need attorneys and do you really need a government like that? Do you really need those things? If you were to wipe those out tomorrow, what would be the challenge of keeping your society together? You are the ones dependent on a weird system, not us.

In talking about economics and recovery, it seems like the Native way of recovery is more revolutionary if you look at it from the point of view of using that word intentionally, with its Western meaning, "to overthrow." We are not inventing something new. We are just relying on what has always been. We are not proposing a new paradigm. The answer has always been here. Economics is the same way; throw that word out, throw all that money out. That seems to be the challenge.

Hózhó nahasdlíí (in beauty and harmony it is finished) thinking comes from the Beauty Way. We come from that ceremony where Changing Woman showed us the nature of beauty, what harmony means to our inner world, as well as how it functions in the outer world. Concepts like these are being researched by Navajo people for Navajo people, not by anthropologists trying to extract concepts for their own purposes. Indian thinking is ours and reflects our needs. We do our own research for our own needs. Scholars come and take what they want and broadcast it in a university. The Indians over here are unaffected by what they do.

These principles are relevant to our needs. They are part of the process of measuring ourselves by our own standards. We want to take those same principles and propose that *A'da'n* circles use them to govern themselves. If there is a dispute among them for defaulting on a payment or not showing up for meetings, we want them to invoke those harmony standards deliberately; not to simulate being Indians, but to use them, because they are the functional reality of our system. They are our laws.

Reintroducing The Sacred Pipe

Back Into Decision Making

CHAPTER TWENTY

An interview with Gerald One Feather

(Lakota)

erald One Feather, Lakota, lives in Oglala, South Dakota. He is a facilitator for the Seven Council Fires of the Dakota-Lakota-Nakota Nations within the United States and Canada which are unifying in common cause through an alliance, Ikce Wicasa Ta Omniciye. The Alliance seeks to bring spirituality back into decision-making. A first priority of the Alliance is the development of an International College for these Nations which will consolidate their knowledge into an institution to concentrate and instruct traditional language, thought, culture, religion, and governance.

This movement started when the Lakotas living on Fort Quapelle in Saskatchewan called for an international meeting of the Lakota, Dakota, and Nakota living in Canada and the United States. Those from Rosebud, Pine Ridge, Sisseton, Shokopee, totaling seven stateside bands attended the meeting. We talked about getting together under one organization and going back to the original seven camp fires.

The whole idea of this movement is to reintroduce the Sacred Pipe back into decision-making. Then we will revive the seven camp fires, as they were originally created and carried out through the centuries. This is a spiritual fire. It is where the people feel the presence of spirit. We hope to rekindle each camp fire. It takes a lot of doing just to do that. Arvol Looking Horse, who is our nation's Pipe Keeper, is involved in all our meetings because he is the one who will unify us. We are making headway, it is just a matter of time.

The purpose of this alliance is to promote and protect sovereignty and peace among the members and bands. The tribal chairman that signs the accord, the holy man of each reservation, and the head men of each *tiospaye* government have an automatic seat on the alliance. There are nine who are members of tribal government and headmen of eleven bands that signed the agreement In Canada, eleven of the sixteen bands signed. We have committee meetings throughout the year where different national issues that affect all the bands are discussed and plans are developed. My job is to facilitate whatever action they have taken. There are four officers of the organization. I am the staff keeper of Paya Bya Band, the pipe keeper is from Standing Buffalo Band, Ranada, the drum keeper is from Sisseton Wampeton Band, and the fire keeper is from Yankton Band.

"THE FIRE DURING
OUR MEETINGS
REPRESENTS THE
PRESENCE OF SPIRIT"

Ikce Wicasa Ta Omniciye operates on what we call opagi; we pray to Wakantanka before the meeting. Decision-making operates on consensus. The spirit is part of the decision-making. We keep the fire from the beginning until the meeting is closed because the fire represents the presence of spirit. In our Indian Reorganization Act tribal governments there is a separation of church and state, majority rule, and geographic representation. These tribal governments are created by the federal government. The Bureau of Indian Affairs has veto power over everything they do. They are the recognized government by the federal system, so we have to deal with them. The only way we can operate is to revive the Seven Camp Fires for a national government.

Several important things were presented at last summer's 1995 meeting. One was this mascot issue. The second was to change the name of the Sioux tribe and substitute our traditional name for ourselves—Dakota, Lakota or Nakota. Also the Alliance discussed national citizenship. You become a Lakota Nation citizen. We cannot agree upon the criteria for being a national citizen which is acceptable to all Lakotas. It is up to the federal governments to deal with Lakota national citizenship. We can do it among ourselves, but you have to get recognition from the federal government.

We are developing two important institutions. One is a national office/embassy for us to have a relationship to all nations. At the first meeting at the United Nations, Arvol Looking Horse spoke for the indigenous people. Officials of the United Nations agreed to set up an office and that has been done. We are working on financing our national office and some of the tribes are willing to support the office from their budgets.

"OUR LANGUAGE
AND CULTURE IS
WHAT MAKES US
LAKOTA"

The second important institution is an international college which will teach our Lakota language and culture. The people are concerned about preservation of Lakota language and culture. That is what makes us Lakota. A person speaking his language sets him immediately apart from the rest of society. The elders say if we are going to survive the next 100 years, we need to revive our language and culture. Our educational system is acculturating and assimilating our young people. We lost several generations of people to the acculturation process. We have got to slow it down and bring in the other side. It is hard to revive your traditional spiritual ceremonies. The former president of Oglala Lakota College left the college and is trying to pull this international college together. Hopefully, in the next couple of years, he should have in place a structure and a delivery system. The international college will teach Lakota language, ceremonies, thought, concepts of what is sacred, land, environment, the way of life, Tiospaye government, and treaty-making.

Traditionally, the whole structure of the Lakota Nation is that each band is self-sufficient, self-governing and capable of assuming all responsibility for protection of all its people. Each fire is independent. The Great Spirit is part of the assistance that is given to the bands when you ask for help. It is up to the leader to speak on behalf of his people, telling the Great Spirit of their problems or needs. Great Spirit helps the people and then people give thanks. We have sun dances to give thanks. This spiritual leadership is what we lost in the last 100 years. It was built into the leader who assumed that responsibility. That is what is coming back. It is a rare and powerful thing.

"IT IS UP TO THE LEADER OF THE BANDS TO ASK GOD TO HELP THE PEOPLE"

The Royal Commission came down from Canada to have a hearing in Kyle, South Dakota. It was commissioned by the Canadian Parliament to research and develop a Federal-Native relationship in Canada. They are studying a new political relationship. We reopened this treaty relationship and also support land claims in Canada. It has been going well. The Canadian government is receptive to the concerns of the Lakota people. One of the Lakota bands in Canada said they wanted the stateside people to be in their treaty.

We are trying to get the United States to look at the treaty process because it is a national problem, especially if some of these people want to join their relatives in Canada under one treaty. One of the things that you have to recognize stateside is that the majority of the Lakota are non-treaty people. The Lakota Nation has asked President Clinton to appoint a spokesman from the White House to look at treaty rights. Some of the leadership told me that the next step would be to ask the Congress to establish a Treaty Commission which would look at all Lakota treaties. Every band has treaties with the federal government. The non-treaties tribes are interested in having a political relationship. They never made peace treaties with the federal government. They were called hostile. This is why the Canadian Lakotas say if they are non-treaty, why not include them in our treaty. We are talking about international trade and investments. We as Lakotas view things internationally because we are across borders.

"LAKOTAS VIEW THINGS INTER-NATIONALLY BECAUSE WE ARE MANY BANDS AND WE ARE ACROSS BORDERS"

We relate to other Native nations through making treaties with them. Oglala Lakota tribe has been visited by the Micmacs of Canada. For treaty relations, the Micmacs will come to a Lakota Summit in the future where we will have a joint trade treaty with them. They want to promote fish, cigarettes and other things they are now in commercial trade with. In return we would be helping them with cultural activities. Oglala Lakotas also signed a treaty with the Native Hawai'ians and are having a meeting with them. We are beginning nation to nation relationships we never had before, but each band is doing this on their own. These will be upgraded to a national level. As resolutions are developed, they go back to each tribe and band to see what they want to do about it. We take action as a nation and the implementation is left up to the bands.

A D D E N D U M

Philanthropic Support For Traditional
Native Peoples And Projects

Native Americans need significant support in the movement to continue traditional lifeways into the contemporary world. Although there is a great deal of interest in Native knowledge these days, and many Native peoples are seriously committed to enlivening language, culture, and religion, there are few tangible examples of what this means in the modern-day world, and few examples of non-Native people extending a true hand to assist Native people in fulfilling their lives as they envision them. We need support which validates the reality of what we know to be true—that the healing and strengthening of Native communities is based upon the renewal and practice of these lifeways which sustain us with the elements of our own identity.

Native communities are microcosms of the choices which confront all contemporary human life. As earth-based peoples, those who follow traditional lifeways provide living alternatives to the direction in which Western civilization is headed. The world view of indigenous peoples is oriented in a direction which many Americans are exploring. The lifeways within each nation of people carry in them teachings which can help all of humanity and, therefore, all of creation. These world view and belief systems are based on respect, compassion, and love for all creation, and are manifested through clear thought and action. As Renee Senogles emphasized, the way we live our lives is responsible for the maintenance or destruction of creation.

Traditional people, who are the living repositories of our language, culture, and spirituality, have not been sufficiently supported within their communities. Many individuals in tribal government programs, or those who have chosen assimilation into the mainstream over affirmation of Native identity, view traditional people as a threat to their choices. As a consequence, very few of the already scarce tribal resources are available to support their work, which is occasionally viewed as opposition to the interests of those in political power. Attention and greater resources need to be directed to traditional Native people in their efforts to maintain their way of life and to develop projects which reflect, strengthen, and enhance living cultural traditions. This will have the effect of validating the choice to live a traditional way of life, demonstrate its application in a contemporary context, and reintroduce its value in day-to-day life.

The challenge before us as Native people is the renewal and revitalization of our ways of life and communities. What little remains, and what hope there is for the future, lies with traditional people. No matter how great the devastation we have experienced, the seeds of traditional wisdom lie embedded within, waiting to grow. The continuum of thousands of years of living persists within us despite the magnitude of the assaults upon us. This process of healing and revitalization can occur through supporting the catalysts within the Native communities who are the living realities of Native thinking people in the 21st century. We are living in a time of chaos and tumult. New projects and organizations, carrying the seeds of renewal which represent the continuum and evolution of Native thought, need to be nourished with resources to make them realities.

Few foundations and individual donors contribute to the revitalization of Native traditions, culture, and language. Below is a brief selection of some philanthropic resources and the ways in which they have supported Native developments. All of the examples given below demonstrate ways in which philanthropy can work more effectively with traditional Native projects. Some examples have come about by the efforts of individual donors, Native or non-Native staff people working in foundations; others have been created by Native people to meet the needs of their communities.

FOUNDATIONS
AND DONORS

EDUCATIONAL FOUNDATION OF AMERICA
35 Church Lane
Westport, CT 06880
(203) 226-6498, FAX (203) 227-0424
Diane Allison, Executive Director

The Educational Foundation of America is a private family foundation founded in 1959 by Richard Prentice Ettinger, Sr. During the late 1970s, the foundation began grantmaking to Native American educational initiatives. The son of the founder, Richard P. Ettinger, was the pivotal force who brought Native issues to the Board and made this a grantmaking area before other foundations began supporting Native peoples. Through Dick Ettinger's leadership, the foundation brought Native grantmaking to the forefront. Since that time, the foundation has continued to invest in Indian organizations that seek to preserve and strengthen culture, the environment, and health and legal services, both on reservations and in urban areas. By primarily sponsoring organizations that are run by and for Native Americans, this area of grantmaking reflects the needs of the Indian community as they define them. The foundation does not predetermine community focus, but allows for the direction to come from Native communities themselves. Projects which have been supported by the foundation include: American Indian Science and Engineering Native Knowledge Series, White Earth Land Recovery Project for strengthening Ojibwe culture and increasing language literacy, Ojibwe Language Project, through the Native American College Preparatory Center, Wabanaki Sovereignty Training Program in Vermont, and Native Action environmental project.

FUND OF THE FOUR DIRECTIONS

8 West 40th Street, Suite 1610
New York, NY 10018
(212) 768-1430, FAX (212) 768-1471
Ann Roberts, President
Ingrid Washinawatok (Menominee), Co-Director
Gary Schwartz, Co-Director

The Fund of the Four Directions was founded by philanthropist Ann Rockefeller Roberts. Ann has been a donor most of her life, but her organized philanthropy began in the late 1970s. Her giving became formalized in 1990 through creation of the Fund of the Four Directions. The overall philanthropic interests of the Fund have included environment, social justice, nuclear issues, women, and Native Americans, including traditional peoples. Ann is one of the first philanthropists to support Native peoples in this country. She is one of the first contributors to the Tribal Sovereignty Program of the Youth Project (now the Seventh Generation Fund). Other support has been given to the traditional Hopi, Hopi-Navajo dispute resolution, Mount Graham Apache Survival Coalition, Navajo Family Farms, and the Western Shoshone Defense Project. In 1992, Ann hired Ingrid Washinawatok as Program Associate, who now serves as the Director of Grantmaking. At present, she is the only Native person directing a private foundation. Ingrid has taken a lead in advocating for Native people throughout philanthropy, insuring Native participation in philanthropic meetings, and moderating/organizing panels. The Fund of the Four Directions co-founded Funders Who Fund in Indian Country, an affinity group of the National Network of Grantmakers (see below). The fund is presently exploring the possibility of totally devoting their grantmaking to Native people.

LANNAN FOUNDATION

5401 McConnell Avenue
Los Angeles, CA 90066-7027
(310) 306-1002, (800) 860-1004 FAX (310) 578-6445
J. Patrick Lannan, President
William E. Johnston, Chair, ICP Board Committee
Barbara Dalderis, Director, Indigenous Communities Program

The Lannan Foundation is the only national private foundation which has developed a significant grantmaking program to fund Native peoples. In 1994, the foundation began the Indigenous Communities Program, a national grant program to meet the needs of rural Native American communities. Lannan is one of the largest contributors in the country to Native peoples, and one of the only foundations which contributes to language and cultural revitalization. It supports Native people's efforts to revitalize their communities through their own institutions and traditions. Priority is given to the revival and preservation of languages and cultures, education, legal rights, environmental protection and economic development which is sustainable and consistent with traditional values. J. Patrick Lannan, Foundation President and son of the founder, was inspired to begin this program after visiting Sinte Gleska University on the Rosebud Reservation. The foundation has actively involved Native people in helping them to define the foundation priorities and approach, and spends considerable time in meeting directly with the projects they fund in their home communities. The foundation staff and board do not view themselves as benefactors, but feel fortunate to have the opportunity to meet with Native people from whom they learn and exchange information and ideas.

NATIVE CALIFORNIA NETWORK
P.O. Box 1050
Bolinas, CA 94924
(415) 868-2132
Mary Bates, Director

The Native California Network is an excellent example of a philanthropic institution created though the efforts of a non-profit organization, the Native community, and an individual donor. The Network was initiated in 1992 through a start-up grant by the Flow Fund, to assist Achumawi and Achugewi writer Darryl Wilson to obtain funds for a project. A more significant grant was subsequently made to form the Native California Network Community Grants Program which would assist Native people in cultivating projects and advising the distribution of these grant dollars. A principally Native Board was created and the Flow Fund has since made an annual $100,000 lifetime commitment for grants to indigenous California groups seeking to support indigenous tribal traditions. Since formed, dozens of community projects have been funded. The Network initiated an Indigenous California Languages Program, which is advised by a board of seven tribal members known as Advocates for Indigenous California Language Survival. The ideas for these projects arose from a collaborative process of discussion among Native California tribal language speakers and others concerned with the continuation of their languages. One of these programs, the Master/Apprentice Learning Program, is nationally recognized for its work in developing new fluent speakers. In addition, the Network has initiated "In Our Midst: A Glimpse into California Indian Life" for Bay area funders through which cultural presentations place Native people in dialogue with philanthropists. The Network expands philanthropic support for Native California people by assisting Native people and those in philanthropy in becoming real to each other. The structure of the Network, a public foundation, evolved from Native people and empowers community activity through linking resources and people together.

AMERICAN INDIAN RITUAL OBJECTS REPATRIATION FOUNDATION
463 West 57th Street
New York, NY 10022
(212) 980-9441, fax (212) 421-2746
Elizabeth Sackler, President

The American Indian Ritual Object Repatriation Foundation is a non-federally funded intercultural partnership committed to assisting the return of ritual material to American Indian nations and to educating the public of the importance of repatriation. Founded by Elizabeth Sackler, the foundation acts as a conduit through which donations of ceremonial materials are accepted and returned to their American Indian nation of origin, or Native individuals, or other entities (clans, societies). Donors receive tax deductions as allowable under law. These returns are done in close affiliation with the recipient, so that they will follow requested ceremonial requirements. Foundation representatives participate as panelists in conferences and seminars addressing repatriation and attendant issues, and as resources to American Indian nations and museums. The foundation has published "Mending the Circle: A Native American Repatriation Guide," clarifying the rights of American Indians under legislation governing the return of ancestral remains and sacred objects. The Repatriation Foundation is not a granting organization and does not purchase art. They hosted a benefit auction for the Kanatsiohake Mohawk Valley Community and the Repatriation Foundation. This was the first benefit supporting traditional Native American culture and repatriation to be held at a major auction house.

JOHN D. AND CATHERINE T. MACARTHUR FOUNDATION

Native American Initiative 1994 and Beyond
140 South Dearborn Street
Chicago, IL 60603
(312) 726-8000
Adele Simmons, President

In 1992, the John D. and Catherine T. MacArthur Foundation, created Indigenous Voices 1992, a special Native American initiative. In total, close to $1 million was contributed in grants and public communication/media projects. Other activities related to, but outside the initiative, were additionally funded. Native people were involved throughout the entire grantmaking process, from conceptualization to implementation, and worked with MacArthur staff in program design, grantmaking, and evaluation. The Initiative was unique and impacted the entire foundation through sensitizing the staff to Native issues and processes, encouraging cross-programmatic support of Native projects, and participation of staff from each of the Foundation's eight programs. A Consultation Forum with Native presenters on a wide range of subjects established grantmaking priorities. Through the initiative, grassroots Native people working on a variety of issues received their first grant recognition from a major foundation. A lasting effect within the foundation has been a commitment to indigenous grantmaking which has continued on some level throughout the entire foundation. The Native style by which the process was conducted was sensitive, open, and unique to the internal process of the foundation. The MacArthur Initiative opened up the opportunity for Native people to become involved on a deeper and more expansive level with other foundations. Louis Delgado (Oneida), Program Officer, Community Initiatives Program, and David Smathers, Special Assistant, Office of the President, provided leadership in the development of this initiative.

W.K. KELLOGG FOUNDATION

One Michigan Avenue East
Battle Creek, Michigan 49017-4058
(616) 968-1611 FAX (616) 969-2188
Dr. William C. Richardson, President
Valorie Johnson, Program Associate (Seneca-Cayuga from Oklahoma)

The W.K. Kellogg Foundation focuses on "helping people help themselves" through the practical application of knowledge and resources. In line with that mission, Kellogg has funded Native communities and organizations working to create social change mainly in the areas of youth development and education, rural development, and health. In 1992, Kellogg hired Valorie Johnson, Seneca and Cayuga, as a Program Associate to the Vice President. She was formerly a Kellogg Fellow, exploring ways in which philanthropy could be more effective in its support of Native peoples. Kellogg is currently involved in an initiative focused on the improvement of higher education for Native Americans. Phase One of the Initiative, "Capturing the Dream," focuses on strengthening tribal colleges with initial planning grants totaling 1.5 million. Phase Two will focus on strengthening tribal colleges and helping them build partnerships with mainstream institutions. Some of these higher education institutions are looking at expanding traditional Native thought into the curriculum. Some other Native projects which have been funded include: Indigenous Women's Network, Eagle Staff Fund, LifeWay Project of the Tides Foundation for People of the Seventh Fire, White Bison Inc., Saginaw Chippewa Tribe (to fund traditional activities that are focused on strengthening the families), the AISES Traditional Knowledge Conference, Americans for Indian Opportunity (efforts for Native leaders in the United States to meet with Native leaders in Bolivia to share indigenous knowledge about leadership), Oglala Community College (for the "Leaders as Warriors Project"), and the Women's Health Education Resource Center.

NATIVE AMERICAN
FOUNDATIONS

SEVENTH GENERATION FUND

P.O. Box 2550
McKinleyville, CA 95521
(707) 839-1178
Chris Peters (Yurok), Executive Director

The **Seventh Generation Fund** is a national Native American intermediate grantmaking foundation dedicated to maintaining and promoting the uniqueness of Native people and nations. Through an integrated program of grants, technical assistance, leadership training and administrative support the Fund facilitates the self-help efforts of Native people to rebuild their communities. The Fund's approach to Native community development is based upon the premise that Native people understand the problems they face and can be empowered to develop solutions consistent with their traditions and values. Founded in 1977 by Daniel Bomberry, the Seventh Generation Fund (formerly known as the Tribal Sovereignty Program of the Youth Project) has supported hundreds of grassroots community initiatives in rights, environment, sustainable community development, Native women and families, and Native traditions. The major current programs of the foundation are Native Sustainable Communities and Native American Environment. The Fund is governed by a seven member Board of Directors, all of whom are Native people active in the revitalization of their communities.

EAGLE STAFF FUND

First Nations Development Institute
The Stores Building
11917 Main Street

Fredericksburg, VA 22408
(540) 371-5615, fax (703) 371-3505
Rebecca Adamson, (Cherokee) President
Sherry Salaway Black, (Oglala Lakota), Vice-President

Initiated by Rebecca Adamson of the First Nations Development Institute, the Eagle Staff Fund is a major collaborative process, in partnership with other foundations, to increase grantmaking and technical support for Native Americans to create, design, and launch their own development strategies according to traditional values and indigenous knowledge. Its purpose is to increase Native people's capacity to control their economic futures by supporting Native grassroots and tribal organizations that are working to create Native controlled reservation economies. The Fund provides seed, start-up, working capital, development capital grants, and technical assistance to Native tribes, institutions, or traditionally structured (family or clan) efforts for Native people to create culturally relevant and sustainable economic development strategies and programs. Other related programs of First Nations include policy reform; the Oweesta Program, which provides assistance in the creation of tribally-based micro-enterprise loan funds and tribal investment strategies; the Oweesta Fund, which provides a pool for loan capital to start-up reservation loan funds; and the Strengthening Native American Philanthropy Project, which promotes Native control and access to private funding. First Nations also publishes "Indian Giver," a quarterly newsletter on effective grantmaking to Native Americans, and "Business Alert," a bi-monthly newsletter on Native economic development issues.

ABYA YALA FUND

P.O. Box 28386
Oakland, California 94604
(510) 763-6553
Nilo Cayuqueo (Mapuche) and Atencío Lopez (Kuna), Co-Directors

The Abya Yala Fund is a foundation for indigenous self-development of communities in South America, Central America, Mexico, and indigenous immigrants from the south in the United States. Abya Yala is the Kuna word for Continent of Life , which includes all of the Americas. Its mission is to foster greater self-reliance by indigenous peoples, and to support community-based initiatives designed to protect land, environment and human rights, improve women's status, realize greater economic self-reliance, and to foster indigenous culture, identity, and spirituality. Of special interest are innovative projects that emphasize the strengthening of spiritual ties with nature and which have potential application for people throughout the world. The Fund provides grants and loans for community projects which Indigenous people initiate, as well as training in administration, communications, proposal writing, and project management. The Fund emerged from and fosters indigenous principles of holistic cosmo-vision. Their goal is to move toward a world in which indigenous cultures, values, and ways of life are protected, shared, and celebrated. The Board and staff are indigenous peoples of Meso and Central America.

HONOR THE EARTH FUND, ENDANGERED PEOPLE-ENDANGERED SPECIES FUND

Indigenous Women's Network
2525 Arapaho Avenue
Suite E-4112
Boulder, Colorado 80302
(303) 786-8262
Winona La Duke (Anishinaabe), Ingrid Washinawatok (Menominee), Co-Directors
Lori Pourier (Lakota), Executive Director

The Indigenous Women's Network and the Seventh Generation Fund co-sponsored an Honor the Earth Tour, featuring the Grammy-award winning Indigo Girls. In 1995, the Fund distributed $200,000 as proceeds of the tour to 38 Native women's environmental and sacred sites protection groups. A CD is being produced and released in 1996, featuring the Indigo Girls and other musicians, the profits of which will also become available for grantmaking. Another tour is scheduled for 1997. Administered by the Seventh Generation Fund (SGF), a separate grantmaking board has been created to oversee distribution of the grants. The Fund is part of a National Honor the Earth Initiative with SGF Environmental Program and the Indigenous Environmental Network.

NATIVE AMERICAN
COMMUNITY
FOUNDATIONS

HOPI FOUNDATION LOMASUMI'NANGWTUKWSIWMANI

P.O. Box 705
Hotevilla, Arizona 86030
(602) 734-2380 FAX: (520) 734-9520
Barbara Poley (Hopi), Executive Director

The Hopi Foundation is a non-profit organization founded in 1985 to promote self-reliance within communities, and to give voice to universal Hopi values, both in concept and through active projects. The foundation grew out of community discussion regarding the impact of Western values and lifestyles upon traditional Hopi culture, and the lack of options and alternatives to deal with these concerns in a pro-active and integrated manner. The Hopi Foundation is committed to implementing projects that provide viable alternatives to poverty or governmental dependence. Priority issues are identified by community members and demonstration projects are designed with the direction of village members. Projects have included: solar electric enterprises, clan house restoration, art scholarships, sexual abuse project, and creation of a fund to assist an elder whose house had been destroyed by fire. Current project emphases are preserving Hopi language, revitalization of clan houses, improving life survival skills, and creating and catalyzing activities that promote good health and well-being.

THAKÎWA FOUNDATION

P.O. Box 1310   2213 West 8th Street
Cushing, Oklahoma 74030   Prague, Oklahoma 74864
(918) 352-3738   (405) 567-3679
Austin Grant (Sauk and Meskwaki), Chairman
Dagmar Thorpe (Sauk/Thakiwaki), Executive Director

The Thakîwa Foundation supports community-based projects initiated by Sauk people to support the continuation of our lifeway, language, culture, and traditionally-appropriate uses of our land. The Thakîwa Foundation was created to perpetuate the Sauk way of life through uplifting the internal capacity of our community to meet our own needs. The objectives of the foundation are two-fold: (1) To strengthen the spirit and the resources of the people to do for ourselves, and (2) To expand the capacity of the people to work within our communities through expanding the external resources available to us. The foundation will work in a variety of ways to support the creative generation of community ideas and projects which support Sauk way of life. The foundation is initiating its efforts through the development of two projects: The Thakîwaki Traditional Agriculture Project, which is reintroducing the growing, harvesting, and storing of traditional corn, beans, and squash, and developing sustainable land use models; and the Enatoneyake Institute, which will perpetuate the Thakîwaki way of life through initiating a process of research, exploration, definition, and practice, intended to take us to the heart of our existence.

NATIVE AMERICANS IN PHILANTHROPY

Drawer 1429
Lumberton, NC 28359
(910) 618- 9749, fax (910) 618-9839
Donna Chavis (Lumbee), Executive Director

Native Americans in Philanthropy (NAP) was founded in 1990. NAP works within philanthropy to expand understanding of Native communities and issues; to build bridges within Native communities which are rooted and respectful of their culture and values with philanthropic institutions; and to provide support for Native people serving on the boards and staff of grantmaking institutions. NAP fulfills this mission by providing information through research and examples of successful projects from our communities, which offer opportunities for grantmakers to intersect with Native people. NAP provides information to Native communities about foundation grants and technical assistance; serves as a presence at the philanthropic table by encouraging and increasing Native people on staff and boards; and participates with other philanthropic organizations through the Council of Foundations and the National Network of Grantmakers. When invited, NAP organizes forums for philanthropic institutions of Native communities; initiates forums including an annual conference and reception at the Council on Foundations; and plans to host regional philanthropic meetings with funders and community projects. In collaboration with the Center of Philanthropy at Indiana University, NAP is revising the curriculum developed by the Fundraising School to train Native people in fundraising. The curriculum can also be used to train foundation people on how to provide the most effective support to Native communities. NAP publishes a quarterly newsletter, News and Notes from Native Americans in Philanthropy. The organization annually awards the Louis T. Delgado Distinguished Grantmaker Award, to recognize grantmakers who have made significant contributions to Native philanthropy and communities. Delgado, a co-founder of NAP, is a former staff member of the John D. and Catherine T. MacArthur Foundation.

FUNDERS WHO FUND IN INDIAN COUNTRY

c/o Fund of the Four Directions
8 West 40th Street, Suite 1610
New York, NY 10018
(212) 768-1430
Gary Schwartz, Co-Director
Ingrid Washinawatok, Co-Director

Funders who Fund in Indian Country was founded in 1992 to educate the constituency of the National Network of Grantmakers (NNG) about Indigenous issues, and to familiarize them with Native community people nationwide. During the annual NNG conference, the group hosts an annual regionally-based panel on Native issues, and in 1995 was instrumental in creating an Indigenous Day. Foundations or donors interested in participating in the Funders group or assisting in the organization of panels for future NNG conferences, are invited to contact them.

A F T E R W O R D

John Mohawk

(Seneca)

This is a unique and powerful book—one that seems should have been written long ago. There have been many books about Native American experiences and culture, and not a few about individuals' journeys seeking knowledge and wisdom among the Indians. Ms. Thorpe's journey is qualitatively different from those which preceded hers. She asks not "what is there in these cultures which I can gain from, which I can learn from, and which I want to know," but the much more introspective and difficult question, "what is it that the people who represent these cultures to their own people want to teach me, and what do they want me and other Indian people to do about these teachings?" She discovers they want her to practice a way of being in the world which is defined by the context of the lived and living experiences of her peoples. It is a profound and insightful discovery, and one which deserves acknowledgment and respect.

People Of The Seventh Fire is not about what non-Indians imagine indigenous peoples' lives and environments to be like. It is a powerfully honest portrayal of the thoughts and aspirations of contemporary traditionalists in North American indigenous communities. Other authors have found it possible to write volumes about these subjects without ever touching seriously on the subject of indigenous identity as it is lived by the people about whom they are writing. A number of books have been written as quests for indigenous spiritual knowledge which do not (or do not adequately) address the fact that these peoples and cultures have suffered more than a century (and sometimes more than three centuries) of systematic repression and abuse. This history, however, forms the foundation of how things came to be the way they are, and it echoes throughout the book.

Ms. Thorpe tackles her formidable task directly, describing her adult life as spent mostly on the margins of indigenous cultures and her recent years as a trek toward a closer understanding and practice of the culture of her Sauk (Thakiwaki) ancestors. She is, if anything, overly modest about her own accomplishments as an activist in both volunteer and professional roles over two and a half decades. To the world outside the Indian Country, Ms. Thorpe has excellent life experiences to claim membership and participation in the world she approaches, and most who have preceded her have stretched less impressive credentials to claim expert status over a wide range of topics including those addressed in this volume. She does not, however, present herself as an appointed expert but as facilitator of the voices of people whose credentials are lived experiences. Few writers on contemporary indigenous people have spent the time to actually interview the people who practice the cultures to capture their voices, and their stories, as this book has done, and no one has done so as comprehensively.

The issue of peoples' cultural identities is, of course, a subject filled with complexity. To her credit, Ms. Thorpe does not flinch from the issue of indigenous identity as she embarks on a quest for meaning in the sense one might seek a meaningful answer to the question, "What does it mean to be Mohawk or Lakota or, in the end, Sac and Fox?" The depth and quality with which she succeeds in bringing this discussion to a new level should help to advance the study of both Native American autobiographical narrative and contemporary Native Studies as well as offer the non-indigenous public insightful views of what most imagine to be an uncomplicated subject. In testimonial to her methodology, I am delighted to report that were she or another writer to approach the traditional community with a list of two or three dozen different individuals, they would emerge with stories and a message from the Indian Country strongly parallel to that told here.

Not everything reported here is necessarily that which a non-Indian audience would like to hear. Indigenous people have been and continue to be damaged by the processes of colonialism and neocolonialism. Their lands are under constant attack, and they are often placed under tribal councils whose members are as acculturated and alien as the Washington bureaucrats who are charged with watching over their interests. Many of the traditional people in Indian Country are profoundly alienated from the major movements of contemporary American (and Canadian) life: consumerism, materialism, "high" technology, economic globalization, and environmental degradation. These things are contradictory to that which Ms. Thorpe and her informants define as a "spiritual" way of life, and remain consistently so across many indigenous cultures and across the whole of North America's geography.

Although defining and practicing an indigenous culture in the context of contemporary society is a daunting task, it is clear some traditionalists are committed to the survival of their cultures through periods of change. Some use fax machines and pickup trucks while calling upon ancient knowledge, some realize that ancient knowledge can be rediscovered, and all know that the survival of indigenous cultural knowledge is more than the sum of its parts, it is crucial to a peoples' identity. The languages are a part of this. Living indigenous languages can only be perpetuated by indigenous peoples who are strong in their ways. The encouraging message is that such people continue to struggle to practice the cultures and sustain the peoples they represent and that indigenous practices relating to the environment, the earth, and community are regaining popularity in the Indian Country. It was enormously important that this book be written from Indian Country to Indian Country, and this Ms. Thorpe has done in the best of all possible ways: with love.